A Northern
Woman
in the
Plantation
South

Tryphena Blanche Holder Fox (courtesy of Mrs. Raymond Birchett, Jackson, Mississippi)

A NORTHERN WOMAN IN THE PLANTATION SOUTH

Letters of Tryphena Blanche Holder Fox 1856–1876

EDITED BY WILMA KING

UNIVERSITY OF SOUTH CAROLINA PRESS

WOMEN'S DIARIES AND LETTERS OF THE NINETEENTH-CENTURY SOUTH

Copyright 1993 University of South Carolina

Published in Columbia, South Carolina, by the
University of South Carolina Press
First paperback edition 1997

Manufactured in the United States of America

01 00 99 98 97   5 4 3 2

LIBRARY OF CONGRESS CATALOGING-IN-PUBLICATION DATA

Fox, Tryphena Blanche Holder, 1834–1912.
    A northern woman in the plantation South : letters of Tryphena
Blanche Holder Fox, 1856–1876 / edited by Wilma King.
        p. cm. — (Women's diaries and letters of the nineteenth-century South)
    Includes bibliographical references and index.
    ISBN 0–87249–850–6 (acid-free)
    1. Fox, Tryphena Blanche Holder, 1834–1912—Correspondence.   2. Plantation
life—Louisiana—History—19th century.   3. Slavery—Louisiana.   4. Louisiana—
History—Civil War, 1861–1865—Personal narratives.   5. United States—
History—Civil War, 1861–1865—Personal narratives.   6. Reconstruction—
Louisiana.   7. Women—Louisiana—Correspondence.   8. Slaveholders—
Louisiana—Corespondence.   I. King, Wilma, 1942–
II. Title.   III. Series.
E445.L8F68   1993
976.3'06'092—dc20   92-39173

To Mother

Contents

Illustrations

Series Editor's Introduction

A Northern Woman in the Plantation South is the eighth volume in an ongoing series of women's diaries and letters of the nineteenth-century South. This series published by the University of South Carolina Press includes a number of never-before-published diaries, some collections of unpublished correspondence, and a few reprints of published diaries—a potpourri of nineteenth-century women's writings.

The Women's Diaries and Letters of the Nineteenth-Century South Series enables women to speak for themselves, providing readers with a rarely opened window into Southern society before, during, and after the American Civil War. The significance of these letters and journals lies not only in the personal revelations and the writing talents of these women authors but also in the range and versatility of the documents' contents. Taken together these publications will tell us much about the heyday and the fall of the Cotton Kingdom, the mature years of the "peculiar institution," the war years, and the adjustment of the South to a new social order following the defeat of the Confederacy. Through these writings the reader will also be presented with firsthand accounts of everyday life and social events, courtships and marriages, family life and travels, religion and education, and the life-and-death matters which made up the ordinary and extraordinary world of the nineteenth-century South.

A Northern Woman in the Plantation South comprises eighty-one letters written from Louisiana by the Massachusetts-born-and-bred Tryphena Blanche Holder Fox. In these letters, nearly all to her mother in New England, Fox recounts her experiences as a small slaveholder and the wife of a physician who cared for the slaves owned by wealthy sugar planters in Plaquemines Parish, Louisiana, near New Orleans. The letters, rich documents of social history, describe Fox's interactions with her domestic servants and neighbors and reveal how quickly she adopted local attitudes and regional customs. The mistress of five slaves and the mother of ten children, her experience was typical of many women of her time.

Carol Bleser
May 1992

Preface

The Massachusetts-born Tryphena Blanche Holder Fox (1834–1912) moved to Mississippi in 1852 and became a plantation tutor. Although she enjoyed her work and the salary allowed her to assist her widowed mother, Anna Rose Holder (1808–1895), back in Massachusetts, Tryphena disliked "depending upon others for her daily bread." She subsequently married a handsome medical doctor in 1856 and moved to a rural Louisiana community along the Mississippi River near New Orleans.

Far from home, Tryphena found solace in a lively correspondence with family and friends. The letters, which were never intended for publication, contain data about southern living and customs before and after the Civil War. As did many northern travelers, Tryphena wrote about social, political, and economic conditions of the nineteenth-century South. Unlike these travelers, she remained permanently in the South and quickly assimilated the regional customs. Those of her letters that recount interactions with domestic servants, black or white, and with neighbors, rich or poor, expose Tryphena's racial prejudices and class biases. Aware of her own foibles, and the caustic nature and acerbic wit of her pen, Tryphena asked her family in Massachusetts to keep the details of her letters private.

The Tryphena Blanche Holder Fox letters form the basis of *A Northern Woman in the Plantation South*. Housed at the Mississippi Department of Archives and History, Jackson, Mississippi, the collection contains 187 letters spanning the years 1852 to 1885. The preponderance of the correspondence is from Tryphena to her mother, with scattered letters to younger siblings Emma and George. Her letters sometimes provide the reader with day-by-day accounts of her activities, as would a journal, since Tryphena frequently made additions while awaiting the opportunity to have a letter mailed.

There are eighty-three letters written from 1852 to 1862. However, when the flow of mail was interrupted by the war, Tryphena's correspondence diminished accordingly; only eight letters written between January 1862 and December 1864 are in the collection. At the war's end, Tryphena resumed a brisk correspondence until December 1869. From that point forward, it is rare to have more than one or two letters per year in the extant collection.

During the war Tryphena kept a diary that tells much about those years through the eyes of a transplanted "Reb." Unfortunately, the original journal no longer exists, though a transcript is housed in the Fox collection. The consensus among the Fox descendants is that Tryphena requested that the diary be destroyed upon her death.

With few exceptions, Tryphena's incoming correspondence was lost, either when she and her children left Louisiana during the war or when fire engulfed her home in 1866. Other letters from Anna Holder between 1866 and her death in 1895 were probably destroyed at Tryphena's request. Despite these losses, enough evidence remains to reconstruct many facets of Tryphena's fifty years of life in the South.

This collection contains eighty-one of Tryphena's original letters, beginning with the one written to her mother in June 1856 in which Tryphena announces her marriage. In deciding which letters from the collection to include, I have tried to keep the focus squarely on events in Tryphena's life and to choose those letters richest in socio-historical detail. The letters written prior to her marriage and those written after 1876 are too scattered to tell much of a story; therefore, they are not included. Another portion of the collection contains correspondence from Tryphena's children. There are nearly a dozen letters written between 1866 and 1885 by Tryphena's daughter Fanny Otis (1857–1918) to relatives in New England that are not reproduced herein. Although they chronicle the growth and development of a young girl in the nineteenth-century South, they present Fanny's story, not Tryphena's.

A Northern Woman in the Plantation South focuses on Tryphena's letters written from June 1856 to January 1876. These letters cover a period of twenty crucial years of war and reconstruction in the South, and they also offer the reader an excellent opportunity to reconstruct the female experience and to hear the voice of a small slaveholder and wife of a physician rather than that of a plantation mistress. Occasionally that voice emanates from a frustrated woman who in manners, education, and style thought she belonged to the planter class, but who never gained full entry into that privileged group because she did not marry a prominent landholder and slaveholder who could have assured her a place among equals.

From the "penitentiary of the U. S.," as her husband dubbed the place where they lived, Plaquemines Parish, Louisiana, Tryphena often penned letters that bear the mark of a writer in search of an appropriate forum. An avid reader with aspirations of writing professionally, she corresponded with Henry Wadsworth Longfellow and Henry David Thoreau. She also admired Fredrika Bremer and believed herself capable of writing about matters of a familial nature with equal aplomb. Tryphena's literary voice surfaces occasionally in ordinary letters, but it is in that correspondence fashioned by special occasions or events that the fullest expression of her gift is realized.

Tryphena fought rural isolation with approved weapons: ink, pen, and paper. The ground rules were to write freely and frequently. In the exchange between mother and daughter, Tryphena's hurriedly written letters were often blunt and occasionally insensitive, yet they never lacked sincerity. Without a significant amount of extant incoming correspondence it is impossible to know what Anna's response was to Tryphena's letters, such as the one of August 20, 1860, when the younger woman complained about the mental anxiety she incurred when comparing their lives. According to Tryphena, her life was one of "ease & almost luxury" while her mother was "struggling for daily bread." Letters of this sort were subject to misunderstanding and likely to create offense; however, the majority of Tryphena's letters were written only when there was "something new, glad, or of great importance to communicate." When unable to keep that promise, she sought balance. "There must sometimes be clouds," she wrote, "but it does not seem best to make them when all is sunshine."

I have kept editorial intrusions to a minimum by retaining the spelling errors, grammatical flaws, capitalization quirks, unclosed quotes, single parentheses, and erratic punctuation in the original. Fox used the dash as an all purpose punctuation mark to set off clauses, abbreviate words, and end sentences. In some instances she used both the dash and period as end marks; in other situations she used neither. In these cases, I retained both marks and left a space to denote missing punctuation.

When faced with limited amounts of paper and time, Tryphena wrote hurriedly about a great number of subjects without paragraphing. The desire to modernize each letter required great restraint. While modernization would make the letters easier to read, recasting paragraphs and deleting signatures would obfuscate the writer's sense of urgency and the need to save paper and interfere with the original thought processes. In short, the disadvantages of paragraphing outweigh the advantages.

I have ignored cancellations unless they changed the meaning of a letter. Other alterations include repositioning dates and place names, indenting paragraphs, and running complementary closings into concluding paragraphs. Bracketed ellipses denote illegible words. Unless other reliable information was available, dates supplied in brackets for some letters are those used by the Mississippi Department of Archives and History.

Acknowledgments

This book would have been impossible without the help of Michael (Mick) Hennen at the Mississippi Department of Archives and History, Jackson, Mississippi, who suggested that I look at the Tryphena Blanche Holder Fox letters—one of his favorite collections.

At the time of her death in 1912, Tryphena lived in Vicksburg with her daughter Blanche Cleveland Fox Birchett, who handed the letters down to her daughter-in-law, Mrs. Raymond (Emma Katherine) Birchett. She answered my queries about Tryphena fully and promptly. She also furnished the photographs of Anna and George Holder with Le Roy and Tryphena, the Fox family home, and the adult Tryphena. My debts to her are incalculable. Descendants of Blanche Cleveland Fox and J. A. C. Birchett exuded much enthusiasm about the publication of these letters and graciously supplied a copy of the Fox genealogy, which aided my work immensely.

The research in Pittsfield, Massachusetts, proceeded smoothly because Ruth T. Degenhardt, department head, Local History and Genealogy Department, Berkshire Athenaeum, and Gladys King, researcher at the Berkshire Family History Association and a distant cousin of Tryphena Holder Fox, rendered invaluable assistance. Carmela B. Lucidi, St. Stephen's Parish secretary, and Peggy H. Sottile, secretary, Pittsfield Cemetery and Crematory, deserve commendations for their help.

Archivists at the National Archives facilitated my efforts in locating records relevant to the Civil War, the Freedmen's Bureau, and the Southern Claims Commission. Staff at the Louisiana and Lower Mississippi Valley Collections at Louisiana State University, Baton Rouge, Louisiana, and at the Southern Historical Collection, University of

North Carolina, Chapel Hill, North Carolina, must also be recognized for their assistance.

I owe special thanks to librarians at Indiana University of Pennsylvania (IUP). They include Mary Sampson, director of the Interlibrary Loan Office, Richard Chamberlin, reference librarian, and Walter Laude, director of technical services. Their student assistants also merit special recognition.

The debts spill over to colleagues and friends. Linda Reed, Irwin Marcus, Howard V. Young, and Robert L. Hall, ever conscious of my research, forwarded pertinent materials to me. Nell I. Painter's helpful comments prompted me to decide what to do with the letters, while Randall Miller, showing an uncommon generosity, encouraged me to edit them. Leslie Rowland's magnanimous editorial advice during the 1991 National Historical Publications and Records Commission Institute, "camp edit," proved indispensable. Barbara Hill Hudson, Ricky Sanders, Vivian Fuller, and Diana Brandi created a forum for discussion along with a supportive environment.

I was fortunate enough to have graduate students from my antebellum South and African American history courses as research assistants. Gary Link, Carol Occhuizzo, James Koshan, and Michael Ruddon earned my gratitude. Undergraduate assistants Andrew Conway and Kellee Durkin also helped in every possible way.

David Lynch, dean of the IUP Graduate School, made funding available for the initial stage of this work. Grants from the IUP Faculty Senate and the Pennsylvania State System of Higher Education Faculty Professional Development Committee supported the research as I retraced Tryphena's journey from Pittsfield, Massachusetts, to Jesuit Bend, Louisiana.

I wish to thank Carol Bleser, general editor of this series, for her editorial comments, as well as Warren Slesinger at the University of South Carolina Press, for his diligence in bringing this work to fruition.

My husband, daughter, and mother maintained the kind of support that only a family can and will. After reading "his half" of the Fox letters, my husband, Alvin Russel Hunter, suggested that I edit them. I argued that it would interfere with my research on slave children, which had prompted our trip to the Mississippi Department of Archives and History. He prevailed, without undue persuasion, for I realized that the

Fox collection was a treasure trove of data about the American South before, during, and after the Civil War. Possibilities abounded.

As I studied the letters, I learned much about mother-daughter relationships. My daughter Andrea, who was then a student at the University of North Carolina, helped as much as her time permitted. Glaucoma is gradually taking away my mother's eyesight, yet she saw more than the rest of us as she listened to Tryphena's letters describe relationships between maids and mistresses in the post-war South. Although I benefited from the comments of family and friends, I must bear the responsibility for all deficiencies alone.

As I complete *A Northern Woman in the Planatation South,* I am far afield from the manuscript on slave children, but I learned much about the conditions of youthful chattel, especially Adelaide, Margaret, and Buddy, having taken this detour with their owner.

Cast of Characters

Brague, Lewis—Tryphena Blanche Holder Fox's (TBHF) uncle.

    Mahala—wife of Lewis Brague and sister of Anna Holder.

    Catherine (Kate)—daughter of Lewis and Mahala.

Cleveland, Tryphena Torry—TBHF's grandmother in Massachusetts.

    Warren—TBHF's grandfather in Massachusetts.

Dewey, Harriet Murray—schoolmate and childhood friend of TBHF.

Fox, Angelina—wife of Daniel.

    Anna Rose (1861–1863)—daughter of TBHF and David Raymond Fox (DRF).

    Andrew Seguin (b. 1832)—younger brother of DRF.

    Blanche Cleveland (b. 1869)—daughter of TBHF and DRF.

    Burt Randolph (1873–1889)—son of TBHF and DRF.

    Daniel—older brother of DRF.

    David Raymond (1822–1893)—husband of TBHF.

    Edward Randolph (1860–1860)—son of TBHF and DRF.

    Eliza (b. 1841)—younger sister of DRF.

    Emily (b. 1834)—younger sister of DRF.

    Emma Cheeseborough—wife of John Angel Fox.

    Emma Catherine (b. 1875)—daughter of TBHF and DRF.

    Fannie (1838–1857)—younger sister of DRF.

    Fanny Otis (1857–1918)—daughter of TBHF and DRF.

    Frank Coleman (1867–1892)—son of TBHF and DRF.

    George Edward Randolph (1863–1939)—son of TBHF and DRF.

    John Angel (b. 1871)—son of TBHF and DRF.

    James Angel (1794–1881)—father of DRF.

    James (b. 1840)—younger brother of DRF.

Lizzie—wife of Andrew Seguin Fox.

Robert (b. 1845)—younger brother of DRF.

Holder, Anna Rose Cleveland (ARH) (1808–1895)—mother of TBHF.

Emma (1845–1922)—sister of TBHF.

George (1847–1935)—younger brother of TBHF.

Le Roy (1831–1864)—older brother of TBHF.

Mary (1840–1851)—younger sister of TBHF.

Semantha (1841–1852)—younger sister of TBHF.

Merrill, Lustus—resident of Pittsfield and friend of TBHF.

Mary—wife of Lustus and friend of TBHF.

Hannah—childhood friend and schoolmate of TBHF.

Messenger, George—TBHF's employer prior to her marriage and owner of Baconham Plantation, Warren Co., Miss.,

Sophia—wife of George Messenger.

Murray, Hattie—childhood friend and schoolmate of TBHF.

Newman, Lucy Fox—sister-in-law of TBHF in Washington, Miss.

Randolph, Sophia—sister of James A. Fox in Warren, Co., Miss.

Reggio, Matilda—wife of sugar planter and neighbor of TBHF.

Stackhouse, Blanche—daughter of Sarah and Haywood.

Haywood—sugar planter and neighbor of TBHF.

Herbert—son of Sarah and Haywood.

Sarah—wife of Haywood Stackhouse.

William—sugar planter and neighbor of TBHF.

West, J. C.—Pittsfield, Massachusetts, merchant.

Abbreviations

ARH	Anna Rose Holder
JAH	*Journal of American History*
JMH	*Journal of Mississippi History*
JSH	*Journal of Southern History*
JSoh	*Journal of Social History*
LaH	*Louisiana History*
MDAH	Mississippi Department of Archives and History, Jackson, Mississippi
NA	National Archives, Washington, D.C.
SHC	Southern Historical Collection
SoS	*Southern Studies*
SQ	*Southern Quarterly*
SW	*Southern Workman*
TBHF	Tryphena Blanche Holder Fox
TTC	Tryphena Torrey Cleveland

A Northern
Woman
in the
Plantation
South

INTRODUCTION

. . . and she brought forth,
and gave to her that she had
reserved after she was sufficed

Ruth 2:18

In 1852 when Tryphena Blanche Holder (1834–1912) became a tutor for the George Messenger family in Mississippi, she could not fathom how that decision would affect the remainder of her life. Teaching at the Warren County plantation offered more than employment. It introduced her to a different lifestyle, where she worked and lived among wealthy cotton planters. Marrying the son of a local well-to-do planter and establishing a home in the South further entrenched her in the world of slaveholders. With her marriage and subsequent move to Louisiana, she exchanged the role of an independent self-supporting northern woman for that of a dutiful southern wife and loving mother.

Tryphena's father, George Holder (1810–1849), immigrated from England, settled in Hinsdale, Massachusetts, in the 1820s, and married Anna Rose Cleveland (1808–1895), who traced her heritage back to John Wilson, the first minister in Boston. Virtually nothing is known of the Holders' early life together other than that they purchased more than one-hundred acres of Berkshire County farm land from Warren Cleveland, Anna's father. In 1841 the Holders moved to Pittsfield, Massachusetts, with their three children, Le Roy (1831–1864), Tryphena Blanche (1834–1912), and Mary (1840–1851).[1]

---

1. See Joseph Gardner Bartlett, "Ancestry and Descendants of Rev. John Wilson of Boston, Mass.," *New England Historical and Genealogical Register* 61 (January 1907): 36–41,

In Pittsfield, an urban industrial center with factories producing writing paper, boilers for steam engines, and iron axles, Holder worked as superintendent for the Pontoosuc Woolen Manufacturing Company. In addition to his work at the mill, which owned scores of looms and produced 130,000 yards of fabric annually by 1850, Holder operated the Washington Hotel, an occupation that allowed his family to interact with many citizens in the community. The Holders joined St. Stephens, an Episcopal church organized in 1830, and sent their children to local schools.[2]

Tryphena studied at Maplewood Young Ladies' Institute, located on a twenty-acre tract a short distance from her home at One North Street. The institute, founded by W. H. Tyler in 1841, offered a wide variety of courses, including English grammar, geography, history, biology, and philosophy. Optional classes in Greek, Latin, German, French, water and oil painting, drawing, and music were also available. The school also touted the availability of a "sedulous moral and social culture."[3]

Maplewood's two academic sessions, which began in May and November, lasted twenty-one weeks each. Officials set aside the last days of each term for comprehensive examinations. Students enjoyed their vacations in April and October. Tuition was ninety dollars per session with further assessments for extra-curricular activities, such as painting and drawing. Students paid an additional twenty dollars per session for music lessons. Greek or Latin lessons were six dollars extra, while French or German lessons were ten dollars more per term. At Maplewood, Tryphena gained proficiency in French and studied the piano.

127–33; *The Genealogy of the Cleveland and Cleaveland Families* no. 438, 2:901; 3:2018, Berkshire Athenaeum, Pittsfield, Massachusetts; Probate Records, March 11, 1831, 94:39, March 14, 1838, 94:359, February 10, 1842, 94:39 Berkshire County, Massachusetts; Records of Birth, Marriage, and Death, 2:28, City Clerk Office, Pittsfield, Massachusetts (hereafter cited as City Clerk, Pittsfield, MA).

2. Josiah Gilbert Holland, *History of Western Massachusetts,* vol. 2 (Springfield: Samuel Bowles, 1855), 560; Probate Records, October 25, 1845, 114:47, March 5, 1846, 113:354, January 15, 1852, 2:28; January 2, 1853, 2:32, Berkshire County, Massachusetts; St. Steven's Episcopal Parish Records, Pittsfield, Massachusetts; "Obituary," *Berkshire Eagle,* December 18, 1822.

3. *Sixth Annual Catalogue of the Instructors and Pupils in the Young Ladies' Institute* (Pittsfield: Hanford, 1847), 11–15. For a comparison of curricular offerings at southern academies for women see Catherine Clinton, "Equally Their Due: The Education of the Planter Daughter in the Early Republic," *Journal of the Early Republic* 2 (April 1982), 48–52.

Her attendance at the institute and the selection of non-required courses offer some indication of the Holder's financial status.[4]

Tryphena was probably a day student rather than a boarder. Many of the other girls who were boarding students came from throughout New England, from southern states, including North Carolina, Georgia, Louisiana, Kentucky, and from the West Indies and Sandwich Islands. The camaraderie among girls at schools such as Maplewood is well known. It warded off homesickness and sometimes flowered into lifelong associations. Tryphena, for example, enjoyed lasting friendships with three of her schoolmates, Sarah Sands, Harriet Murray, and Hannah Merrill, who lived in or near Pittsfield.[5]

The Holder family's financial status changed for the worse in 1849 when George Holder died. By 1850 Le Roy was working as a clerk and Tryphena was completing her education at Maplewood, but the younger children, Semantha (1841–1852), Emma (1845–1922), and George (1847–1935), born after the Holders moved to Pittsfield, were entirely dependent upon Anna. In addition to the death of George Holder and subsequent financial problems, the family would soon suffer more tragedy. Eleven-year-old Mary Holder died of typhoid fever September 8, 1851, and Semantha died of congestive fever August 9, 1852.[6]

Tryphena, who was at Gaylord's Bridge, Connecticut, perhaps away working as a teacher to help support the family, learned of the extent of Semantha's illness too late to return home and assist with her care. Try-

4. *Sixth Annual Catalogue*, 16. See Clinton, "Equally Their Due," 54–55.
5. U.S. 7th Census, 1850, Population, Berkshire County, Massachusetts, NA; Family History File, Berkshire Athenaeum, Pittsfield, Massachusetts; *Sixth Annual Catalogue*, 6–9. For related discussions see Clinton, "Equally Their Due," 56–57; Steven M. Stowe, " 'The Thing Not Its Vision': A Woman's Courtship and Her Sphere in the Southern Planter Class," *Feminist Studies* 9 (Spring 1983), 115–18; Carroll Smith-Rosenberg, "The Female World of Love and Ritual: Relations between Women in Nineteenth-Century America," in *Women's America: Refocusing the Past* 2d ed., edited by Linda K. Kerber and Jane De Hart-Mathews, (New York: Oxford University Press, 1987), 170–71; Steven M. Stowe, "The Not-So-Cloistered Academy: Elite Women's Education and Family Feeling in the Old South," in *The Web of Southern Social Relations: Women, Family, and Education*, edited by Walter Fraser, Jr. (Athens: University of Georgia Press, 1985), 92–93.
6. City Clerk, 12:112, 2:2, 2:20, Pittsfield, MA; ARH to TBH, August 9, 1852, MDAH. U.S. 7th Census, 1850, Population, Berkshire County, Massachusetts, lists Semantha's age as fourteen, while City Clerk records give her age as eleven. See City Clerk, 2:28, 2:32, Pittsfield, MA. The Holder's fifth child, George Warren Holder, born June 13, 1844, in Pittsfield, died two days later. City Clerk, 2:2, Pittsfield, MA.

phena, a young, unmarried, educated woman, had not found it difficult to find employment. Approximately 20 percent of the white women in antebellum Massachusetts between fifteen and sixty years of age worked as teachers at some stage of their lives. Women ordinarily considered teaching to be temporary employment. In the 1840s they remained in the public schools an average of only 2.1 years. Nearly all women gave up the profession once married. Although their salaries were lower than their male counterparts, teaching offered an opportunity for financial independence in the interim between adolescence and marriage. Anna could use any earnings Tryphena sent to help with her ongoing expenses.[7]

After 1850 Le Roy moved to New York to take a job "firing an engine between Niagara and Buffalo." He and Tryphena helped fill the family's financial void. The family's survival depended upon Anna's ability to persuade local merchants to extend credit until Tryphena or Le Roy could help pay the debts. If either child failed, Anna was in distress. This precarious financial structure demanded continuous subsidies and Tryphena emerged as the sustaining mainstay when Le Roy failed to honor his commitment.[8]

In August 1852, while still in Connecticut, Anna informed Tryphena that George Messenger, a Mississippi planter visiting his mother in Egremont, Massachusetts, wanted to hire a tutor for his adopted daughter Lucinda, commonly called Lui or Lucy. Northern teachers frequently worked as plantation tutors. Afterward, Messenger contacted Tryphena and she readily accepted the position. The eighteen-year-old woman began the journey to Baconham Plantation in Warren County, Mississippi, in the fall of 1852.[9]

The plantation South was vastly different from what Tryphena experienced while growing up in Pittsfield. She moved from an old established New England town with a population of 5,587 in 1850. Pittsfield, located on the Boston and Albany Railroad, offered such social amenities as Congregationalist, Baptist, Methodist, and Episcopal churches,

---

7. See Richard M. Bernard and Maris A. Vinovskis, "The Female School Teacher in Ante-Bellum Massachusetts, *JSoH* 10 (March 1977): 332–39; Clinton, "Equally Their Due," 45.
8. TBH to ARH, October 15, 1855, MDAH.
9. ARH to TBH, August 9, 1852; TBH to ARH, November 11, 1852, MDAH.

as well as the Pittsfield Young Ladies Institute, the Pittsfield Gymnasium for boys, and the Berkshire Medical College. Pittsfield also had a newspaper, the *Pittsfield Sun,* which had been in operation for decades.[10]

The nearest town to Baconham, the cotton producing plantation owned by George and Sophia Messenger, was the cotton exporting town of Vicksburg—less than twenty-five miles away—with a white population of 3,678 in 1850. One church, Featherstone Chapel, was located several miles from Baconham, but there were no public schools in the vicinity. These were not the most glaring differences. In 1850 there were 12,096 slaves and 5,996 whites in Warren County. The average slaveholder in the county owned 20.2 slaves in 1850. The Messengers owned ninety-seven bond men, women, and children in 1850. The value of Messenger's real property and personal property in 1860 was $100,000 and $130,000 respectively. Among the county's planters who held more personal property was Jefferson Davis.[11]

Slaves in her midst was new for Tryphena, but she had some familiarity with African Americans. There were 285 blacks in Pittsfield in 1850 and Maplewood Institute employed at least six as servants that year. The contrast between Tryphena's life in Massachusetts and Mississippi prompted her to write: "There is more than two thousand acres in this plantation and Mr Messenger and his lady own about one hundred negroes besides a large place and many hands sixty miles above here. Then they have here forty yoke of oxen, and more horses and hogs and everything to correspond; perhaps you will think I have stretched the story a little when I tell you that since I came here they have killed hogs, to amount to sixteen thousand pounds and salted it down."[12]

Knowing that the young tutor was in unfamiliar surroundings, the Messengers welcomed her into their social circle when entertaining sea-

10. Holland, *History of Western Massachusetts,* 547–60; U.S. 7th Census, 1850, Population, Berkshire County, Massachusetts, NA.
11. U.S. 7th Census, 1850, Population, Berkshire County, Massachusetts; U.S. 7th Census, 1850, Population, Warren County, Mississippi; U.S. 7th Census, 1850, Slave Schedule, Warren County, Mississippi; U.S. 8th Census, 1860, Slave Schedule, Warren County, Mississippi, NA; Jonathan Beasley, "Blacks—Slave and Free—Vicksburg, 1850–1860," *JMH* 38 (February 1976), 3, 7.
12. U.S. 7th Census, 1850, Slave Schedule, Warren County, Mississippi, NA; U.S. 7th Census, 1850, Population, Berkshire County, Massachusetts, NA; TBH to Tryphena Torrey Cleveland (hereafter TTC), January 25, 1853; TBH to ARH, November 11, 1852, MDAH.

sonal guests, visiting friends, or shopping in Vicksburg. Tryphena accompanied Sophia Messenger to a church fair and magic show in 1856. Another member of the household, the octogenarian Lucinda Vaughan, Sophia's mother, was especially kind to the teacher, who found several contemporaries, including another plantation tutor, to visit and interact with at social gatherings. Tryphena developed warm friendships with Fannie, Emily, and Eliza, daughters of James Angel Fox, the Connecticut-born Episcopal minister who owned nearby Woodburne plantation.[13]

As the tutor at Baconham, Tryphena taught Lui and two other pupils, Sarah and Laura Billingslea, who boarded with the Messengers Monday through Friday and returned to their home, a nearby cotton plantation, each weekend. There was little comparison, according to Tryphena, between Lui's abilities and the Billingslea girls. Sophia Messenger praised Tryphena's work and declared that she should remain at Baconham until her daughter was old enough to study all Tryphena knew. "You need not think of going home," Sophia Messenger asserted, "Lucy and I cannot spare you possibly."[14]

The curriculum taught by Tryphena included arithmetic, geography, and grammar, and did not differ greatly from that offered by other tutors of the period. Although they never met, Amanda Worthington, a Mississippi planter's daughter and a contemporary of the Messenger and Billingslea girls, studied the basic rudiments of "quite a few subjects," including history, science, literature, religion, drawing, "besides reading, writing, and arithmetic" at a Washington County, Mississippi, plantation. Amanda and the other children attended classes for six hours per day Monday through Friday from January to July. Both Amanda and Lui studied the piano.[15]

Work as a plantation tutor was probably less strenuous and better paying than teaching in the public schools of Massachusetts or Connecticut. Moreover, in a study of one hundred tutors in plantation society during the nineteenth century, Elizabeth Brown Pryor claims that

---

13. TBH to ARH, November 11, 1852; January 9, 1856, April 5, 1856, MDAH.
14. TBH to ARH, November 11, 1852, MDAH; TBH to TTC, January 25, 1853, MDAH; U.S. 7th Census, 1850, Population, Warren County, Mississippi, NA.
15. TBH to TTC January 15, 1863, MDAH; Clifford C. Norse, "School Life of Amanda Worthington of Washington County, 1857–1862," *JMH* 34 (May 1972): 107–16.

having a tutor was a "symbol of prestige, indicating both a respect for high intellectual achievement and the attainment of a comfortable financial position." Planters ordinarily paid between $250 and $500 per year in addition to room and board.

Less than a year after she began the work, Tryphena sent $100 to Anna.[16] Although Tryphena was conscientious about helping her mother, on one occasion she jeopardized Anna's credit by not paying a debt in a timely fashion in 1856. The Pittsfield merchant, J. W. Davis, raised questions that cast doubt upon his willingness to further extend the family's credit. The anxiety created by the matter taught Tryphena "a good lesson" and she promised to "never do the like again." She settled the debt, but the apprehension persisted. Anna's financial condition and Tryphena's sense of obligation placed both women in an awkward position. Undoubtedly Tryphena loved and wanted to assist her mother and the children as much as possible, but to help them meant she either "neglected" herself or felt guilty about any apparent indulgence. Like many young women her age, Tryphena admired fashionable clothes, but she could not buy them easily if she bought necessities, such as wood and food, for her family.[17]

Although comfortable in the Messenger's household and fascinated by their wealth and social status, Tryphena remained anxious about Anna and the children. "A thousand thoughts of all things dear, Like Shadows o'er me sweep," she mused. Describing herself as "a stranger in a strange land," she often sat alone, thinking about her mother, sister, brothers, and childhood friends. In short, she was homesick.[18]

In 1855 Tryphena visited Pittsfield. Before returning to Mississippi, she located Le Roy in Rochester and "made him promise" to send five dollars to Anna by the first of November. He also agreed to do as much as possible, but "actions," she wrote "would be better than words." Le Roy, however, had greater financial responsibilities than Tryphena be-

---

16. TBH to ARH, October 15, 1855, December 7, 1855, MDAH; Elizabeth Brown Pryor, "An Anomalous Person: The Northern Tutor in Plantation Society, 1773-1860," *JSH* 47 (August 1981), 363. See also the Launcelot Minor Blackford Diary, SHC; D. D. Hall, "A Yankee Tutor in the Old South," *New England Quarterly* 33 (March 1960): 82–91; Robert C. McLean, "A Yankee Tutor in the Old South," *North Carolina Historical Review* 47 (Winter 1970): 51–80; James A. Padgett, ed., "A Yankee School Teacher in Louisiana, 1835–1837," *Louisiana Historical Quarterly* 20 (July 1937): 651–63.
17. TBH to ARH, February 18, 1856, MDAH.
18. TBH to ARH, October 15, 1855, TBH to TTC, January 25, 1853, MDAH.

cause of his travel with the railroad, which required him to board in several towns. Her circumstances were different. She received room and board in addition to a salary, which had grown to $300 per year by 1855.[19]

The visit to Massachusetts alleviated much of the young woman's loneliness, but seeing her mother and younger siblings in such financial difficulties merely deepened her apprehension about their well-being. She returned to Baconham and comforted herself with the knowledge that she could not remain in Pittsfield and aid them as much as she could from Mississippi, yet sending money home also created uneasiness. Never confident that it would not be stolen, lost, or delayed, Tryphena eagerly awaited an acknowledgment. The arrival of the mail was equally disturbing. She feared reading her mother's letters since they often told of illnesses, deaths, or the urgent need for more money.[20]

Tryphena experienced a "little fit of homesickness" in the spring of 1856. She had a hard time readjusting to her routine after going North the year before. Baconham was no longer as pleasant as before. The novelty and variety were gone. Besides, in a letter to Anna dated May 25, 1856, she complained that she had "become somewhat tired of teaching" and said that she was "very unhappy and undecided." Tryphena only hinted here at whatever bothered her and apologized for troubling Anna, who had her own "perplexities." Toward the end, the letter contained a glimmer of optimism. "Things seem smoother now," she added, "all will be right again I hope."[21]

In a June 1, 1856, letter Tryphena, without any forewarning, announced that she was to marry David Raymond Fox (1822–1893), a physician who practiced among the wealthy slaveholding sugar planters in Plaquemines Parish, Louisiana. During a month's visit at his family's plantation, Woodburne, the thirty-four-year-old physician frequented nearby Baconham. To buffer the shock of her sudden marriage, Tryphena made excuses for not telling her mother sooner. "He did not propose," and "I did not like to write uncertainties." To be sure, she did not know if he were "just flirting or in earnest." Tryphena told Anna

---

19. TBH to ARH, October 15, 1855, MDAH.
20. TBH to ARH, December 7, 1855, MDAH.
21. TBH to ARH, May 25, 1856, MDAH.

that she had not given her consent thoughtlessly. "I am much pleased with him and I knew him well previously, by reputation," she wrote. In a confident tone, she described the doctor as "intelligent, refined, of noble sentiments," and believed he had high moral values. Tryphena included other pertinent details in her letter. "He has a nice home of his own," along with "an extensive practice and consequently a large income." To dispel any misgiving, Tryphena wrote that everyone at Baconham thought she was doing "so well." Sophia Messenger delighted in her "good fortune." Well wishes aside, Tryphena later admitted that her marriage was a rather "wild move."[22]

The brevity of the Holder-Fox courtship raises the question of whether the marriage was based solely on Tryphena's desire to improve her social status and assist her impoverished mother. In her study of plantation mistresses, Catherine Clinton argues that "wealth was as great an influence on women's decisions to marry as it was on men's choices." After "marrying up," Tryphena wrote, "I am so glad that I am no longer dependent upon this one or that for food & shelter." She now committed herself to "constant attention and kindness" to greatly increase her husband's comforts and happiness and "to compensate for the happy change." It appears that she based this vow upon a calculated sense of obligation, rather than sentimental attachment. She wanted protection from "the hardships and trials of the world and its selfishness."[23]

The marriage held out the potential for affluence; however, Tryphena did not understand that her husband's income was linked directly to the successful production of sugar and the vigor of the slave workers, whose owners hired him annually. The weather could be as devastating to sugar planters as disease. Slaveowners had no control over the weather, but they could determine who attended to their chattel. The prolonged illness or death of slaves raised questions about the doctor's abilities and the feasibility of retaining him.[24]

---

22. TBH to ARH, June 1, 1856, November 18, 1856, MDAH.
23. Catherine Clinton, *The Plantation Mistress: Woman's World in the Old South* (New York: Pantheon Books, 1982), 60; Steven Mintz, *A Prison of Expectations: The Family in Victorian Culture* (New York: New York University Press, 1985), 103–46; TBHF to ARH, June 29, 1856, April 26, 1857, June 28, 1857, November 18, 1856, MDAH.
24. See Martha Carolyn Mitchell, "Health and the Medical Profession in the Lower South, 1845–1860," *JSH* 10 (November 1944): 424–46; David O. Whitten, "Medical

Immediately following their early morning wedding on June 3, 1856, Tryphena and David Fox left Baconham for their home in Louisiana. She made the adjustment to her new home along the Mississippi River, but she sorely missed "society" after living in Pittsfield and at Baconham, with its proximity to Vicksburg. Jesuit Bend, Plaquemines Parish, Louisiana, a tiny settlement along the west bank of the Mississippi River, paled by comparison with Pittsfield or Vicksburg. The 1850 population for the entire parish was 7,490. Of that number 4,779 were slaves. Sugar cane and rice plantations dotted the landscape. The requirements for cultivating cane and producing sugar differed greatly from what Tryphena had seen of Mississippi's cotton fields. Although cane was produced in Mississippi, in 1850 Louisiana produced 91.28 percent of the sugar in the United States whereas Mississippi produced only 7.24 percent of the crop.[25]

The differences in the natural environment were also sharp. Tryphena missed the amicable coolness of old Berkshire with the scenic Hoosic, Taghcanic, and Saddle mountains. Louisiana's malevolent weather was unsettling. Her new home was hot, damp, overrun with ants, and thick with mosquitoes. The intellectual stimulation of the academy and the consolation of churches were also missing. There were no schools and the nearest church was in New Orleans, approximately thirty-five miles away. Besides her correspondence, her only link to the world she had known was the *Pittsfield Sun*, which Anna arranged for her to receive.[26]

She dismissed neighbors, planters, and plantation manager alike if they were not "very intellectual or refined." The geographical isolation, coupled with this disdain for the less well educated, mired Tryphena in loneliness. She viewed the Guythes, the family of a local plantation manager, as "good hearted," but admitted that one did not "gain much by visiting them." To be sure, some of her social calling was to "keep on the right side" of neighbors because of the doctor's practice.[27]

Without family nearby and friends of her choice the new bride con-

Care of Slaves: Louisiana Sugar Region and South Carolina Rice District," *SoS* 16 (Summer 1977): 153–80.

25. U.S. 7th Census, 1850, Population, Plaquemines Parish, Louisiana, NA; U.S. 7th Census, 1850, Agriculture, NA.
26. U.S. 7th Census, 1850, Population, Plaquemines Parish, Louisiana, NA; Holland, *History of Western Massachusetts*, 561.
27. TBHF to ARH, June 24, 1860, March 3, 1858, January 4, 1857, MDAH.

centrated upon letter writing and household matters. Settling into the
new home, which they called Hygiene—possibly alluding to Raymond
Fox's practice as a medical doctor—proved exasperating, and southern
housekeeping tested Tryphena's domestic capabilities. Shopping for basic
necessities required trips to New Orleans over rough or muddy roads,
which took several hours of traveling time in each direction. The cooking
was not too much of a chore since slave women prepared most meals,
but Tryphena often taught them to make dishes "her way" after obtaining
recipes from her mother. She plunged into gardening and raising poultry, the pride of "Southern ladies," to add variety to the daily fare. Hired
laundresses or slaves did the washing and ironing. Since Tryphena did
not spin or weave she often sent back to Pittsfield for fabric to make
clothes for the family, white and black. The sewing, because of her frugal-
ity and the needs of the doctor, who had to "keep up a certain style,"
turned her into a human machine. Tryphena achieved degrees of success
as she directed domestic routines and was confronted with births, illnesses, deaths, and cantankerous servants.[28]

Dr. R——, as Tryphena referred to her husband, did not know the
full extent of his mother-in-law's financial status until several weeks after his marriage. He then promised to assist Anna as much as possible.
To help him, Tryphena devised numerous plans and schemes, including
selling her gold watch, having Anna open a boarding house in New
York, or even to "break [the family] up entirely" by boarding Emma
with a family in Pittsfield, sending George to live with Le Roy in New
York, and moving Anna to Louisiana. Parsimoniously she decided not
to buy ice during the summer of 1857 in order to help her family in Massachusetts. She kept expenses to a minimum by feeding the family,
white and black, vegetables and poultry grown at Hygiene. Her overall

---

28. TBHF to ARH, December 7, 1855, May 22, 1866; November 5, 1866; February 13,
1867; May 25, 1867, August 16, 1858; February 5, 1868; April 13, 1869, MDAH. See John
Q. Anderson, ed. "A Letter From a Yankee Bride in Ante-Bellum Louisiana," *LaH* 1
(Summer 1960): 245–50. The bulk of Tryphena's sewing was for practical use rather
than ornamental purposes. She relied upon her sister for tatting, which she added to
garments. For discussions of clothing see Gerilyn Tandberg, "Decoration and Deco-
rum: Accessories of Nineteenth-Century Louisiana Women," *SQ* 27 (Fall 1988): 9–31;
Susan Strasser, *Never Done: A History of American Housework* (New York: Pantheon
Books, 1982), 130–37; Anita Stampler, "One Woman's Work: Clothing the Family in
Nineteenth-Century Mississippi," *SQ* 27 (Fall 1988): 95–104.

objective was to assist Anna, and to furnish and beautify her home without placing the doctor in a financial bind.[29]

Despite these efforts, there were too many factors beyond her control. Notwithstanding the outward differences in their circumstances, she and Anna had much in common. Both were mired in a cycle of dependency. The mother was financially dependent upon a daughter who in turn relied upon her husband, a good provider and caring spouse, but one who was not wealthy. As Fox's livelihood depended upon planters whose financial fortunes were "tied closely to the unpredictable and uncontrollable forces of nature," intense heat, an early frost, or too much rain could be catastrophic. A crevasse or break in the levee along the Mississippi River could be equally ruinous. The growing season was not long enough in Louisiana for cane to ripen completely; therefore, planters delayed the harvest until the late fall, thus subjecting the crop to frost, which could ruin the entire harvest. Any of these factors could determine a planter's ability to satisfy all debts, and the doctor collected his annual fees accordingly.[30]

Anna Holder depended upon her children, yet she tried to maintain a sense of independence by working occasionally at a local hotel. The fact that her mother had to engage in menial work embarrassed Tryphena, who acknowledged the personal conflict with her mother's poverty and her own pride. Whatever help Tryphena gave was a stopgap measure; therefore, Anna's financial condition remained essentially unchanged. The most exasperating part for Tryphena was her inability to help aside from getting money from Dr. R——, who was also subjected to economic forces beyond his control.[31]

Fox, although a planter's son, did not have the means to invest in real or personal property. He owned a body servant, and subsequent to his

---

29. TBHF to ARH, November 18, 1856, June 8, 1857, February 19, 1858, September 20, 1858, MDAH.
30. TBHF to ARH, November 18, 1856, June 8, 1857, May 16, 1858, MDAH; Lewis Cecil Gray, *History of Agriculture in the Southern United States to 1860*, vol. 2 (Gloucester, Mass.: Peter Smith, 1958), 748; Paul W. Gates, *The Farmer's Age: Agriculture 1815–1860*, vol. 3 of *The Economic History of the United States* (New York: Holt, Rhinehart and Winston, 1960), 123–24; J. Carlyle Sitterson, *Sugar Country: The Cane Sugar Industry in the South, 1753–1950*, (Frankfort: University of Kentucky Press, 1953), 13–14, 18–21; Walter Prichard, "Routine on a Louisiana Sugar Plantation Under the Slavery Regime," *Mississippi Valley Historical Review* 14 (September 1927), 169–71.
31. See TBHF to ARH, August 28, 1859, August 20, 1860, MDAH.

marriage hired or purchased slaves to assist his wife with housekeeping chores. Without difficulty she assimilated the habits and ideals of slaveholders. Her marriage and their investments in the "peculiar institution" removed the tenuousness from the social status of a propertyless, unmarried woman. She blended in with the other northern-born slaveholders in Warren County, including the families of George Messenger, John A. Fox, his sister, Sophia, and brother Elisha.

Unlike Fanny Kemble, Anna Matilda King, Ella Gertrude Clanton Thomas, Mary Boykin Chesnut, and other slaveholders' wives, Tryphena never spoke out or wrote against slavery, nor was she an "abolitionist at heart." There was too much at stake. Rejection by her husband's family and friends or the loss of her financial security would have been disastrous for Tryphena. Her new way of life was tied into the slaveholding society in Mississippi and Louisiana.[32]

As a slaveholder Tryphena relished her new status, but it proved equally vexatious. Like many other slaveholding women and men, she failed to understand that material well-being did not placate slaves for their loss of freedom. When the doctor's waiting man ran away she felt a personal affront, and she showed no sympathy for the newly married Reuben wanting to be with Phillis, his partner in an abroad marriage. Tryphena did not believe the slave could be dissatisfied or that he acted alone.[33]

Susan, a slave whom Fox purchased in 1858, raised Tryphena's ire at every turn. Tryphena had fair warning about Susan's recalcitrant behavior, but the attractive sales price blurred her vision. Susan defied the mammy image, was given to falling ill, working at her own pace, and disobeying orders. She was "troublesome property" indeed for Tryphena. Unlike some women in slaveholding families, Tryphena showed

---

32. Burr, "A Woman Made to Suffer and Be Strong," 219–20; Sudie Duncan Sides, "Southern Women and Slavery," part 1, *History Today* 20 (January 1970): 54–60; Mary Boykin Chesnut, *A Diary from Dixie*, ed., Ben Ames Williams (Boston: Houghton Mifflin, 1950).

33. TBHF to ARH, August 12, 1856, MDAH; Elizabeth Fox-Genovese, *Within the Plantation Household: Black and White Women of the Old South* (Chapel Hill: University of North Carolina Press, 1988), 334. See Jo Anne Sellers Huber, "Southern Women and the Institution of Slavery," (M.A. thesis, Lamar University, 1980); Jane Turner Censer, *North Carolina Planters and Their Children, 1800–1860* (Baton Rouge: Louisiana State University Press, 1984), 135–49.

no special concern for the condition of slave women; consequently, there was no basis for sisterhood between the two women. The exact nature of this disaffection is open to question, though it was probably related as much to Tryphena's race and class as it was to her age. Susan appears older.[34]

Tryphena could not abide Susan, but her appreciation of children was too great to allow Susan's youngsters to suffer. Her ambivalence about whether or not slaves were persons or property was greater when dealing with children than with adults. Her concern about the illness and death of her slave children occasionally transcended race without focusing upon pecuniary matters.[35]

Infant mortality rates were high in antebellum America and communicable diseases are colorblind. Slaveowners and slaves lived with sickness and death. Planters' diaries and overseers' records teem with notations of illness and death. Fevers, intestinal worms, measles, whooping cough, and other maladies took their toll. After the death of a neighbor's child, the southern woman Mrs. A. C. Griffin lamented, "I hope she bears it with fortitude. . . . It is very seldom a family as large as hers can be raised."[36]

Tryphena, as the mother of ten children born between 1857 and 1878, also knew illness and death. Four of the children predeceased her, and she did not bear the loss of her infant son Edward Randolph (1860–1860) or young daughter Anna Rose (1861–1863) with calm resolution. In 1863 despair over Anna Rose's death moved her to write the following poem:

34. TBHF to ARH, December 27, 1857, December 16, 1860, MDAH; Burr, "A Woman Made to Suffer and Be Strong," 219; Frances Anne Kemble, *Journal of a Residence on a Georgian Plantation in 1838–1839,* John A. Scott, ed., (Athens: University of Georgia Press, 1984), 214–39. See Sudie Duncan Sides, "Southern Women and Slavery," part 1, *History Today* 20 (January 1970): 54–60; part 2 (February 1970): 124–30; Jo Anne Sellers Huber, "Southern Women and the Institution of Slavery"; Joan Reznen Gundersen, "The Double Bonds of Race and Sex: Black and White Women in a Colonial Virginia Parish," *JSH* 52 (August 1986): 351–72; Carol K. Bleser, "Southern Planter Wives and Slavery," David R. Chesnutt and Clyde N. Wilson, eds., *The Meaning of South Carolina History: Essays in Honor of George C. Rogers, Jr.* (Columbia: University of South Carolina Press, 1991), 104–20.
35. See J. Thomas Wren, "'A Two-Fold Character': The Slave as Person and Property in Virginia Court Cases, 1800–1860," *SoS* 24 (Winter 1985): 417–31; William Cohen, "Thomas Jefferson and the Problem of Slavery," *JAH* 56 (1969–1970): 503–22.
36. A. C. Griffin to Mrs. B. F. Richardson, August ? 1848, Caffery Family Papers, SHC. See Nancy Schrom Dye and Daniel Blake Smith, "Mother Love and Infant Death, 1750–1920," *JAH* 73 (September 1986): 329–353; Robert A. Margo and Richard H. Steckel, "A Dreadful Childhood: The Excess Mortality of American Slaves," *Social Science History* 10 (Winter 1986): 427–65; Everard Baker Green Diary, SHC.

For spirits round the Eternal Throne
How vain the tears we shed!
They are the living, they alone
Whom thus we call the dead.

Fold her, oh Father! in thine arms,
And let her henceforth be
A messenger of love between
Our human hearts and Thee.[37]

Tryphena's apprehension about the possible death of a child, or her own death in childbirth, surfaced with each pregnancy. The reasons for such trepidation were gynecological and psychological. Childbirth in antebellum America was frightening and dangerous regardless of the expectant mother's race or class. Much of Tryphena's anxiety hinged upon not having her mother or sister present. Tryphena, however, was not alone. Her sisters-in-law generally made the trip to Hygiene for the birth of her children. David Fox, husband and doctor, was also present.[38]

Tryphena's growing family and her desire to make a comfortable home claimed so much of her attention that she rarely made trips away from Hygiene. Because of his work, Dr. R—— was not free to make the rounds of a seasonal visitor and Tryphena did not travel without him, preferring instead to send any extra income to Anna. Consequently, the visits of friends and family assumed an added importance. In 1860, Tryphena began a massive renovation and refurbishing project at Hygiene in preparation for guests. Dr. R——'s idea was to treat them as well as they could afford and "not be too penurious." The coming of the Civil

---

37. TBHF to Anna Holder, February 1, 1860, March 17, 1860; Tryphena Blanche Holder Fox Diary Transcript (hereafter cited as TBHF Diary Transcript), April 2, 1863, MDAH.
38. TBHF to ARH, June 16, 1861, June 28, 1861, March 29, 1861, MDAH. See Natalie Shainess, "The Structure of the Mothering Encounter," *Journal of Nervous and Mental Disorders* 136 (February 1963): 146–61; Natalie Shainess, "The Psychologic Experience of Labor," *New York State Journal of Medicine* 63 (October 15, 1963): 2923–32; Catherine M. Scholten, " 'On the Importance of the Obstetrick Art': Changing Customs of Childbirth in America, 1760 to 1825," *William and Mary Quarterly* 34 (July 1977): 426–45; J. Jill Suitor, "Husbands' Participation in Childbirth: A Nineteenth-Century Phenomenon," *Journal of Family History* 6 (Fall 1981): 278–93; Judith Walzer Leavitt, *Brought to Bed: Childbearing in America, 1750 to 1950* (New York: Oxford University Press, 1986), 36–40, 58; Clinton, *The Plantation Mistress*, 151–54.

War received less attention in Tryphena's letters than her arrangements for house guests.[39]

After the 1860 presidential election, Tryphena began to make occasional comments about the threatening sectional crisis. As early as her marriage in 1856, she had been critical of northern newspapers, especially of the *Berkshire Eagle,* and of northern abolitionists. After the war began and the South's decisive tactical victory at Manassas on July 21, 1861, she voiced the strong opinion that "Southerners can *never* be conquered; they may all be killed, but conquered, never." Her remark reflected both her allegiance to the South and to the Confederate belief that "one Southerner could whip ten Yankees."[40]

Dr. R— moved his family to Woodburne Plantation in Mississippi near Vicksburg immediately before the fall of New Orleans on April 25, 1862. While there, Tryphena saw inflation erode her buying power. She made tallow candles for the first time in her life. Conditions there further deteriorated, and her correspondence ended abruptly, along with her ability to send money back to Massachusetts. By March 1863 her bill of fare consisted mainly of "hominy & ham or pork gravy & cornbread with molasses." The war threatened her existence. She buried one child and she prepared for the birth of another—George Edward Randolph (1863–1939)—with the bombardment of Vicksburg in the background.[41]

Tryphena's abhorrence of the Union grew as she saw Northern soldiers "doing much harm through the country—burning dwellings & outhouses, freeing negroes, stealing stock & provisions, & laying everything waste." They ravaged her husband's family home, Woodburne. Among James Fox's losses were fourteen horses and mules, one hundred hogs, one hundred sheep, sixty-five cattle, and the entire poultry lot. The soldiers also took fodder, corn, and molasses, in addition to thirteen bales of cotton and miles of fencing. Union victory at Vicks-

---

39. TBHF to ARH, October 28, 1860, MDAH; Joan E. Cashin, "The Structure of Antebellum Planter Families: 'The Ties that Bound us Was Strong,'" *JSH* 56 (February 1990): 59–60.

40. TBHF to ARH, August 8, 1861. See James M. McPherson, *Ordeal by Fire: The Civil War and Reconstruction* (New York: Alfred A. Knopf, 1982), 210.

41. TBHF to ARH, December 27, 1861, MDAH; TBHF Diary Transcript, December 14, 1862, March 9, 1863, March 24, 1863, April 22, 1863, MDAH. For a discussion on candle making see Mary T. Dyer Diary, Alderman Library, University of Virginia, Charlottesville, Virginia; Clinton, *The Plantation Mistress,* 24.

burg nearly silenced Tryphena's pen. She wrote: "July 4th, 1863—
Memorable for—*The Fall of Vicksburg*."[42]

The war exacted much from Anna and Tryphena, for its divisive nature set families against families. The older woman endured "unkind remarks" and had her feelings "cruely hurt" regularly by townspeople
who had "such a bitter feeling against the south." She had a Confederate daughter and a Yankee son. Dr. Fox joined the Confederacy after
the fall of Vicksburg as a surgeon and medical examiner in northern
Mississippi. Le Roy enlisted in the U.S. Navy on February 21, 1863, and
served as a fire man, or engineer, aboard the U.S.S. *Sassacus*.[43]

At the war's end, Tryphena did not easily accept the results. The Confederacy would be "counted as part of the Old Union," Tryphena
wrote. In her opinion that fate, readmission to the Union, was worse
than defeat for the Confederacy. The South was "not subdued, only
overpowered," she insisted. Although bitter, Tryphena saw a "gleam
through all the darkness," the resumption of free and frequent correspondence with Anna. The war was a leveling agent between the two
women and left little basis for an unequal comparison of their lives.
There were losses and damages that could not be recovered or repaired.
Both women suffered deprivation and death. Le Roy died December
27, 1864, a little more than a year after Anna Rose Fox.[44]

Returning to Jesuit Bend after the cease-fire, Tryphena worked to restore Hygiene to its former comfortable condition, only to have it razed
in 1866. In the long run, however, neither the fire nor the war destroyed
her mettle. She talked of rebuilding her home in the same letter chron-
icling its ruin—deliberately painting optimistic scenes. Instead

---

42. TBHF Diary Transcript, May 14, 1863, MDAH; TBHF to ARH, July 3, 1863,
    MDAH; McPherson, *Ordeal by Fire*, 332–33. James A. Fox, who opposed secession,
    received compensation for his losses that mounted to nearly $10,000. See "Claim of
    James A. Fox," no. 10,663, Southern Claims Commission, NA.
43. ARH to TBHF, July 18, 1863, MDAH; "Enlistment Rendezvous," Rendezvous
    Records, vol. 24 (1863), 94, NA; Muster Roll of the U.S.S. *Sassacus*, 1863–1865, U.S.S.
    Satellite, 1863, U.S.S. *Saugus*, 1864–1865, U.S.S. *Keokuk*, 1863; U.S.S. *Keystone State*,
    1861–1865, U.S.S. *Kenwood*, 1863–1865, NA.
44. TBHF to ARH, June 12, 1865, MDAH; TBHF Diary Transcript, May 9, 1865,
    MDAH. See Nancy T. Kondert, "The Romance and Reality of Defeat: Southern
    Women in 1865," *JMH* 35 (May 1973): 141–52; Burr, "A Woman Made to Suffer and Be
    Strong," 222.

of lamenting about the losses, she looked beyond the shadows and saw the stable, kitchen, and storehouse undamaged.[45]

During Reconstruction Tryphena Fox began anew. Dr. R—— continued his practice among ex-slaveholders while she filled her days with housekeeping chores and child care, aided by newly freed men and women who did not meet her expectations any more than had slave men and women. When they proved unsatisfactory, Tryphena hired white servants, preferring either Irish or Dutch. At other times she toyed with hiring Chinese immigrants. Regardless of their races, servants came and went with rapidity. She understood the basic nature of the problem and longed to live in a place where she could either "control or command labor," or where it was "the fashion for ladies to do their own work."[46]

With the passage of time, the relationship between the Holder siblings Emma and George changed as they all matured. It appears that Tryphena erased Le Roy from her consciousness. She did not mention his name in her correspondence after July 26, 1864. Perhaps this was the result of deep-seated feelings about Le Roy not fulfilling his obligations to the family, or perhaps it stemmed as much from Tryphena's hatred of all things Union. In any case, one brother filled the shoes of the other. George was different from Le Roy. He remained in Pittsfield with their widowed mother and unmarried sister. He was attentive to them and solicitous to Tryphena, readily filling her shopping orders for clothing and other items not readily available in Louisiana. Of greater importance, George relieved her uneasiness about Anna and Emma.[47]

After Emma obtained a job at the Pontoosuc woolen mill, Tryphena gradually accepted the fact that her younger sister was no longer a school girl and had no choice but to enter the labor force. Always class

---

45. TBHF to ARH, February [17], 1866, February 20, 1866, MDAH.
46. TBHF to ARH, August 7, 1866, February 13, 1867, October 2, 1868, October 9, 1868, August 6, 1869, MDAH; Jacqueline Jones, *Labor of Love, Labor of Sorrow: Black Women, Work, and the Family, from Slavery to the Present* (New York: Vintage Books, 1985), 53, 68–72. See Daniel E. Sutherland, "The Servant Problem: An Index of Antebellum Americanism," *SoS* 18 (Winter 1980): 488–503; Daniel E. Sutherland, "A Special Kind of Problem: The Response of Household Slaves and Their Masters to Freedom," *SoS* 20 (Summer 1981), 161–63, 165; "Dr. [Booker T.] Washington on the Servant Problem," *SW* 34 (May 1905): 200–201; "The Servant Question," *SW* 40 (July 1911): 394–95; Virginia Church, "Solving the Problem," *SW* 40 (July 1911): 402–9.
47. TBHF to George Holder, August 22, 1865, MDAH.

conscious, she cared no more for Emma "working out" than she did for their mother having to do the same. One advantage of Emma's job, from Tryphena's perspective, was its proximity to Pittsfield; she could help George care for their mother in her declining years. Tryphena felt pains of daughterly guilt in the early postwar years because she was not in Pittsfield and could offer her family no permanent solution for overcoming their poverty. Things did change, however. George became the head of the Holder family and Emma was by his side. Perhaps it is coincidental, but letters to Pittsfield tapered off as her sister and brother accepted a greater share of the financial responsibility for Anna.[48]

In the postwar years Tryphena focused more of her attention upon her own family. She recognized that childhood and adolescence were special times in the growth and development of youngsters. Her children experienced the joys of growing up in the rural Louisiana South. They filled their leisure hours in comfortable surroundings with a variety of pets, ranging from cats and dogs to ducks and rabbits, with toys and games, such as back-gammon and euchre, and with books and music. The children frolicked in the bath house at the river's edge and occasionally traveled into New Orleans for day trips. They also studied rudimentary lessons under their mother's direction.[49]

Aside from her children, Tryphena was also devoted to her husband. Dr. R——, as Tryphena portrayed him to Anna, was affectionate, polite, and tried to make her happy. He did not commit marital infidelity, abuse alcohol, or stay away from home for excessively lengthy periods.

---

48. TBHF to ARH, October 3, 1866, MDAH. Visits from Emma and George in the 1870s may account for the paucity of letters in the 1870s. Additionally, Tryphena and her husband traveled to Pittsfield in 1877.
49. See Daniel T. Rogers, "Socializing Middle-Class Children: Institutions, Fables, and Work Values in Nineteenth-Century America," *JSoH* 13 (Spring 1980): 354–67; Bernard Mergen, *Play and Playthings: A Reference Guide* (Westport, Conn.: Greenwood Press, 1982), 22; Blackford Diary, April 12–20, 1848, March 13–14, 1849, June 7, 1849, SHC; D. D. Bruce, Jr. "Play, Work and Ethics in the Old South," *Southern Folklore Quarterly* 41 (1977), 37–38; Melvin G. Herndon, "The Unemancipated Antebellum Youth," *SoS* 23 (Summer 1984): 145–54; Bruce Bellingham, "The History of Childhood Since the 'Invention of Childhood': Some Issues in the Eighties," *Journal of Family History* 13, no. 2 (1988): 347–58; Ross W. Beales, Jr, "In Search of the Historical Child: Miniature Adulthood and Youth in Colonial New England," *American Quarterly* 27 (October 1975): 379–98; Joseph F. Kett, "Adolescence and Youth in Nineteenth-Century America," in Theodore K. Rabb and Robert I. Rotberg, eds., *The Family in History: Interdisciplinary Essays* (New York: Harper , 1972), 95–110; Vivian C. Fox, "Is Adolescence a Phenomenon of Modern Times?" *Journal of Psychohistory* 5 (Fall 1977): 271–90.

She praised the doctor as "a husband, in every sense of the word." Tryphena, however, portrayed herself as the stabilizing factor in their marriage. "It is I who keep *him* up though you may think me boasting to say it." If Dr. R—— brooded, she cheered and encouraged him to look on the lighter side. Whether it was losing a part of his medical practice in 1858 or losing his fortune for a third time in 1873, she tried to remain optimistic. "I bear it resignedly though I feel it is *hard*," she explained.[50]

To be sure, Tryphena ostensibly endured trials for her husband or children's sake. There were private moments of depression, especially after the death of George Randolph in 1860 and the loss of her home in 1866. At times she was extremely restless, unhappy, and ill tempered. There were other times, if alone, when her spirits were low and she was "tempted to have a good cry," but she was too reserved to yield to her own feelings. She cried only if "all traces of the *storm*" were gone before the doctor returned. This raises questions about the true source of her unhappiness.[51]

Subtleties in her letters and diary make readers aware of a pervasive enigma. For example, there are hints about some tension between Tryphena and her former employer, George Messenger, but it is never explained. Following an afternoon visit to Baconham in 1861, Tryphena wrote: "It was perhaps the thought that I should never see him again which induced me to go—deeming it best that the *past* be forgotten." It is clear from her letter that Messenger was ill, but the reference to the *past* is not elaborated upon.[52]

Nearly five years passed and brought many changes in both the Messenger and Fox households. After his wife died in 1864, George Messenger married Emily Fox and became Tryphena's brother-in-law. During a brief December 1865 visit to Hygiene, Messenger, who was already ill, grew progressively worse. He returned to Baconham accompanied by Dr. Fox. During her husband's absence Tryphena turned to her diary to write about George Messenger: "Last Friday Rev. Mr. Goodrich came from town and baptised him—was it not strange that it should have happened here beneath my roof? He spoke of both marry-

---

50. TBHF to ARH, December 22, 1865, January 17, 1858, December 18, 1873, MDAH
51. TBHF to ARH, June 24, 1860, June 12, 1866, MDAH.
52. TBHF to ARH, January 22, 1861, MDAH. Emphases in the original.

ing into the same family—of leniency on my part—of his foolishness and how I did what I thought was right— Should he die while Dr —— is gone, I shall tell Dr—— all on his return, if not, I will tell D—— when we shall hear of his death—it will make me a happier and better woman when my husband knows all." Messenger, whose parting words to Tryphena were "Farewell, Sister," died in February 1866. We do not know if Tryphena ever divulged her secret to her husband, or if it in any way influenced her hasty marriage. The extant sources do not yield the answers, but they show that Tryphena forged ahead with the same philosophy that carried her through more than a quarter of a century. "It is never good for us to look on the dark side," she wrote, "Every cloud has its silver lining & though we cannot always see it . . . we must remember it is there."[53]

53. TBHF Diary Transcript, December 11, 1865, MDAH; TBHF to ARH, July 14, 1856, December 13, 1865, December 22, 1865, MDAH.

PART I

Before the War
1856–1860

Read this first[1]

FRIDAY JUNE 6TH 1856. ST. CHARLES HOTEL. N. O.

At last Dear Mother, I have a little time to devote to you. You have doubtless received my last informing you of my intentions. I was married Tuesday morning by the Rev. Mr Fox—now father.[2] Can you see the ceremony performed, in imagination if I give you a slight sketch of the scene. It was as bright and beautiful morning as ever shown upon a bridal pair; the sun had but just peeped above the horizon and threw now and then one of his brightest rays through the dense shade of the China[3] upon the gallery, making golden streaks upon the silvery hair & white robe of the aged pastor, who stood there with numerous others to solemnize and witness the marriage. A door on his right opens and the groom and bridesmaid followed by the bridal pair walk out and form a semi-circle in front of the clergyman. He commences the solemn ritual of the Episcopal church for Matrimony and all is so hushed one might hear a sigh. You know how the bride looks as she stands repeating the vow, which binds her for life to another, but of the bride groom I must tell you. He is just six feet tall, straight and slim, with a finely proportioned form, small feet & hands. He has a high white forehead, a thick suit of dark brown hair, very dark hazel eyes, regular features and a heavy goatee. His complexion is sunburnt from frequent exposure. His figure is commanding, yet not stiff and he has an air of refinement which is very prepossessing, showing him to be much accustomed to good society. So much for *my* husband and *your* son-in-law. The ceremony over, the bride receives the congratulations of his friends; a warm kiss and welcome "Dear Daughter," from the old gentleman, and a series of new titles—as Dear Sister, Dear Niece, & Dear Cousin from the others. The breakfast-table was spread and taking for form's sake a cup of coffee with the company, and bidding good-bye to all—mistress, pupils, & servants, T——left Baconham where she had spent many happy hours, and some unhappy ones, especially since her return from the North; *his* visit being the almost only pleasant days for

1. Two letters were included in the same envelope; Tryphena included this note to establish sequence.
2. Tryphena Blanche Holder and David Raymond Fox married June 3, 1856, at Baconham Plantation, Warren County, Mississippi.
3. It appears that Tryphena dropped a word here. Perhaps she refers to a Chinaberry tree.

memory to fall back upon. There were present, Uncle Elisha Fox[4] his wife and a sister of hers, Miss Wardlow, Aunt Randolph—a sister of Father Fox's—a widow lady who lives with Aunt Sophia Fox of whom I have written, Emily, Fanny, Eliza, & James & Bob,[5] half sisters and brothers of the Dr's, and a Dr Wilkinson from his neighborhood on the coast whom he met in Vicksburg, the day before & invited out. You will see from what I shall write you that all the Dr's acquaintance are of the 'hon.'— Mr Messenger was not present; he had been gone to Deer Creek[6] some days and was not expected home for some time and the Dr. did not seem disposed to wait; it will probably surprise him as coming off so soon. Mrs M——Mrs Warren,[7] Lui and Laura made up the number. Mr Daniel Cameron was invited but did not start soon enough, so that we met him as we were going to the Depot. Mrs M——sent us in her carriage   We stopped at father's and there I was greeted on every side, by the servants who came to congratulate their new mistress and tell her how glad they were that Master Raymond has got her & she must make him a good wife— he is a great favorite among them. At Bovina, I met several acquaintances and it sounded so odd, to be addressed as Mrs Fox and every one seemed so surprised to find that I was such for we had kept it as secret as possible on purpose.

At the Depot in Vicksburg we were met by Aunt *Soph* (as she likes to have every one call her, who greeted me very cordially as her niece, Miss Lu Fox from Yazoo & a Mr Egleson[8]—all relations. Aunt Soph, had ordered her carriage for us, so Father, Dr—— & I rode up to see Mrs McGruder—a sister of the late Mrs Fox,[9] a very pleasant lady indeed, whom I had met quite often before.

From there, we rode to Major Roach's whose wife[10] is a niece of Aunt Soph's; she came out and calling me Dear Cousin, told me she fell

4. Elisha Fox, a cotton planter in Warren County, Mississippi, and younger brother of James A. Fox.
5. Emily Fox (b. 1834), Fanny Fox (1838–1856), Eliza Fox (b. 1841), James Fox (b. 1840) and Robert Fox (b. 1845).
6. Deer Creek, a second plantation owned by George Messenger, some sixty miles north of Baconham.
7. The mother of Sophia Messenger.
8. O. T. Eggleston, a resident of Vicksburg, Mississippi.
9. The third wife of James A. Fox, Catherine, died in mid-March, 1854. See TBH to ARH, March 9, 1854, MDAH.
10. Mahala P. H. Roach, wife of James Roach, a Vicksburg banker.

in love with me the first time we met & was much pleased with the match — Of course Mother, my head was nearly turned at all these flatteries & would have been quite, had I not remembered, it was my wedding-day. As we left there to go to the boat, Aunt Soph says "now Raymond, take good care of *her*, for she is the most precious charge you can have"—and bade me Good Bye, so kindly that I could hardly keep from tears. When she takes a lilking to any one she cannot do too much for them and she is very wealthy & has no children, and I am glad she is not prejudiced against me. Emily told me, that Aunt Soph. always liked me, but as I lived at Mrs M——s and they were not friendly she could not notice me. We were accompanied to the boat by quite a gay party of young people, where we had champagne & cake, and my health was drunk until I feared I should have but little left, for excitement was all that had kept me up, for the two weeks previous. About two they left us — all but father Fox. I was sorry to part with Fanny, she is such a dear good girl and is Raymond's favorite sister. She & Emily came & sewed for me all day Monday & she stayed with me that night, helping me pack, for I was very much hurried. I disliked to have it known on board the boat that I was a bride, because I thought I should be an object of curiosity and perhaps, remarks, but I got along very well and was shown every attention. Wednesday, as the boat stopped at Natchez all day, Raymond hired a hack and we rode out to Washington six miles from Natchez, to visit his sister Mrs Lucy Newman. She also greeted me very cordially and sent for Mrs Monette & her daughter — aunt & cousin by marriage to come & spend the day with us.

□ □ □

My Dear Mother,   HOME." JUNE 29 "56.

Three weeks have rolled rapidly and pleasantly away since last I wrote. The only thing that could bring a shade to my happiness was the thought of you — for until last night, it was a long time since I have heard from you and I was becoming extremely anxious about you. But yesterday evening I went to ride to the P. O. four miles distant with Dr Raymond, and found there a letter from you enclosed in one from Mrs M—— and how my heart throbbed to see the familiar handwriting, but

---

11. "Home" or "Hygiene" was now at Jesuit Bend, Plaquemines Parish, Louisiana.

it was directed to Miss Tryphena Holder, and perhaps it was with a sigh (though not of regret) that I thought it was probably the last that I should ever receive directed to the good old name. I also had one jointly with Raymond from father Fox, and a good affectionate one it is too, but I must notice yours first.

You probably little thought when you penned that of the great change in my condition, and I half wished I could be behind the curtain and see you, when you read the one which tells you of my intentions, for I know it will be very sudden to you. I wish to see whether a look of regret and sorrow sweeps across your features or a smile lights your countenance and you rejoice that your daughter has found a protector, who will shield her with his love and a haven which promises fair to be a "home" when she may rest secure from the hardships and trials of the world and its selfishness.

I am glad to hear that Mr Root is friendly to you; I hope he will continue so. It seems that you have not moved;[12] it is a matter of some surprise to me, but I suppose you will tell me in your next. I hope *now*, our correspondence will be kept up on the old plan—letters free and frequent even if they are not long, for by my new position I have gained several new correspondences, who will expect to hear from me occasionally, particularly father; I will just quote a few lines from his letter and you will see that I have reason to love him and wish to retain his regard. "Dear Raymond & Dear Blanche"—"A letter from Raymond reached me a day or two since, written the day after you arrived at home and it informed me that Dear Blanche had written to me but *that* letter has not yet come to hand" (I sent it in the next mail and I would copy for you what I wrote to him, Mother, if I had time) A letter from Seguin informs us that "Blanche seems happy and that Raymond is perfectly delighted" which very important information was received by me with much satisfaction and I most ardently hope that so pleasant and agreeable a beginning may continue unalloyed to the end. Young people just married are usually very attentive and very civil and obliging to each other; continue the same course of conduct and the happiness of

---

12. Anna Holder had toyed with the idea of moving to Rochester, New York, to open a boarding house to support herself and her family. See TBHF to ARH, October 15, 1855, MDAH.

your married life will continue undiminished. But remember that the first unkind word spoken by either to the other, will cause a breach that can never be perfectly repaired. In nothing that happens in the world is it more necessary to strictly observe the maxim "Obsta principiis!". As you had not much time to *court* before marriage, my advice is, that you court each other after marriage and continue to do so, to your lives end." Then after some family matters, he signs himself—"with much love & good wishes, Your Father, Jas. A. Fox."— He is going North as delegate from Miss. to the Episcopal convention at Phil—and will probably visit you. You will like him I think, I need not say I hope you will try to make his visit a pleasant one, and such as will leave good impression for him to bring back into the large family circle here, for you know too much of good society and how to make persons at home, to need such a wish on my part. I shall be proud to have him as my father-in-law visit you—as my mother.

LATER

Since writing the above I have been quite ill, with an attack of bilious fever. I am not able to sit up yet, but am recovering fast under the Dr's prompt treatment and kindness of nursing and Mary's (the new servant)[13] attentive care. I was imprudent in doing too much about the house myself not being accustomed to housework for some times and unwilling to wait for Mary's arrival from N. O which I feared would be two or three weeks yet & the house wanted fixing so badly as far as dust and smoke & dirty windows was concerned. And I was having callers every few days and it annoyed me to see things look so, and I went to work myself & this is the result.

MONDAY JULY 7TH

I am quite well this morning, so that I am able to go about the house, and such confusions, as I find things in, you can hardly imagine, for my sickness has not been all. The negro girl Mary who came last Sunday waited upon me & did considerable housework until Thursday when she began to complain. Friday morning while the Doctor was gone she was taken with a violent cramp in her stomach, which lasted all day in spite of all his efforts on his return to lessen it. That night there was no

---

13. A slave hired out to Dr. Fox by the owner, Mr. Salvant, a Plaquemines Parish sugar planter.

sleep for any one and the next morning he thought she would die, and sent for her master; he came and said if she was well enough or better by night, he would take her away for there was no one here to wait upon her and she needed constant attention. During the evening, after cupping her & giving her powerful medicines, she became better and a waggon was brought & she was lifted into it upon her bed & taken home—four miles distant. she is so much prostrated that it will take her a long time to recover her former strength. That is the way with all diseases in this country, they must be cured quickly or they kill quickly, and if one recovers from a short attack, they find it has been so severe as to leave but little strength. A three days fever here prostrates a person as much as a three weeks fever at the North. But Mary's sickness, coming just at that time, was not the only trouble, for Wednesday Henry—the Doctor's waiting man—came in sick with a fever, thus leaving Phillis all the work and waiting upon, to do. She is Seguin's negro and is only to stay until he begins to keep house in Algiers opposite N. O. and we expect they will send for her every-day, but I hope Henry will be well by to-morrow; he is taking quinine to-day and has no fever. Poor fellow! I pity him, for I know what bitter stuff it is. I think I shall be very well after this—as it is my acclimating sickness—if I am careful, but you do not know what a scare-crow I am—all bones and *big ones* at that, and in danger of being bald—a pretty looking bride! *you* think. But I do not care, so long as I am not *loved* for appearance, if I were that would all be gone and I should not have had the kindness of attentions.—the most watchful care— But let me tell you a little of my house affairs— The orange trees are growing finely, one has eight upon it, about the size of a large peach. I have ten little ducks, all healthy and growing fast and I love to watch them when Phillis feeds them. Southern ladies in the country take great pride in raising poultry, and I am going to see if I cannot have a nice variety for my table next winter. There are eight old hens, who are laying well now, so that I have plenty of eggs for the Doctor buys one or two extra dozen every week. But we have no cow and it is quite inconvenient to cook without milk, or send to the nearest neighbor every time I wish for any, and often when I send to the plantation above—about three quarters of mile—at noon, the cows are not milked; the gentlemen who own it do not reside upon it, but leave it to the care of an overseer and he is intoxicated half his time, so that the negroes do about as they please. They have holiday on Saturday and the Dr. hires one or two of the men to come and clean the yard, but they have not done much at it yet. Negroes are so slow that they put me out of patience, not doing in all day what a good white man would do in an hour. The front part of the yard is in very good order now; there are no flowers in it, but it is covered with grass which is even and free from weeds and looks very pretty; the back part is filled with pieces of lumber, brick, weeds and rubbish of all kinds; you know how a place looks after building. I am waiting for Henry to get well, and then I am going to have him lay some plank walks from the house to the kitchen, which is about twenty yards to the west, and from the house to the store-room, about thirty yards to the south. In this country all provisions are kept under lock and key and one of the principal duties of a southern lady's housekeeping is to carry the key and give out the proper quantities of groceries for each meal, otherwise the cook would waste twice as much as was needed and pilfer as much more.[14] So I have to go to the store-house with Henry or Phillis twice a day and sometimes get my feet wet, but the brick store-room underneath the house will soon be done, and then I shall only have to go downstairs. I like housekeeping and shall be delighted when the back part of the house is finished and I can arrange things to suit me. The front rooms look very well and if Mary had not been taken sick I should have had every-thing in order directly. Now everything will have to remain in 'status quo' for Dr Raymond says I shall not do another thing in the way of housework, so how comfortable do you suppose I shall feel to sit and sew or read and see so many things around me out of place? I am trying to make out to you I am a model of neatness! I forgot how well you knew me—

The sun has been very oppressive for the last few days, and we have had frequent thunder-showers too. This morning the sun shines very warm but there is a good breeze in fact it blew upon me so strong I was obliged to shut the window blind. The river is quite low now and still falling. I walk out on the levee evenings with Raymond and it would be *very* pleasant did not the mosquitoes annoy us so much. He has two

---

14. See Alex Lichtenstein, " 'That Disposition to Theft, With Which They Have Been Branded': Moral Economy, Slave Management, and the Law," *JSoH* 21 (Spring 1988): 413–40.

good boats, the river has left one quite high up, on the bank, the other is yet in the water. Tow boats or steamers or sails are passing every hour up or down the river, and carriages or horse back rides in the road so that it is almost like living upon a street. The tow boats come so near, that I can see the sailors among the masts of the vessels and almost distinguish their countenances. Of course the sight of a vessel is a great novelty to me and I love to have the Dr. tell me the names of the different parts, as they pass.

The neighbors what few there are, (for we do not associate at all with the Creoles) are very kind to me. Mrs Stackhouse, whose husband is a rich sugar-planter about three mile below, called upon me last Saturday and Thursday morning sent up a negro-girl with a large waiter full of ripe peaches and figs. Mrs Pickens who left for the North with her husband, last Tuesday, sent me a great quantities of vegetable such as ochre, eggplant, squashes, &c, which were very acceptable, for there is but little in our garden this year— Henry neglected it while the Dr. was gone, and he laughs and says his wife cost him his garden. I have found the right side of Mr Martin too, the overseer above here, and when he is sober, sends me vegetables and a variety of things so that I am selfish enough to wish him *to keep sober*. Mrs Urquefort,[15] before she left, gave the Dr. six large bottles of orange syrup, to drink with water, and a jar of orange preserves. The Dr. is gone every Monday and Tuesday morning from seven to eleven or twelve, then Wednesday he is at home unless called for extra visits. Thursday and Friday morning he is again absent and Friday evening he goes to Mr Stackhouse's, I generally ride there with him, sitting in the buggy while he visits the hospital—for all these large plantations have one, with regular nurses. Saturday morning he is generally at home, in the afternoon at twilight we ride to the P. O. four miles away. Last Saturday I was not well enough to go, so he went alone and brought me two letters—one from father Fox—all to myself and one from Fannie, and one from Lucy—near Natchez to both of us. Next week I hope to get one from you. Father Fox writes me that he starts for the North next Monday; I have invited him to visit you. But

---

15. Possibly Alisa, wife of the sugar planter Robert Urquhart, who appears in the U.S. 7th Census, 1850 Population, Plaquemines Parish, Louisiana, NA. It is possible that Tryphena misspelled the name.

here comes Phillis for orders and my paper is almost used up so I must close. If Mr Davis speaks about the remainder of that bill, tell him it will be there soon—the letter has been written and I am waiting for a chance to change the five gold pieces into a bill. If no other opportunity Raymond goes to town soon and will fix it for me, so he must not think I have forgotten it. Tell Emma & Georgy I send them a kiss and much love—also much to yourself, from both of us. Compliments *to any, who inquire—Dont show this to any one it is all for you.* Good Bye. and believe me always Your affectionate daughter

T. B. Fox.

Raymond calls [me] Blanche entirely, he does not like the other name and the negroes call me "Miss Blanche" too.

□ □ □

Dear Mother,   HYGIENIA JULY 14TH [1856]

Your fresh letter to Mrs D. Raymond Fox has been received and perused by both son and daughter, also the one previous. We read it coming home from the P. O. and it afforded much for conversation and *thought.* Mother you say that you feel my husband does not like you; you do him injustice. could you see the care-worn, thoughtful expression to his countenance all the evening after reading yours and about your affairs, and hear his inquiries about them and his plans, you would feel that you have indeed a son who took an interest in your welfare and would assist you immediately were it in his power. Could he do so without too much sacrifice of his practice, which some other Dr might step in and take from him while absent, we would visit you and he would attend to your affairs. If it had not weighed upon his mind, he would have read his papers and journals during the evening & retired as usual, but he was talking about you till very late and told me he slept but little & the next morning resumed the same conversation. He says that if you will see Father Fox—if he visits you—about your affairs, he can probably show you some way to better them. Of course you can do as you think best about that—no one of the family except Raymond knows any thing about them. Did you not see his name at the end of my letter. He remarked to me that he did not feel at liberty to write to you, as I do to his father because he was not acquainted but hopes to be, and I was, with his father. He subscribed for the N. O Delta and said as he brought me the receipt, "now we will read it and then send it to Mother," and I send you a pamphlet, in which is a piece written by him. He did not wish to send it to you on that account, but because it would tell you something of the place he has brought me to. Now, after this, do not think such a thing as that, for it makes us both feel bad. We shall come to see you as soon as practical [. . .]. I could leave very easily and he tells me that if I wish, I may go next summer whether he can or not, but I do not think I should be willing to leave without him or enjoy my visit, so you must not expect me very much, unless *both* can come. I told him, I did n't believe you would care to see me unless he were along and so he says well we will wait and go together unless you get so homesick and tired of me that you can not stay. I know I have settled far from you but, I feel that had you been with me at the time he was in Warren,[16] you would have advised me by all means to accept him and I used to say to myself, how foolish Mother would call me if I should refuse so good an offer for I shall not probably have another such. You say, you hope I will make a good wife. If wishes and resolutions so to do and a good husband make a good wife then I have fair prospects of being such. I fear I am sometimes too enthusiastic and this happiness will not last, for I remember how many married couples I have seen, happy and devoted at first, but gradually becoming distant toward one another and finally being miserable in one another's society. I have no other grounds than these for such fears, yet I have my faults like all others and they may govern me, instead of I, them. But I did not give my consent to this without mediation and reason, and my marriage vows were not lightly pronounced with the mere moving of the lips. I never felt more solemn than as I stood and promised to love, obey, serve, honour; and keep in sickness, and in health, one who hath offered me heart and home, on a short acquaintance. I know that I have been a good wife so far, but that is only six weeks to-morrow, and the earnest desire is to be one through life. Our tastes are very similar, our education equal as far as a man's and woman's can be, when the former has a profession to which he has devoted twelve years, and both willing to give up to the other. He tries to gratify my every wish and make me happy; he is affectionate and as polite to me now as the day we were married. Considering all these things,

---

16. Warren County, Mississippi.

does it not seem Mother, as though we might get along well together? There must sometimes be clouds, but it does not seem best to make them when all is sunshine. Poor little Georgy! Tell him I love him very much yet and he must be a good boy, and someday he will see that he has not lost his sister. I am glad to hear that Emma's health is better; tell her I send her my love and a kiss and want her to learn very fast, so that she can write to me. Now a word about our affairs. Do you think the debts, aside from the mortgage, are over a thousand dollars; or can you tell the exact amount brought into the suit; if those debts were paid before September would the church let the mortgage run until you could sell the other place?[17] Please write me carefully as Raymond asked me & I could not tell him. Do you think any one there would lend you a thousand and if so would it clear up every thing but the mortgage? Then you could pay that as soon as you could sell the other house.

Raymond looks at your miniature and says you look as if you had seen a great deal of care and trouble and pities you, regretting that it is not in his power to help you himself immediately, and then he looks at Semantha's & thinks she was beautiful and ought to have been saved. His hair & eyes & eyelashes are just as hers were and I often think of her when I look at his eyes— Now a little about myself— I am quite well now though not very strong yet. You & Hattie wonder what I am doing; not much of anything lately only sewing, reading & writing. Having two servants to do the work, I do but little myself and that, particular things which I do not like to trust to them, but I have to watch them and tell them every little item to be done, for a negro never sees any dirt or grease, so if a Southern lady does not do much manual labor, she has head-work enough to keep her busy. I could not help thinking of you this morning when I cleaned my *lard lamp* with the globe & chimney; you know, you always do that, and so I thought I must do as mother does. It needed a new wick and I had quite a time fixing it, but know how now.

It is a very pretty one which Raymond bought with many other things while we were in N. O. The parlor looks beautifully—so cool &

---

17. It is not clear which property Tryphena refers to. The Holders owned property in New York state in addition to land acquired in several purchases made between 1831 and 1845 in Pittsfield. See Probate Records, 94:39, 94:359, 103:421, 114:47, 113:354, 135:183, 138:183, 139:427, Berkshire County, Massachusetts, Pittsfield, Massachusetts.

clean. The matting more suitable than carpeting here for summer, is red & white—a very pretty piece. The new curtains of green & white damask with gilt cornices & holders, extending to the floor, on the door-windows that open on the gallery are very rich looking. The trimmings and all cost forty dollars. The centre-table spread is to match. I suppose you have my ottoman and footstool; have the moths eaten them yet? I shall probably send for them next fall—& have them fixed for the parlor. I suppose you have not many vegetables yet, while we have had every variety for some time and the neighbors keep me supplied with fruit. Mr Urquefort—a wealthy sugar planter above sends me a basket of fine peaches every time the Dr. goes there and Mr Martin sends me figs and yesterday morning a Creole lady, whom I have never seen, sent me a basket of figs, she is the first Creole who has ventured to send me any thing, but they are a very respectable family, having no negro blood in them, while most of these Creoles have. As you will see in the report there are a great many free negroes in this Parish[18]—one old mulatto man who lives three miles below here is worth a hundred thousand dollars. His father was an Englishman, his mother a black slave. He lives with a negro woman and has several children; I saw two of the girls who came down on the boat with me. They have every thing that money can procure for the body, but no education and of course they are mere nothings, neither white or black, illegitimate and shut out from all grades of society— This may be taken as a specimen of much of the population of this part of the U. S. Many of the Creoles with negro blood are very wealthy but devoid of principle and illiterate. The majority however are merely independent—owning a small piece of ground one or two negroes and a house. Some work out by the day, and some receive their living from the oranges which they raise for the N. O market. As you ride by these Creole settlements you will see that nearly every yard is filled with orange trees. The men are generally indolent and none of them have the least respect for the Sabbath—playing cards, dancing, shooting matches, and hunting being their amusements for the day. On the whole I consider them as a class only one grade higher than the negroes and that owning to the little Euro-

---

18. In 1850 there were 390 free black persons in Plaquemines Parish. See U.S. 7th Census, 1850, Population, Plaquemines Parish, Louisiana, NA.

pean blood in them   But I am writing too much— Phillis comes in with a large basket covered with leaves larger than this note, & says "Miss Blanche, here is a present for you from a lady across the river—a boatman brought it over & on opening it it proves to be ripe figs—large & of two kinds   the White & Purple called the 'Celeste'— I should like to send you some. I received the paper— Write often if it only be a few lines. I have several more correspondents now as all his sisters write to me. One thing more, Please tell me how you made those nice biscuits last summer, I want to learn Henry how, for I do not like his way. The sun is very warm this morning; we have frequent thunder showers, and I have not suffered from the heat yet. The Dr is absent this morning and two boys have been here for him since he left, so he will have to go again as soon as he comes— His practice is very extensive, besides that for which he is paid by the year—to visit plantations weekly. Good Bye with much love from

Trin—

The Dr says what makes Mother think I dont like her? give my love to her and tell her she must not think that; perhaps she won't like me— but *I* know you will like *one another* and I am so anxious for the time to come when you can meet him and become acquainted.

▢ ▢ ▢

My Dear Mother,   HYGIENE, SEPT. 8TH 1856.

Though I have not written to you for two or three weeks, it has been neither from want of inclination or time; perhaps a feeling that I had nothing to write about but trifles and every-day occurrences kept me from it and perhaps I was waiting to hear from you but have been disappointed. As I glance at the date, it strikes me that it is just five years ago to-day since our Mary left us and my pen is involuntarily laid aside and I find myself musing on the many changes since then. How widely we are separated now, we—who met around the home hearth-stone that night after we had laid [Mary] in her last home.[19] We, who then met, have seen afflictions since then and have felt the world's selfishness

---

19. Mary Holder is buried in the Terrace Grove section of the Pittsfield Cemetery, Pittsfield, Massachusetts, along with her father, George, mother, Anna Rose, sisters Semantha and Emma, and brothers Le Roy and George. See Pittsfield Cemetery and Crematory Records, Pittsfield, Massachusetts.

more in these five years than in all our lives before and perhaps it *was* best that she was taken, that she might not need to face the storms.

But where is Le Roy? it seems as if I had no brother; and past correspondence when we heard from one another once a fortnight can not have been reality, when now nearly a year has elapsed and I hear not one word from him. When you have an opportunity   Give him much of my love   tell him I am the same sister Triphen as ever, and would be *so* pleased to hear from him. Tell him to write and assure me it was not a long dream of twenty years, that I had a brother who loved me and shared the same interests with me. Dr Raymond and *his wife* are both well. There has been but little sickness in the parish this season. Dr Raymond has now several cases of dysentery—all on the other side of the river. It is endemic on one plantation. He has lost no cases yet, though the disease is very violent. A daughter of the planter has been very sick with it; she has recovered from the disease but is much debilitated and is of so delicate a constitution that it is doubtful if she lives long. She is a very pleasant and interesting young lady of nineteen and leaves a fortune of forty thousand dollars in her own right. Her younger sister— Miss Mary Grant, was an old sweet-heart of the Dr's. On the other plantations there is no disease excepting occasional attacks of the common chill & fever. For the past three or four weeks we have had some quite warm days but very cool nights. The wind blows too much to be pleasant and I often am obliged to shut the windows and doors to keep things from blowing into chaos! Judging from my complexion you would pronounce it a fine breeze for *tanning*. I am nearly a mulatto & expect to be *black* by the time I am ready to visit you, and then if I was only a slave, would I not be caressed and petted, by those Fremont fanatics of Old Mass. I get angry every time I read the Eagle[20] with its coarse wit and coarser arguments. Fremont *may* be President, but I dont think he will owe his elevation to the Editor, or boss of that paper. Do you know who sends me the Pittsfield Sun?[21] Two copies of it came last Saturday direct from the printing office. If it is you, as I suspect, I am a thousand times obliged, for it is like a gleam of sunshine from my

20. The *Berkshire Eagle*, one of Pittsfield's two newspapers, began publication in 1855.
21. The *Pittsfield Sun*, founded by Phineas Allen in 1800, continued publication until 1906.

native land, now so wrapped in the *blackness* of Abolitionism. Aside
from the annoyance of these high winds the mosquitoes are very troublesome to-day — more so than I have ever known them before. It is just
the weather for them, cold nights, when they cannot move about much
and warm, damp, or sultry days when they can bite the hardest. It is like
having some one near you, touching you every now and then with a
coal of fire. You jump and it is gone, to be applied in some other place.
Even my shoes are no protection to my feet or kid gloves for my hands.
They are not large, but black & fine. Ants, are another source of annoyance. They are everywhere, in the fields, forests, houses and barns. Anything eatable weather flesh or vegetables attracts them. I have learned
by the dear experience of having a great quantity of clothing ruined by
them, to put everything carefully away at night, if I do not care to see it
full of little holes in the morning. All my provisions have to be carefully
wrapped up or stowed away into the safe, the legs of which stand in
little basins of water and into which they cannot penetrate. As I have
commenced telling you of my *weighty grievances* I might as well finish at
once and make a *clean breach* of it. Now dont think I am going to "fess"
how many quarrels I have had with a certain Dr. because we have not
had *one* yet, and I am only going to *tell you* about — *rats.* They infest the
cornhouse and stable, destroying great quantities of corn; but I would
not care so much for this if they would only let my *ducks* alone, for out
of twenty-five of the last brood, only nine are left; they are getting big
enough to defend themselves. All the rest of the poultry are doing well
and are much pleased with their new residence, into which they were
ushered Saturday night by moon-light. — I must go & see what Mary is
about and of course my pet goes with me, of course. — I find Mary
singing as loud as she can bawl and washing off the wheels to the
buggy, which the Dr. is going to have painted. We are doing something
toward improvement all the time and yet we do not get fixed. yesterday
he hired an old negro man to white wash the outside of all the buildings
in the yard. I believe I told you we had a new room built for the servants. It is added to the kitchen; it stands two feet from the ground and
is large, airy and comfortable. Mary occupies it at present and some of
the abolitionists ought to take a peep at the poor slave's quarters. She
has a nice high-top walnut bedstead, with a good mattrass, pillows,
sheets and white counterpane, a white mosquito bar, Russia[n] matting

on the floor, a trunk of good, & *fashionable* clothing, pictures hung
upon the walls, some glass-ware & chairs. White muslin curtains shade
the window which opens to the south and the door to the East. She is
a very good servant and cooks almost everything in good order, excepting light-bread   I have let her try *twice* & she has brought me in, both
times heavy, sour bread, not fit to be eaten in any way. I am so sorry I
do not know more about housekeeping or rather cooking for, if I
showed her once it would be enough. Your recipe for biscuit proved to
be such an excellent one, can you not tell me how to make milk-yeast
bread, such as you *used* to. We have no baker near us. Or ask Hattie to
write to me how she used to make that nice light bread she had when I
was at home. At present we have not much of a garden, but are plentifully supplied with vegetables. The oranges are very large now, but not
yet ripe.[22] I had some large green ones sent me a few days ago; they are
good eaten with a little salt. *My pet,* is a little Scotch terrier, given to Dr.
Fox by Mr Grant. It is ugly, but so playful & sagacious that I think it
powerful pretty, particularly as it takes off my slippers, drags at the bottom of my dress & allows herself to be petted by no one but me. Mr
Reggio one of the Dr's wealthy patrons sent me some pomerganates
last week. They look very delicious but have not much eating matter in
them. His son, Lucun whom the Dr has been attending for the last two
months, since his arrival from the Hydropathic institution died last Saturday. He was about fifteen. He has had a chronic diarrhea, for a long
time. He is the only patient who has died since I came here, out of a
practice among two thousand people in the sickliest season, so dont you
think *my* doctor is a successful one? I have three letters to answer received last week, one from Lucy & one from Mr Daniel Fox—a
brother—who is in Texas—he wrote me such a good, long affectionate
letter that I should like to let you read it. He is trading in stock among
the Indians & gives me fine accounts of them. Lucy is very kind to me;
she sent me various recipes, for cakes & nice jellies & preserves & some
[. . .] melon seeds to plant.

I will try not to have so long a time gap again without writing to you.

---

22. Tryphena wrote "The oranges are getting very large now, but not yet ripe," but then
    cancelled the word "getting."

Answer this soon   Give my love to E. & Georgy. Do they grow very much? Remember me to any who may inquire & with much love believe me as ever— Yours

T. B. F.

Dr Raymond was gone when I wrote this, but is at home now. He sends his love to you. We have been talking about you all through breakfast. Good Bye.

T.

□ □ □

My Dear Mother,   HYGIENE, NOV. 18TH 1856.

I have received your letter of "the 6th," which has given me no little trouble and anxiety.

I have told Dr Raymond of your affairs, and through his kindness my mind is somewhat relieved; it cannot be wholly at ease, when knowing his circumstances as well as I do, I see the sacrifice which he makes to assist you. But no one will appreciate his generosity more than yourself, when you have seen so much selfishness among friends and acquaintances, so much oppression and utter neglect, while *he* a perfect stranger, steps forward and offers you *real* aid. Our plan for you, after much conversation is this; to lend you (dont be frightened at the word *lend*) money to move to Rochester or some western place, and open a boarding house on a medium scale. His money comes in from the first of Jan. to the middle of Feb. With the first payments, he has to meet some liabilities of this year, so that he could not send you the ready money until the *middle* of Feb. or first of Mar. Then you may rely upon him for whatever amount you think necessary, within his limits, say two hundred or two hundred and fifty dollars. By the first of April you could be settled and ready to commence anew, with new associations and acquaintances and under obligations to no one, that will trouble you for notes and payments, —but one who sees his way clear, and will not break his promise. In the meantime, can we depend at all, upon Le Roy? he is the very one whose assistance you need, to find you a house and engage boarders somewhere in his vicinity. If he is not ready & willing (though I presume he will be *now*) can you not write to *Mr Up-*

ton[23] & make your arrangements through him. Until Dr Raymond can send you the funds, which will only be eight or ten weeks from the time you received this, can you not go to grandpa's and stay or let the children go there, if you have other views for yourself? Write to Le Roy and see if he will not assist you *to go* & to stay where he is until then, when you can be making arrangements and acquaintances for the spring.

If I had ready funds of my own, I would send them, but I have nothing excepting my watch. I have been thinking how that could be disposed of here, but see no way. If it will do you any good and I presume you can sell it there, I will send it to you, *as soon as* you answer this. I can do so with perfect security, and actually have no need of it now. I never wear it and Dr R——would have no objections. He has one.

It would pay for the children's board, for this winter.

What do you think of the plan? With Le Roy's assistance and not his money, it is an excellent one, and without him it is passable, and far better than anything else that can be seen. Perhaps, you do not think so; if not, you must write and tell me, and let me know *what you* think would be best. You do not know how anxious I am to hear from you again. I presume I am much blamed, because I have married, but I could not have helped you as much as this, if I had not. By the first of March, I should have had only a hundred and fifty due to me and clothed myself out of that, so you are better off, than if I had remained single. And do you not think that after you are away from Pittsfield and fairly started that you can get along? We think so, for I have told the Dr. what a business woman you were until you became discouraged & the Pittsfield people, took so much pains to help you down hill instead of giving a little timely assistance. Perhaps I can help you still more, by and by, by taking Emma with me, if we get along well here, but I should dislike to ask this of Dr Raymond, if you are at all successful, and with what he offers now. He would send it on immediately if he had it, but I told him I thought you could not very well commence out west without some time to make arrangement and could get along this winter, and he would be obliged to hire it and pay interest. Still if you can com-

---

23. A friend of the Holder family in New York. Possibly an employee of the New York and Erie Railroad, for which Le Roy Holder worked. See TBH to ARH, October 15, 1855, MDAH.

mence now as well as in the Spring, he will make an effort to get it for you. He is very kind, but I do not wish to ask too much of him; if he was rich and did not work hard night and day, I would not care. But I will try to make up for it, in dressing very economically and not going to N. O. any this winter and not buying a piano, which *he* wants very much. He is not very well, and had to go away to night though it is dark and raining very hard. I am not quite well, but presume it is more mental than bodily sickness.

Write to me immediately, if not more than four lines, and remember that what I have said about helping you is not *all talk*. One thing I have forgotten; how long is your house rented to the present tenants? and can you not find some one to take it as soon as he leaves, so that the rent of it will partly pay for the one you hire "out west"? Or can you not make out the property in your own name & sell it by Spring.[24]

Later—

I received your letter of the 11th last night, and you have no idea of the relief it gave me— For the whole week, I had not taken my place at the table, or laid my head upon the pillow, without being inexpressibly anxious to know where you & the children were, and how you were faring. I would have sent this sooner, but the mails have been very irregular and I could not get it aboard the boat. I know how you will be relieved at the contents of it; you say you wish you could see my husband. If you cannot see his face you may his mind, nobility & generosity are the traits. And Mother he is so good to me—not an unkind word or look has ever been given me, and my only wish is, to make as good a wife, as he is husband. He thinks you had better not borrow money from Mr Root, by involving the other place, if you can possibly get along until he can assist you. And I am so glad that Le Roy has shown himself, for I have now much hope, that you can rely on his influence & knowledge to help you settle elsewhere. that is, if you wish it. Dr Raymond also thinks that it would be useless to attempt to retake the other place, and that it would give you more trouble and anxiety than it is worth. He says if he had known you two years ago, he would have

---

24. Anna Holder had relinquished all claims to property purchased by George Holder for ten dollars. See Probate Records, March 5, 1846, 113:354, Berkshire County, Pittsfield, Massachusetts.

helped you to the money, if possible, so see the difference between a Northern & Southern man—one of Massachusetts' & one of Mississippi's sons.[25] His health is a little better than two or three days ago, but he has some fever yet, evenings——. Housekeeping affairs have troubled me some lately; the negroes get out of tune sometimes, but do pretty well as a general thing. I have learned Mary to make very nice soda biscuits and from a new cook-book which Dr R——gave me, have taught myself how to make *light bread,* and I am as proud of my first my *first* light loaf in the safe, as a girl is of her first beau. Oranges here are as plenty as apples there, and the *new* sugar is excellent. I can stand upon the gallery and see the tall chimneys of nine sugar houses on different plantations, puffing their black smoke, at once. A week ago Friday we were invited to a wedding dinner at Mr R. Wilkinsons, seventeen miles below. There was a large company present—all strangers but old friends of the Dr's, so I soon was made perfectly at home among them. After a fine dinner at *five,* which kept us at table about two hours, we had music & dancing. The bride was an old flame of Dr R——'s, but has married a Dr, far inferior to him in looks, intellect, & deportment—a real but, but, my pen talks too much. We remained over night, passed a very pleasant day and returned about four, as we came by the P. O. I felt a presentiment that I should have bad news, & he brought your letter out which completely stunned me. I suppose Hattie M——is married by this time, I received her wedding card some days ago.[26] Last night we had a letter from father Fox enclosing his wedding card—— He was married to a Miss Cheeseborough,[27] just before leaving the North. Sister Fanny had been very sick, and was then but little better. She is Dr. Raymond's favorite sister & will probably come & spend the winter with him to regain her strength. Sister Lucie near Natchez had lost her youngest babe—six months old, so you see, we have both had news to worry us.

---

25. Although Tryphena makes much about her husband's southern birth, his father, James Angel Fox, was born in Connecticut and his mother, Sarah Otis, was born in New York.
26. Harriet Murray married R. H. Dewey on November 12, 1856, at the South Congregational Church, Pittsfield, Massachusetts. See Family History File, Berkshire Athenaeum, Pittsfield, Massachusetts.
27. The Louisiana-born Emily Cheeseborough became James A. Fox's fourth wife in November 1856.

I read in the Pittsfield Sun of Mrs Richard's[28] death; I was sorry and surprised to see it— I presume it is Mr Richard's Mother. What has become of Uncle Bragues' people & Grandpa's?

I have heard nothing from Baconham lately. Father brought on a teacher for his children, but there is much opposition to Northern teachers, in the leading papers of the South; particularly since Freemont attempted to run.[29] When I think of my former position, I am so glad that I am no longer dependent upon this one or that for food & shelter and hope that by constant attention and kindness I can so far increase his comforts or happiness as to compensate for the happy change. It was rather a wild move, but all for the best so far.

But he has returned from dressing a negro woman's arm, which he had to cut off, about a week ago & will wish to write so I must close. Give much love to Le Roy, & tell him to write to me soon. I hope he will help you as much as he can. Dr Raymond joins me in love to yourself & the children. Your daughter

T. B. Fox.

□ □ □

My Dear Mother—   SUNDAY JAN 4TH '57 HYGIENE, 3 P. M.

As I am a little lonely, it will make the time pass pleasantly to write to you though I mailed a letter to you last Tuesday. The day is a very pleasant one, with warm sunshine and a slight breeze. I have been reading most of the morning; Dr Raymond went away about twelve o clock to dine with Mr Pickens and a physician from Natchez— it is a gentleman's dinner, as Mrs Pickens left home last week to be absent about a month. I am very sorry as she is so good a neighbor & the only person I visit familiarly; there is no ceremony between us and she does many little favors for me. I probably told you before, that she was not an educated woman; but their wealth has enabled them to travel and mix in refined society, so that she has acquired good manners and taste from observation. It is said that they are about to "sell out". Then my nearest neighbor will be Mrs Stackhouse & Mrs Brooks her mother. I do not like them at all, for though the Mssrs Stackhouse are the wealthiest planters

---

28. This was a relative of Robert Richards, a childhood friend of Tryphena.
29. Tryphena refers here to John C. Frémont, who ran for president on the newly formed Republican party ticket in 1856.

here, the whole family is exceedingly illiterate. All the visiting I do there is to call occasionally, just to keep on the right side, on account of the Doctor's practice there. Perhaps you would like to know who lives next door, just across the intervening acre; Mr Sarpy—a creole & overseer, on a very large plantation above has bought the house and ground, and is now repairing and arranging it for his—let me see—not negro *wife,* but his *negress,* and his four mulatto children. They have been living upon the plantation where he oversees, but are now to remove to the "new place". The occupant of the next house is known as "Old Bru"—a fugitive from justice in France who has been here for the last three or four years. He lives by the *very honorable* and profitable calling of receiving stolen goods from the negroes, for which he pays them a mere trifle and which he sells after getting a sufficient quantity of each kind, at a good profit in N. O. The family below are quite respectable—the man a native of France, an honest & industrious carpenter, who works on the plantations. Then comes a widow of some sort. Her husband disappeared one morning very *suddenly,* was last seen going back through the fields toward the swamp, and has never been heard of since. They are Creoles. Below these, is a family of the name of Geoffrey, also Creoles—a good for nothing lazy set. Then there is the grocery, kept by Madame Pauline Safore; her husband died a year or two ago; he amassed a fortune, some twenty-thousand dollars by trading with the negroes, "receiving stolen goods—such as sugar, molasses & corn & paying in bad whiskey and mean dry goods. Although it is unlawful to do this, without the negro can show a written permission from his master, yet no one molests the offenders and the Madame still "makes money". Two creole brothers live below, who are quite well off, having small farms & neat little houses. They raise vegetable for the market & buy & sell stock, as many of the Creoles do below. Although these people live so near, yet I know no more of them personally, than as if I lived in Pittsfield; only seeing them as I ride by in the buggy with the Dr. Then comes Mr Pickens' large plantation & then Mr Stackhouse's, and farther on another settlement of Creoles.

I did not go to town as I thought I should; the roads were very muddy & bad & after much deliberation I concluded to stay at home. But the time seems long when "the Dr." is gone and I am a little timid among such a rabble of negroes & Creoles as surround us & no decent white person within a mile. But I make Reuben lock up all the house and Boze, the watch-dog, stays in my room, so I get along very well. I dont believe I have told you lately about my housekeeping. We have no cow yet, but I occasionally send to Mr Martin's above & get milk. Mary does tolerably well, though I am obliged to watch her or she will "shirk", and Reuben—our new negro man, proves to be very trusty and industrious. He is from Virginia and the greatest talker in the country, but very respectful withal. Frank, the Creole negro boy, whom we hired & who annoyed me so much, we sent away about a month ago & I was glad to get rid of him. I tried in vain to make a good dining room servant of him, but he was too slow & stupid. He had been badly managed & would steal everything he could lay his hands on. He seemed so remarkably fond of *pilfered* eggs and my nests were often robbed.

I have now forty chickens, & twenty-two ducks. There is nothing in domestic affairs that interests me more than my chicken-house & its inmates & I visit it every day & allow no one in there without my permission. I have about 8 or ten eggs a day & find them a great addition to the table, as we cannot get fresh meat often. I should like to send you five or six dozen, but they *might break,* so I will or rather Dr Raymond will soon send you that which will buy them. He was making out his bills Friday to hand in, & counting up what was due during the next month; and, said I, "what are you going to do with all your money when you get it after paying your debts?" Well, the first thing, said he, "I am going to send your mother fifty of it." You can imagine how happy this made me as he had seemed down-hearted & spoken of you but little lately & I hardly expected it when I asked him. So if you can get along with Mr Morey, with that note I sent you, until then, I shall be much relieved, you must write soon & let me know.

I have been very busy sewing lately—too busy for my health & now that my hurry is over, shall not do so much. I owe Hattie Murray, or I forgot, Mrs Dewey, a letter, but have not felt like answering it, since I have been much worried about your affairs, thought I wrote part of a one to her one day & could not finish it. I shall write soon.

[unsigned]

My Dear Mother   SUNDAY APR 26TH 1857.

I received your letter last night and hasten to answer, while I have so good an opportunity. The news that Le Roy had not assisted you, made me feel very badly, for since I last wrote help from him, for you had been my only hope. And now, it is a question whether I can help you or not; for I have not yet let Dr Raymond see your letter or told him the worst of its contents, and it is worrying me so much, for the taxes ought certainly to be paid. He is very much fretted at present and I dont know what to do about troubling him. For the last two weeks he has been constantly *away*; every day besides his regular visits elsewhere he has had to go to one of his yearly plantations eight miles below on the other side. The owner[30] purchased about a hundred & fifty unacclimated negroes & sent them all down at once. They have had the measles, and the dysentery & now a diarrhea has made its appearance. Of course "the Doctor" must *cure* everybody & everything or he is "of no account," and in spite of his constant attention several have died — but from improper diet & want of care in the managers of the plantation. Dr Raymond gets five hundred dollars a year for attending it & he now fears that the owner will be dissatisfied and discharge him & it would be no small loss from his salary. He thinks too that the overseer is a deceptive man & will use his influence with Mr Doyal, against him. Mr D—lives on one of his plantations above N. O. & only comes down once in two weeks or so. He is probably the richest sugar-planter in La—and has always been very kind to Dr R—but he is easily prejudiced & rather whimsical, so our chance is rather uncertain. Being up so much nights & traveling so constantly, together with anxiety to save the negroes, & trouble about losing the place,[31] by the year, have all combined to make him rather low-spirited. You will know then how I feel about telling him of your affairs, and sympathise with me situated between two such anxious points — desire to assist you and yet a wish

---

30. Tryphena refers to Henry Doyal, the Ascension Parish sugar planter who owned 2,454 acres of land and 282 slaves. He also owned more than one plantation in Plaquemines Parish, along with 194 slaves, in 1850. J. Carlyle Sitterson, *Sugar Country: The Cane Sugar Industry in the South, 1753–1950* (Frankfort: University of Kentucky Press, 1953), 163; U.S. 7th Census, 1850, Slave Schedule, Plaquemines Parish, Louisiana, NA.
31. By February 1858 a new physician in the parish, Dr. Greenwood, had taken over at a plantation where Fox previously practiced.

not to worry him. Another thing too, he subscribed twenty-five dollars last *June* towards building a parsonage twenty miles below here, when we have not the least benefit from the church or minister & this week, that was handed in for payment. Not that he grumbles about it, only things come just at the worst time. I am all alone to-day. He went to town this morning with Mr Penrose, an old friend of his, who came early this morning and breakfasted with us. I expect him back about sundown. The day seems rather long and it would make me so happy to step in and see you & talk & tell you all about my Southern life & hear about your affairs since I left you. But this paper & pen shall do the best they can towards telling you of my affairs & the time slips away fast when I am writing to you. I was foolish enough to take a good hearty cry after the gentlemen left, for I have been alone so much lately, that I could not bear the idea of trying to get through the day by myself, and it looked so selfish in me to wish him to stay when he has done nothing but doctor sick negroes and ride in the rain & sun & wind for the last month. The buggy only holds two or I would have gone & visited Lizzie. It looks like rain now & the wind is very strong. There have been two severe frosts here lately; one the twelfth & one on the twenty-third of this month. The last one cut down all the corn & injured what cane escaped the first. Much corn will have to be replanted; it was "knee-high;" our garden was considerably injured by the last; still we have quite a variety of vegetables. New Irish potatoes, two inches through, green peas, beets, carrots, lettuce, spinach and artichokes.

Often, as we set down to dinner, I cannot help but wish that you & the children could come in & dine with us, for what a long cold time, there is, before vegetables will be eatable in your latitude. Flowers are in bloom in the greatest abundance, and the mantle is plentifully supplied with bouquets, sent by the Dr's numerous friends, old & young, black & white. Wild flowers grow here on the levees & sides of ditches, in the greatest luxuriance & many which we cultivate at home with care grow here by the road side — the verbena, spider-wort a large delicate purple-flower, the crimson fleur-di-lis & others. Perhaps I told you, we had been setting out more shrubbery. The evergreens do well, but the rose bushes seem to fade. Mr Urquehart gave us the cuttings from his beautiful yard. It will take us some time to make ours look nicely, but we are doing something to it every week & hope to have a pretty home one of these days. Hedges are very common here & grow nicely with a little attention. We are going to plant one running from each front corner of the house as it stands in the centre of the acre, to . . . each side fence, and thus separates the front from the back yard. It is an evergreen, resembling the sweet orange so closely you can only distinguish them by the fruit, & with proper training can be made of any height. we wish to have ours, four or six feet high, so as to entirely hide the back yard & garden, from the road.

Mr Stackhouse would not sell Dr Raymond the acre of land behind us, but has let him have it for an indefinite period provided he fences it. This costs him over a hundred dollars at the cheapest; it is partly finished. Reuben is at work on it a little every day, so I hope soon to see the horses turned in there out of the front yard. Old Grey, is quiet & dignified & does no harm but Dick, is such a frisky dandy of a horse that everything is in danger, either from his teeth which he is very fond of prying on the bark, or his feet, which he often lifts very high. The kitten is making so much noise for her dinner that I must go & feed her, for she is all the pet I have & don't like to be slighted & Reuben & Mary are off— I gave them the day & have no dinner cooked— the first day it has been omitted since I came here. But I was telling you about *Dick*; he is of a light bay, bob-tail, rather small, yet well formed, & and as round & as slick as a butter-ball" & goes at the rate of "two forty" or a *little* less *perhaps*. He knew how well he looked this morning and was in a hurry to get off. Old Grey is as lonesome without him as I am without Dr Raymond & I am not sure but I shall have to go & sympathize with him. The kitten jumps in my lap & says "thank you marm" for the dough-nut I give her.

My health is very good and I have been attending to domestic affairs a great deal lately & sometimes am conceited enough to think myself quite a nice housekeeper. Monday I made some dew-berry jam & about a quart of cordial; both of which are pronounced very nice. Dew berries are ripe & very plentiful now; and are much better even than the blackberry.

[unsigned]

My Dear Mother,   HOME, MONDAY JUNE 8TH 1857.

I have not answered your last received two weeks ago, because I have been too much perplexed to do so, unless I could at the same time give you assistance. Now, that the letter enclosing *twenty five dollars* in *bills* was put in the mail for you Saturday I feel more like writing. If you have not received it when you get this you must let me know immediately, as it has at least three days the start of this. You will not think it negligence, that it was not sent sooner were I to tell you how much I planned & tried to think of some means, by which I could help you. Our expenses have been very heavy this year & we shall have to practice the strictest economy to get through to the first of Dec, when payments *come* in again, to avoid running in debt. We go without ice, this summer & send you the twenty-five instead. I know I can get along without it and Dr Raymond says he can, if I can. We drink river water; the mud settles by bringing it over night and stirring a little alum into it. Then I dip two or three bottles of it from the barrel & hang them in the well, so that with a little care, we can have cool water all summer, unless the water in the well dries up. It is hard & full of earthy matter, not like the clear crystal well water found in New England. It has a brackish taste & sometimes a strong smell; but it does very well for the horses & poultry & watering the garden   We have to do this a great deal although there is a heavy dew every morning; the sun is very hot now & soon dries it up. Our vegetables are looking very well & we have a good variety, but it keeps Reuben busy to prevent the weeds from choking everything. A kind of grass called cocoa which grows here everywhere in abundance, is the worst garden enemy, for it is almost impossible to uproot it. It has a bulbous root & grows rapidly to two feet or so in height and is not fit for fodder.

I have experienced no inconvenience from the heat yet; this is our warmest month, but the delightful sea-breeze that springs up about ten prevents the sun from *demolishing* us with his fierce rays. The moonlight nights are cool & pleasant & the mosquitoes have been quite moderate for the last few days. This is only a breathing spell & a new swarm will soon make its appearance & bite & buzz with new energy. You don't know what a draw-back they are to an otherwise delightful country. Our mosquito-house is again in order & were it not for that, I should sometimes be really miserable. It took me two days to make it &

took both Dr R——& myself a part of two days to put it up. As I go
through the house, I feel that it is in tolerable good order for the summer, though it needs the closest watching to keep down the cob-webs
& dirt-dauber's nests. Flies & ants trouble me some but by making
Mary clean the rooms thoroughly once a week, I manage to keep the
house in as good order as most persons here do, with three or four servants. I expect it will be rather hard for her this summer to do all the
washing, ironing, cooking, and housecleaning, but I cannot help it, for
we cannot afford to hire or buy another at present. We have large wash-
ings for Dr Raymond is obliged to dress genteely & riding so much in
the dust & on horseback soils his clothes very fast, so he has to have a
clean suit of white or *light* pants & vest & shirt every morning nearly
besides his under clothes once or twice a week.

We have five in the family now, ourselves, Reuben, Mary, & a sick
boy, belonging to Father Fox;[32] he is here for Dr R——to treat & what
makes it worse for us he is perfectly helpless with his lower limbs &
needs a great deal of waiting on. He has [a] spinal complaint with pa-
ralysis of the legs, though otherwise he is very healthy & eats as much as
anybody. I give him all his medicine & see that he is properly attended
to, which is a little care at least on my mind. It is doubtful if he ever gets
able to do anything, excepting such work as requires only his hands. I
am going to teach him to sew. he is eighteen & a very bright, good
natured boy, never complaining in the least.

The worst of my sewing is completed; I finished a dress & the last
pair of drawers for Dr R——last week Friday & you cannot imagine
how relieved I feel. I hope I shall never get such a quantity to be done
again for I have sewed as if my bread depended on it. Saturday, just one
year from the day I first came to Hygiene, Dr R & I went to N. O. We
started from here just at sunrise (five) & were only an hour & forty
minutes going in. We breakfasted with Seguin & Lizzie; Seguin is very
unfortunate; he gets little practice & no pay & is now struggling along
with his drug-store which was much damaged by fire [one] week ago
Sunday. Dr Raymond had to help him too by a loan of cash, which we
shall not be able to get again for the present. Seguin is already deeply in
debt there, but is going to try through the summer, then if he cannot

---

32. The sick boy was named Osborne.

succeed, I dont know what he will do. I spent the day with Lizzie until about four when Dr R——took me over the river, to do a little shopping & look around a little. I did not go so much because it was necessary, as to break up the monotony of life down here, for I see very, very few persons indeed & were I differently situated should probably be very discontented   I am often unhappy, but it is only on your account, when I reproach myself for marrying. Had I married a rich man I would not feel so, but I wont trouble you with *my* troubles, it is enough you have, of your own. Do you think Le Roy will help you any more this summer? I cannot bear to think what will be done unless he does. Dr Raymond speaks very kindly about you & is willing to help you, but he has got his affairs into such a condition, that he may not be able to do so & it makes me quite miserable half of my time. Last week I hardly slept at all, for besides all this there is another subject to occupy me & of which you will probably *not be* surprised to hear & I think you ought to have a hint in due time, so you will not be hurried in supplying yourself, (should you deem it necessary to the new dignity) with a grandmother's caps & spectacles! The time is not far distant & I cannot but be sad to think how alone I am to be with no mother or sister or even old friend or acquaintance.

Hope whispers that his sister Lucy may be able to be with me & another cheering thought is, I am in such kind & experienced hands. There is no wardrobe commenced for the little expected one yet, though the articles were purchased some time ago, fearing I might not be able to go to the city again, but I have so little else to do, now there will probably be ample time during the next three months. The fact was, I did not know what or how to begin & was as ignorant about cutting out anything as a child and there is not a person down here to whom I would apply. no one suspects me yet, though all the Creoles have been on the look-out ever since we were married. You know one can dress admirably with, hoops & crinoline and I went to town feeling that I was not exposing myself in the least. Lizzie gave me a few hints & some patterns & Sister Lucy sent me a long letter full of advice, so that I am not quite so much of an ignoramus as I was. There are many things that I ought to know now, and you cannot tell how I long to see you sometimes. I suppose Mrs Dewey is not so smart as I am; I expected to hear from her last week.

As a young housekeeper, there are a good many things I need especially in the way of bedding but I suppose I shall have to try to get along with what I have, rather than run in debt for anything. But if I have any money to spare would you like to sell me your lenin sheets & pillow cases, I paying you the full value of the material & for the sewing on them. It would be helping you, instead of paying out the money in town, & then they would be ready made. If you should wish to do so, and the expense of sending them will not be more than I can afford, tell me what you appraise them at, and I will see what Dr Raymond thinks about it. Could you find out from the express office there how much it would cost. I write this because I see that the sheets & pillow cases which he had before I came are giving out very fast & we shall be obliged to buy new ones in the Spring any-way, if not sooner, though if I am careful with them perhaps I can get along without any new ones until spring.

Enclosed you will find a violet; I have very few flowers, four bushes of these & three pinks in a box on the gallery constitute my garden, and I take good care of it. I have a hundred young chickens, three little turkeys that follow me all about the yard, tell Emma & Georgy, & ten little ducks. The turkeys have no mother & I feed them often as well as the little ducks. Tell Georgy there are three young puppies running all about here & I would send him one if I could. They are very playful sometimes & very quarrelsome sometimes & would soon learn to know him. Now I have written you a long letter & it is *all* for yourself, I will write again soon & shall expect to hear from you in a short time. Give my love to the children & accept much for yourself from   Yours as ever

Tryphena B. Fox

□ □ □

My Dear Mother,   HOME, JUNE 28TH 1857.

I received yours of the 19th, last night, after being very anxious about you all the week. The money was a longer time than usual in reaching you, your letter came through very soon—eight days. Hattie's was a longer time coming.

Dont think it a sacrifice for us to help you; I would rather submit to any deprivation, than to feel the anxiety I did, before I could send you that last. Now if Le Roy can help you until Dr R——gets his affairs

arranged again, I shall be so glad & relieved & then he will be happy to
assist you again. I keep regular account of every cent we spend & to
show you that we are not *extravagant* & that our expenses are necessarily heavy, I will *make* out a list of them for you, & it will be a little guide
for you to know more my housekeeping affairs too. — Now that I have
taken my bath (one of the daily indispensables in this country) dressed,
given out dinner & seen it under headway, I will try to finish. Dr Raymond writes to his brother Seguin to go & see about the box, to-morrow.[33] I shall feel anxious till we hear of its safe arrival. But Mother, you
have robbed yourself, and I am sorry that I mentioned the things at all,
however acceptable they may be; it will seem a little like home to have
home things around me. If you were only to be with them! Dr Raymond had plenty of silver when we were married, six large spoons &
forks & six dessert spoons & forks; so I shall not need those you have
sent, and will keep them all for Emma.

Many thanks for everything & I will say more when I get the box.
Emma's mat will be highly prized. I have been wishing to embroider
something for her, but have found so much other sewing that I have
had to put it off. The little earrings enclosed, were Mary's and I send
them, as she is the one to have them now. Tell her to have her ears
bored & wear them to remind her of the former wearers. Dr Raymond
spoke of buying her some pretty ones, last spring, but he has had so
many other things to get, that he has not mentioned them lately. It is
the warmest day we have had yet; he has just returned from a ride of
fourteen miles, tired and hungry & had to go up the road to open a
negro man, found dead in his cabin this morning. It is Mrs Reggio's[34]
waiting man—a very valuable & trusty servant; he was up all night
dancing & playing cards. I suppose he had disease of the heart. Is it 'nt
a nice job, for such warm weather as this? At noonday, too. The Dr. will
probably not be at home until three or four o clock so you see, there is

33. Between June 8, 1857, when Tryphena first mentioned the bedding, and June 28,
   Anna apparently agreed and wrote to tell Tryphena that she would send the bedding
   along with other items mentioned herein. See TBHF to ARH, June 8, 1857, MDAH.
34. Several sugar planters with the surname Reggio appear in U.S. 7th Census, 1850,
   Population, Plaquemines Parish, Louisiana, NA. Perhaps she refers to Matilda, the
   thirty-year-old wife of the sugar planter Auguste Reggio, whose name appears near
   that of David Raymond and Tryphena Fox in the U.S. 8th Census, 1860, Population,
   Plaquemines Parish, Louisiana, NA.

one great draw-back to my housekeeping nicely, — irregular meals. The table often stands half the day. Ther has been a great change for me since a week ago yesterday. Mary had been harboring her boy here — feeding him & letting him sleep in her room; he had run away from his master Mr Salvant. She did it for a whole week; we asked her if she had seen the boy & forbade her giving him anything. She stoutly denied having seen or heard of him, all the week, but her master suspected her & came & took her away very suddenly Saturday morning, bringing me another to fill her place. She is an excellent servant & though I have done nothing all the week but teach her my ways, it has been a resting-week for me. Mary had tried my patience for the last month & we should have had to do something with her if her master had not taken her away. On searching her room, we found *the* reason of her laziness & impudence — a jug of whiskey. I knew very well that [a] Northern woman would do all the work she did for us & have every afternoon to sew or do light work, but Mary had got so, that she was never through the washing or the ironing & it seemed impossible to get the kitchen cleaned & everything was getting behindhand. Very often I worked right hard thinking to help her along & the more I did the more she *shirked*, until I was fretted nearly to death & would rather not had any servant at all. She used to do so well that I thought perhaps the warm weather was affecting her, but I know now, that she was often nearly drunk, and I did not think of such a thing at the time. Her master will keep her a month or so to train her. The very afternoon she went from here, she ran away too, & had just come back yesterday of her own ac-cord. All the people, on the coast have always thought her one of the worst Negroes here, & wondered how I got along so well with her, but she has always done well for me until this last month. This woman Ann, I like so much that I shall be very sorry when they are changed again. She is quick & ready, — talks a great deal but is never sullen. She fin-ished the washing in one day & the ironing in two besides the cooking & housework — a thing Mary never did; she could never get the ironing done until late Saturday night & pretend to be ironing every afternoon too. She shall toe the mark when she comes back. This woman too gets up very early in the morning & does a number of little things before breakfast, while Mary never thought of stirring until called & then would often be late about her breakfast, which was very annoying to the Dr, when he wished to go away early, in the cool of the morning; the sun is extremely hot here at mid-day. In the shade one does not feel it as there is generally a good breeze. You write as though you thought I had poor health. and it has been remarkably good, excepting that one sickness I wrote you about. Of course, I am all the time *complaining* but presume the little ailments of first one thing and then another are the every-day occurrences of any one in my condition. The first two months I *did suffer*, so I cannot bear to think of it now, but since have got along tolerably well & hope to do so. My looks have not improved much, & I hardly think you would own such a scare-crow for a daughter; for with all the rest of the changes I have become almost *black*— Hattie writes me of her new house & things, which must be very convenient & pretty & then adds that she is very happy, in her new relation, which I am glad to hear for I feared the match would not be at all suitable. When I think how I would have married & how I have, I am very thankful that there is a future seeing, future planning Eye, watching over us, & preventing our following those inclinations which if pursued, would lead us & others with us so far astray. Dr Raymond is indeed a husband, in every sense of the word and if all who bear the name, were like him there would be far less misery, especially among our own sex, who are naturally dependent in disposition & sensitive in mind. I know I do a great many things, wrong & make many failures in housekeeping, but he has never fretted or scolded me, yet. He is gone most of the time & I try to make everything as pleasant as possible for him when he is here. The evenings we spend in the mosquito house. I fixed up his big bachelor arm-chair last week, which has been broken a long time; he has that, I have my sewing chair our little table, with the lamp, books, papers & my work-basket. I sew & he reads aloud to me— you can imagine what my sewing is, and how my heart throbs with pleasure as I finish one little article after another & put it carefully away. There are painful moments too, when I fear I am not fit for such a responsible duty as is a mother's, even if everything turns out well and the same doubts haunt me as I suppose every woman feels at such a time. Dr R——cheers me up & tells me there is not the least ground for apprehension & I do hope for his sake "all will be well"; I can see how great a source of joy it is to him, he is so domestic in his habits and feelings.

But I have written enough about myself and my affairs & know you must be tired of them.

I was telling Dr Raymond of the land in [New] York State and he inquired if the taxes were paid on that. I did not know, but promised to ask you in my next & how much land there is, & in what township & county it is. Do you know if it is improved any in value as it was some-time ago? Please tell me also where you direct Le Roy's letters. I would like to write to him again.

The peony leaf & myrtle I put away in my Bible; it is now almost five years since Samantha[35] died and how much like a dream everything since then seems. I often dream of her yet & always see her in health and beauty, just as she was when we parted— I seldom dream of Mary but often find myself thinking of her. Dr Raymond says you *picked* for that lock of hair, he knows, trying to make yourself out so young, when he has plenty of grey hairs. I will send a lock of his—from the top of his head— it is very thick, inclined to curl, & generally smooth & glossy.

I did not hear from sister Lucy last night as I hoped. I fear she cannot come, her husband's health is so feeble.

Mr Richards must be thinking seriously of the matrimonial state— buying carpets looks suspicious. I hope he will get a good wife; he seems to be the only old friend who has stood by you, in your troubles If you were near, we could help you, in a great many ways. I could share my fine big Shanghai chickens with you, send you a dozen eggs occa-sionally & plenty of vegetables from the garden.

I would have sent you some of the money Dr R——gave me for clothing, but I had to be very moderate in my own dress, so to get what little things I needed & then he had to give me fifteen more. I have bought no laces or embroidery all is plain— the flannel costs a great deal more than I expected. For the same money I could have got twice as much at the North.

I believe I have written all now— The Dr has not returned; every thing is very still & I should have been quite lonely if not writing.

I should not know how to behave in church now, it is so long since I have been in one— There has been no company here lately, & I do not go out any excepting to ride a little ways. A lady sent me a basket of ripe

---

35. Tryphena variously refers to her deceased sister as "Semantha" and "Samantha."

plums, Tuesday & another a dish of honey — which I can't eat & would send over to you, if possible. My appetite is good, but every thing I eat, disagrees with me, so I am tired of all eatables. Write to me soon, give my love to the children.

I will write again when I get the box. With much affection — believe me yours as ever

Tryphena Fox.

I came near writing Tryphena Holder.

□ □ □

Dear Mother,   HOME, JULY 31ST 1857.

I presume that it is almost unnecessary to remind you that this is my birthday — twenty-three years old. Five years ago to-day I wrote to you from Mr Hubbell's parlor at Gaylord's Bridge, little dreaming, I should have settled so far from you, now. Like all the rest "I'm growing old, *growing old*," and already begin to feel quite staid and matronly. It is yet very early for Dr Raymond was sent for at daylight, to visit a man with lock-jaw, so I jumped up too, had some breakfast for him in true Yankee style, that is, "in a hurry." For the last four weeks we have had rain every day, generally a hard shower coming up about noon. You cannot imagine what a difference it makes in my housekeeping affairs, to have such weather; every thing gets mouldy & muddy & out of order & the washing is around from one week's end to another; it is impossible to get the clothes dry only by piecemeal, and they look so yellow & dirty, that I am nearly discouraged. Perhaps I fret, more than is necessary, but how can one help fretting when everything goes wrong? If Ann was as slow & faithless as most negroes are, I dont know what would be done, but fortunately, she is of some account.

Last Saturday Dr R——went to the city, found the box & shipped it to me by that day's boat. I found it full of *home* & unpacked the things, laughing & crying at the same time. A regular 'haw, haw' greeted the old iron spoon, as I pulled it out. The lamp-mat from Emma is very pretty & shows a great deal of taste for such a little girl. I think she bids fair to beat her older sister's at fancy articles. The miniatures I prize very much but fear you have robbed yourself in sending them. The six silver forks, spoons, and tea spoons, I do not need at present so I shall pack them away & take good care of them to return to you, when I have a good opportunity or to Emma. The flannel sheet is just what I wanted & very acceptable indeed, also the six linen towels & dozen diapers. The pillows are very different from any of Dr R's little ones & make my bed look very much better. They smelled badly & have to be put out in the hot sun every morning. Besides these I find, 3 pr linen sheets, 8 pr. pillow cases (4 wide, 1 fine narrow pr, & 3 coarser) 12 small napkins, one large one & 1 odd towel—2 pr curtains, 1 sugar shovel, butter knife, salt & mustard spoon & the ottoman, footstool, & piece work, which Dr R——laughs at me about, & says I had better finish *now*. It gives me as much pleasure to go & sit down by the old box & take the things out & look them over, & put them away again as if I were a child with my first hoard of toys. I am waiting for pleasant weather, so to have the things whitened & done up, for their long voyage has made them quite yellow & musty. It cost five dollars to N. O. & a little more down here from the express Office.

Dr. R cannot assist you any more at present; his brother Seguin has had to borrow money from him and with some expenses, not calculated when the money was lent, he finds himself in rather an embarrassing position. One item alone—corn for the horses—has cost *fifty-five dollars* for last month with enough until the 1st of Sept. It is ninety-five cents a bushel in N. O. Everything is so dear, that I can't see how people are to live without plenty of money.

Some days I am quite well, and hope to stay so, when the next perhaps I cannot sit up half an hour. I have faint turns in the morning which last about *two* hours—no pain, but such a nervous weakness.

Write to me often & let me know how you are getting along, for I worry so much about you.

Tell Mrs Gabriel I have not forgotten her & would like to see her very much

I cannot write more, the boat *will* be along soon. Shall send you short letters, *often* now. With much love to yourself & the children   I am, Yours affectionately

T. B. Fox

I hear that Mr Messenger has gone North. Those ladies who call on you, will do so from curiosity—not out of any kindness to me particularly.

My Dear Mother,   [AUGUST 31, 1856][36]

You must excuse my not writing sooner; I have felt so little like doing anything, that even a short letter to you looked like a task. This morning I feel quite well, but how long it will last, is the question.

The weather has been oppressively warm for the last few days, with frequent thunder showers as usual. Everything has gone wrong for the last three weeks, but I am done fretting now, since there is no use in it. You will doubtless be astonished & think Dr Raymond & myself the most cruel & hard hearted of *wretches,* when I tell you that our negro man Reuben has *run away*; he took leave three weeks ago yesterday, without the least provocation or punishment beforehand to make him dissatisfied. So we have only one servant to do the work of two— She attends to the horses, harnessing, & unharnessing & feeding, brings her own wood, chops it, feeds the chickens & brings all the water, besides doing the housework. This I let go at loose ends as much as possible & everything looks *so nice,* just at this time too, when I anticipated having everything in such good order.

I could tell you a long lingo about the purchase of Reuben, his fidelity for about six months, then his taking a wife from the next plantation, her ruining him putting him up to steal, & lie & drink & finally persuading him to run away, *she going at the same time,* but it would be too long a story. It would show you though, that he has not run away because he has such hard task-masters, or such quantities of work to do, or because he is not properly clothed & fed & cared for when sick. But I know what those ranting abolitionists will think that *Triphen Holder,* has turned out to be a Southern monster, so you must keep my troubles to yourself. We don't know when we shall get him, but Dr Raymond will probably dispose of him as soon as possible after he returns. His wife, Phillis, was caught some time ago & it is very probable that she feeds him. He has been tracked in various places, with other negroes. There are three or four out, besides him from this neighborhood. His conduct for the last three months shows that he is a grand old scoundrel & was probably sold in Virginia for some rascality.

---

36. This date was assigned by MDAH based on an inscription, not in Tryphena's hand, on the envelope. The letter is difficult to place accurately, though 1856 is obviously incorrect.

Mary came back about two weeks ago, & has done so well that she hardly seems like the same servant.

Dr Raymond is somewhat out of health & very much "out of spirits." He is so mortified & angry to think a negro would run away from him, when so many around here on the plantations, would be glad to have him for master & envy Reuben his place so much. He has so little to do & so many privileges.

The horses, stables, yard, garden & poultry are the things he has to attend to & his whole work, is what a white man at home calls "chores", so you may know, it is nothing very heavy. The garden has grown up with weeds since he left, & the vegetables are mostly spoiled from these continued rains. Fruit is scarce now, we have a few melons, but they are not very good   The mosquitoes have been very bad since I last wrote, so you see—the last three weeks cannot have been very pleasant. Monday Mrs Stackhouse & Mrs Brooks[37] called on me—the only white ladies I have seen Since July.

Sometimes I am in quite good spirits but there is so little to interest me with no company & no chance for riding out & so many things to worry me, that it is the greatest effort for me to be cheerful at all.

Dr Raymond went to town to hire a woman to take care of me, but did not find any, as he could only stay one day. Seguin is to hire one & send her down on the boat next week. I dread having a stranger about me, but it is the best that can be done. Lucy's husband is in such poor health, she cannot come & Aunt Randolph whom I did *hope* to have with me had to go to Father Fox's to take charge of things there. He & his wife have gone North again. His health was so poor, he had to go. Mrs Reggio inquires often about me & will come herself, when I wish her & has promised Dr R——to let her negro nurse stay a week with me. I consider it a great compliment, for there is no one else about here, that she would do so much for. There are some garments to make for myself yet, then a "heap of mending" to do & then all the wearing apparel will be in pretty good order. I wish I could say the same for the house, but there is no use fretting & one thing I am certain of, there cannot be much company here to see the disorder. There are but few

---

37. Lydia Brooks, the forty-eight-year-old mother of Sarah Stackhouse. U.S. Census, 1850, Population, Plaquemines Parish, Louisiana, NA.

ladies in the neighborhood. Dr R——says he can keep house for himself, & "I reckon" he can as he had such good experience in that line, before he was married. The little pins came safely; I think the "heir apparent" will be well provided for; not a letter comes from any of the relations, but it contains something for the little line. Lucy has been exceedingly kind in sending me patterns of every description, & Aunt Randolph sent a very pretty linen lawn shirt trimmed with valenciennes lace in her last.

I told Hattie what I had been doing, so if you have any curiosity to know about such *trifles,* she will read it to you.

Write to me soon & I will write again next week, if I can. My love to all, with much to yourself from Yours aff—

T. B. Fox.

□ □ □

Dear Mother,   Sunday P. M. Sept. 20th '57

I was taken sick last Sunday night about twelve o clock and safely delivered of a little girl in about *two hours.* My confinement so far, has been unusually free from the maladies attending that of most women. I have had no milk fever or trouble with my breasts. As this is my seventh day I hope soon to get up & attend to my household duties & the claims of the little one. It is a fine, plump child & weighed about nine pounds! It is not decided yet who it resembles, but I think its father, as her little eyes are very dark & she has plenty of very dark hair. Dr R——is well. I will write more when I can sit up. The mails must have failed for I have heard nothing from you in a long time. Write soon-

With much love to yourself & the children from both Dr R——& myself & "ma petite" I am   Affectionately Your Daughter

T. B. Fox.

To, a *"Grandmother.*
written flat on my back!

□ □ □

My Dear Mother,   Hygiene, Nov. 1st 1857.

Now that the baby is asleep, & I have sent Osborne his medicine (a thing I have to attend to three times a day) and given out breakfast & looked to the milk and cream, there are a few spare moments which can be called mine & I will give them to you. 'Pet' is moving, so I cannot write long; she is still quite well & only cries now & then from colic which troubles her occasionally. For the last three days she has been in my arms almost constantly. Marie[38] had to be sent home, having stuck a nail in her foot so she could not walk & I have got the baby into the bad habit of sleeping in her arms & now she won't sleep on the bed in the day-time so I am obliged to hold her—great business is nt it? She was just named when we received your letter— we were four weeks about deciding, but at last concluded on *Fannie Otis*[39]—after Sister Fannie Fox and the maiden name of Dr Raymond's mother. I thought it proper she should be called that, as she is the only granddaughter of the first wife—(the Dr's Mother) and he never had any [of his own] sisters to be named after her. He & an older brother, Daniel, are all that are living of hers & this & Daniel's one son, the only grand-children. Fannie was very dear to Dr R——so dear that I am sometimes jealous of even the memory of her & it was by her that the match was made—so I thought it no more than right that his first daughter should have her name. I wished to name her after you or Mary; sometimes I fancy she looks very much like Samantha, who will ever be as dear and whose memory will ever be as sacred as if I had named my first little one after her. I gave the preference to the Dr's side of the house, as he is so much older & presume my side will not be left out when the *other eleven* are to be named. I hear that Aunt Randolph with whom the Dr is a great favorite, is very much disappointed that it is not a boy, so it could be called Edward Randolph, after the Dr's twin brother, who died when quite young. I reckon, she can bear the disappointment if we can.

My health is very good; I am not very strong yet, but hope to gain when I can go about some. It is now *five* months that I have been confined to the house & it begins to be very tedious to me. Dr Raymond had the horse harnessed this evening to take me to ride but was called away *ten* miles below just as the buggy was ready. The influenza still prevails, & he is absent most of the time, so that I cannot help feeling lonely sometimes and wish you could be here with me. One would think I ought to have an easy time with only *us two* & the babe, & three

---

38. A hired servant.
39. Tryphena initially used the spelling "Fannie" for her daughter's name, but later settled into the consistent use of Fanny. Fannie Fox died in 1856. See TBHF to ARH, December 29, 1856, MDAH.

servants— but I can tell you mother with the sick boy Osborne making four negroes here, it is just as if they were so many children to look after! It requires more watching & telling & running after them to get the work done, than to do it oneself. Mary has annoyed me more than I can tell you for the last few weeks & the better I treat her, the more impudent & lazy she grows. If she would only do right, and she can do so well when she pleases, I might have quite an easy time, & grow *fleshy,* but this constant worrying keeps me poor. We have bought a cow since I last wrote & Mary has the milking to do & she lets the pans stay unwashed, & her milk pail & strainer & the milk would all be sour, if I did not look after them every time; then she steals the cream, & butter when I tell her to do the churning & grumbles & dawdles about all the time. Reuben is very good in intention but needs directing just like a boy of ten. Talk about *freeing* negroes, some of them could n't take care of themselves *ten* days.

SUNDAY—TWO WEEKS LATER.

I am very sorry that I have allowed the time to slip by, in this way without sending this & hope it will not happen so again, even if I do not write more than half a page. My time is so much occupied with the babe, when she is awake and with mending & making & household affairs when she is asleep, that my pen has been wholly neglected lately and I owe all my correspondents a letter. I was much disappointed in not hearing from you this morning; I was sure there would be a letter for me; but I know as well as if you had written that you are in distress and it only makes me more anxious to know how you are getting along. When I think of the money 'panic' at home, the thousands who are thrown out of employment & the hard winter coming on it makes me very unhappy & anxious about you. Hattie wrote me that you & the children were well & I was very thankful to hear that little.

My health is excellent, but I am not good for anything, for it takes but little to tire me. The baby has an attack of colic regularly every evening which lasts about two or three hours. I have the whole care of her so that by night I am very much worried and for the last week or more have been obliged to go to bed with her very early, thus taking away much of my writing & sewing time. The little negress whom we have hired is not good for anything, as nurse; she is very handy in waiting upon me, but I believe it is more work to look after her, than she is worth as waiting maid.

This last week I have been out visiting twice & it has really done me good. Wednesday evening to Mrs Stackhouse, taking the baby, along, & Mary to nurse her, & yesterday started for a short ride & unexpectedly spent the day with Mrs Goodin while the Dr went on to town with Mr Goodin as he found him just starting as we arrived there. The sugar houses are all in operation now & it gives the coast a very lively air. A boiler burst last Tuesday, in one of them, seriously burning the fireman—a negro. Dr Fox, has been attending on him twice a day, but it is hardly probable that he will live No others were hurt. The weather has been quit cold but we have had only one or two white frosts. It is so changeable here that you cannot tell one hour, what it will be the next. This morning it is warm & foggy, but is turning cold every moment. We had a letter from father yesterday; he was on his way home & will visit us soon, I look for them next week, so will have to be busy this week preparing for them.

I have made no preserves or cake in a long time; we seldom eat any & company is scarce. Oranges are ripe now & quite plentiful. A Creole Woman sent me nearly half a bushel of large fine golden ones last week, but they are too nice for preserving. Every time I look at them, I wish I could send some to the children— What do you think we had to pay for the cow? An enormous price to New England ears for a common creole cow—55.00, while I know that Grandpa has sold better ones for twenty. She has a young calf which gets one half the milk—a gallon the other, is enough for us. I suppose you have noticed that the banks in New Orleans suffered as well as in other places. Fortunately Dr R——lost nothing by the failure of the one he generally deposits in for we had used it out. He gave his note for the cow. His business has been very good this year, so that the cash will begin to come in soon after the first of Jan. He looks worried & tired & I wish he would have a respite, but there is little hope of that.

I believe I have told you all, for this time, & I must close for fear the boat will come before I can get this ready.

Give my love to the children & accept much for yourself & I believe that I often wish you could sit at my table & share my fireside & can only hope that your trouble will not last always.

Your daughter,

T. B. Fox.

□ □ □

Dear Mother,   HYGIENE SUNDAY, DEC, 27TH 1857

It gives me great pleasure to enclose, the check of twenty-five dollars to you. I hope it will help you at least, a little, towards getting through the Winter. I consider it my Christmas present from Dr. Raymond. — After this, we are obliged to save every dollar he can "rake & scrape" to pay for a negro woman, whom I told you in my last, he thought of purchasing.[40] She has two likely children (girls) the oldest, five years of age, and is soon to have another, and he only pays fourteen hundred for the three. It is considered an excellent bargain, at the present high prices of negroes, and he would not sell her & the children for less than $2,000. She came & worked two days, so we could see, what she was capable of doing, and I find her a good washer & ironer and pastry cook & able to cook plain, every day meals. She was sold by a Frenchman; who like most foreigners, is very hard on negroes. He has a family of ten & she had all the work to do besides getting her own wood & water from the river— She was not used to do this, & gave them a great deal of trouble, and besides, they could speak but little English & she did not understand French so her mistress found it impossible to get along with her. She came from Mobile last Spring. How much trouble she will give me, I dont know, but I think I can get along with her, passably well any how. Of course it increased my cares, for having invested so much in one purchase, it will be to my interest to see that the children are well taken care of & clothed & fed. All of them give more or less trouble. We get along very well with Reuben now, since *Phillis'* visits here, are forbidden. She made him ugly & idle. Mary has her periodical sullen fits as usual & I put up with a great deal from her. I suppose we shall keep her until after this woman (Susan) is confined which will be about the last of Feb. In the mean time I am going to make Mary

---

40. Susan, a slave woman and mother of Adelaide and Margaret.

take care of the baby & do coarse sewing for there are suits of clothes to be made for both Reuben & Susan & her children. I shall take the time to do up what fine sewing I can for the summer. Dr R——said last night, when I was up tossing the baby, trying to quiet her, that I was the greatest slave on the coast for I never had a moment's time for myself & he would not submit to it any longer. The baby grows finely and has learned to coo in good earnest. For the past week or so she has troubled me some at night, though on the whole she is a pretty good baby.

Christmas did not pass very pleasantly with me. Dr R——took an early dinner with me & then was obliged to go to town; so I was very lonesome in the afternoon & evening. If it had been any other day I should not have felt so, but it was such a calm sun-shiny afternoon, & such a bright moon-light evening, that I would have given a great deal to have been in town with him. But these women with babies must make up their minds to stay at home, unless they are rich enough to have a carriage & can take a servant along to nurse the baby. I do not expect to go to the city this winter, though we could borrow a carriage, but I have no bonnet or cape, only the one I bought when I left home. Dr R——offered to get me both but it looks extravagant when I go so seldom & there are so many other things really needed & I wanted to send you this. Spring will be along by and by & then I can go.

Father Fox made us a flying visit last week; he came Wednesday evening & returned Saturday morning. I enjoyed his visit far more than I could tell you. It seemed so nice to have Somebody here, to talk with us & relieve the monotonous life. He asked me to go back with him but I could not think of leaving Dr Raymond by himself & he is completely tied to his practice.

Friday evening, about twilight he Christened the baby; there was no one here but ourselves. It would have been *so* pleasant to have had more of his friends & some of mine, (though I believe *you* are almost all on my side) but we stood up, as we are, alone, and presented our first-born, for the blessing of Heaven & promised to bring her up, according to the requisitions of our Maker & the Church, as far as lay in our power.

Do you ever hear from Le Roy, now-a-days? give him much of my love & tell him what a nice little niece he has, & for the sake of our happy childhood days not to forget his old maid sister Triphen who did not quite turn out an old maid for all. Tell Georgy & Emma I should like to see them very much but I expect it will be a long long time now, before we meet. What has become of Hattie D——and why dont she answer my last? It is now four yrs five winter's since I left Old Berkshire, and it almost seems like a dream that I ever lived there.

I have time to write a little more & so give you a P. S. I forgot to tell you what a quantity of nice things were sent to baby & myself from Woodburne. Sister Emily made her a beautiful little white frock, *trimmed* with cambric edging and five sets of tucks, four in each set. The[n] she sent me a bundle of Sister Fanny's things—they were divided among her friends; it consisted of a checked silk dress but very little worn, a nice large cape, trimmed all around with linen lace, two inches broad, and a quantity of other lace & edging suitable for the baby. I shall keep the clothing, as it is, as a memento of her. To her little name-sake, they sent a beautiful box, containing many of her toilette articles—two fancy shaped bottles of perfumery, and a quaint little jug, with "Jockey Club," some nice soap, her *silver* powder box (which is a *valuable*) a little emery stand, some new Turkey red trimming for a morning dress & a fancy crocheted bracelet. All these I have put away for her, till she is old enough to hear about her Aunt Fanny, & take care of them herself. Besides these Aunt Randolph sent her a new crib quilt, three wrappers—a white, yellow, & purple one, four little sacks embroidered on the edge, two green gingham, one buff cambric & one yellow flannel with a little red dot in it. This is worked with yellow silk floss & is a dressy little thing. Besides these, I found in the bundle two pairs of little white socks, one with a pink stripe in the foot the other with a blue, a little pincushion, and a little *holder* all for the baby. For me there was an embroidered collar, Aunt R——'s work, a large blue figured satin pincushion and two crocheted lampmats, and another one for Dr R——. So you see they think a great deal of us at Woodburne & far more of me than I deserve, *I guess.* It is said that an addition is expected to the family about the first of March; four sets of children! just think of it; so much for old men taking unto themselves young wives.

But I am at the end of my paper again, so with much love I am as ever   Your aff. daughter

T. B. Fox.

If you have any trouble in collecting this, let me know & Dr——will try to arrange it.

You [. . .] his endorsement on the back of the check.

T.—

□ □ □

My Dear Mother   [Hygiene Sunday Night May 16th 1858]

I have not written for the most miserable reason imaginable — because I could not help you, and it is with the greatest reluctance that I send this. I know how disappointed you will be on opening it— I see you throw it down in despair, exclaiming "what shall I do"? I hoped if I put off writing something might happen so that I could enclose at least a small sum of money, but I cannot. Dr Fox's collections this year with money lent out which he cannot get fall short by $900; He will be obliged to borrow $200, to get through the year & pay current expenses—provisions, horse & cow feed & other necessary out go. *He would help you if he could.* The reason of his not getting his expected dues is the total loss of crop to all the planters on this side of the river, by the *crevasses,* which have completely submerged all the plantations in this vicinity. Messrs Stackhouse upon whom he depended for $170.00, the first of May are ruined. Their fields, sugar houses, quarters & dwelling are in under water—in some places four feet deep; We have the river very high one side & the overflowed land like a lake on the other. Fortunately our house is high off the ground—& our yard slants up to the river, so that our front yard is dry yet, but the lower end of the garden & the cow-lot are under water. A little draining machine & ditches which Dr R——has been making will probably save the garden from being entirely submerged.

We are on the highest point of land here. In some places the water has filled the fields & crossed the road to the foot of the river leevee, making the bridges float & the roads almost impassable.

I would have written this before I received any answer to my last, but I was quite sick. I had two chills with high fever, followed by an obstinate diarrhea which made me very poorly. All are quite well now. Baby is growing very fast   she sits alone on the floor & creeps a little with her *heels.* Dr R——threatened sending me up to Mississippi to recruit, but I can get well here faster by taking the travelling money, & sending it to you. He has not the money to spare now, but if anything happens — if some delinquent pays a bill, and he says I can go with that, I will ask him for it, for you.

You do not write as though you wished Emma to come — I have thought of another plan — How would you like, (provided all can be done which I shall write presently) to break up entirely, place Emma with Mr Spear,[41] Georgy with brother & *you* come out here with me; — *If* — Mr Spear would be willing to board & educate Emma, for what rent he could get for the place — say $100, per year, & if Le Roy would be willing to take Georgy with him. You may think [it] strange that I make you such a proposition as to leave your two young children at the North & you come here, but it is the only way I can think of, unless you let Emma or Georgy come. Then you would have only one to support & perhaps could get some kind of employment. I know it would be best if Le Roy & I could now & then send you money for you to remain where you are & as you are & live on what we send you — but *that* is so uncertain, that it must keep you all the time watching & hoping & waiting & making you very miserable & often unhappy. If Le Roy can continue to assist you through the summer Dr R——says he will send you money in the fall — but that is so long. If you still wish to send Emma — how would it do to let her return with Miss Abby that was; she can put her in the care of some[one] on the boat after she leaves it from her place down to N. Orleans & I could meet her there. Tell me what you think of it & I will write to (Miss Abby . . . as soon as I get yours. *Think well* — of my propositions & let me know — for I am worried & cannot enjoy anything feeling as I do now about you all.

I cannot write any more to night — as you see my pen is a mere scratch — & the mosquitoes are like bees — stringing and buzzing incessantly.

I am afraid that Emma will be put down & have all her independence of spirit destroyed if she goes to the Institute under the present circumstances[42] — I know how poor girls are treated by a crowd of thoughtless girls who can wear finer clothes & have richer parents.

41. Reverend Charles V. Spear, A. M., administrator, and teacher of moral and natural sciences at Maplewood Institute for Young Ladies in Pittsfield.
42. Emma Holder attended Maplewood in 1858 and 1859, but did not graduate.

With me I could dress her very well from things too small or not needed for myself. Good night. Give my love to her & Georgy — & dont think me careless & neglectful because I have not sent any money. If I was single, you know it might be different — though Dr R —— is not to blame now. With much love I am as ever Your daughter

T. B. Fox.

□ □ □

My Dear Mother,   HYGIENE *ISLAND* July 9TH "58

As you have not heard from me in some time, you may be anxious to hear how the times go with us — At present we are living very unpleasantly and have had much anxiety all this week about the baby. She was taken suddenly with vomiting last Saturday which continued at intervals, Sunday and Monday with drowsiness & weakness.

Dr R —— gave her calomel which relieved her and she seemed better; yesterday she again showed much prostration and coughed a great deal. Towards night I think she had a chill, so that I shall be obliged to give her quinine to-day. Her cough is very bad this morning though looser than yesterday. I cannot tell you how anxious I am about her & fear she will not recover very soon, situated as we now are. As you will guess by the date above, we are entirely surrounded by water & since Wednesday morning. it has rained almost incessantly. The atmosphere is very damp and at times so close we can hardly breathe. The water stands twenty inches on the back yard & a foot & more in front. There is not a dry spot of land in the yard   The levee which you know is like a raised railroad is the only terra firma visible for miles. In some places the back water is so high that it runs over the levee from the fields into the river. We can go to the kitchen & out houses, only by paths of staging built up two feet high. Fortunately the house stands on brick pillars six feet from the ground so we shall not have to move or put false floors in as many of our neighbors do. The kitchen is two feet from the ground but I expect to see the water in it every day. The stables are under also the corn house & Reubens cabin. The water has risen rapidly for the last few days from the heavy showers; we thought as all of our out-buildings were built up from the ground we should suffer no inconvenience, but Dr R —— had to have the corn moved yesterday & has the stables to fill up with dirt — Many of the people have gone away, some to the city, others to the other side for a time. Most of the cattle have been sold and what few are left are in an almost starving condition — it is truly heart-rending to see the poor creatures standing upon the bare levee with hardly a blade of grass to appease their hunger. Dr R——told me he saw two dying yesterday as he came up the road. Many planters have hired their negroes out elsewhere so that the coast is almost depopulated & has a very desolate appearance   I am sorry for the poor Creoles, who depend upon their little patches of ground for sustenance. — many of them live by supplying the N. O. market with vegetables, & fruit, all of which are destroyed. I expect all of our orange trees will die; we have taken up the arbor-vitaes and magnolias and set them out in half barrels, out of the water, but they look badly. The Fates seem to be against us in adorning our place & making a pretty home of it. The old oak on the South & the three young pecans on the North which are growing rap-idly now will probably be the only shrubbery left. We have some of the curiosities of Natural History brought to our very doors by the back-water — alligators, a variety of snakes & craw-fish. One gentleman killed an alligator on his back gallery — it had just taken possession of a goose. Snakes glide about in the water as numerous as the grass-hoppers were on the land. We have killed a great number   some very venomous. Ann amused me the other morning — she came in very much excited to tell that she had "just killed one of them big red & yellow snakes what draws the thunder & lightening you know" that's what made it rain last night" — a negro superstition.

The craw-fish are miniature lobsters — red with red claws & belly & dark reddish brown back— They are almost innumerable and do untold damage to the levee by making their holes through— In fact it is to the craw-fish that we are *indebted* for all this great loss & trouble. Where the crevasse occurred, the levee was completely undermined by them — The Creoles make use of them as an article of diet — eating the white flesh on the tails & claws. We have plenty of fresh-fish now as Dr R——has set a long line in the river, one night he caught a cat-fish three feet long & fourteen inches through. The meat was very white & firm & made a delicious dish for breakfast. Besides he had caught a large number of smaller blue cat-fish, so we had as much as we wanted last week. Another article of food which we have is *the shrimp* — which is very much like the *prawn* of the North, only smaller. We make sacks with a hoop for a rim & suspend them into the river, with meal inside for bait. The shrimp come in, for the meal & in a few moments a large quantity will collect in one bag. This is pulled up, the water strains through the sack leaving the shrimp behind. Sometimes, we let the sacs down three or four times before we get enough for our family   say half a peck. These are washed & boiled in salt & water about ten minutes. There is only a little morsel of food in each one, which is white & delicate like lobster & makes a very good salad. The Creoles almost live on them. I have them caught more for the negroes as a variety for them, for I am obliged to feed them mostly on salt pork & corn meal. You can imagine that it is rather difficult to find a great variety—without fruit or vegetables. I forget when I say fruit, for I am not wholly deprived of that— John—a negro man living on the next place brings me a large dish full of fresh figs every morning   They are very nice peeled & eaten with milk & also make a good preserve. I often say— "now if I could only send these to Mother"—sometimes I am almost sick from wishing to see you—probably being so confined, so like a prisoner makes me think more of you all & of "old times," than if we were differently situated. Dr R——is perfectly disgusted with the country & we have long talks about "how nice it would be to move into some neighborhood where we could enjoy some society"—but those long talks always end in resolving that we will stay where we are until we are *sure* of doing better.

MONDAY A. M.

I am happy that I can tell you that baby is better, before mailing this. Last Friday she was so sick, that we hardly thought she could live   she showed symptoms of quick pneumonia & Dr. R——was obliged to apply a blister to her breast & give her broken doses of calomel all night— We sent for leeches but could not get any. The blister relieved her and she has been recovering slowly since. Her cough is better but still holds on. The little thing requires constant nursing and looks so bad & puny to what she did two weeks ago that I cannot bear to have her put down a moment. She has no teeth yet! and is ten months old day after tomorrow.

Dr. R——has lost some patients lately with congestive fever. It is said that the yellow fever & typhoid fever are in N. O, but are not prevalent.

The water rises on us every hour— the levee below at Mr Stackhous place is in danger of breaking   If this high wind continues through the night, it cannot stand & we shall have a foot more of water piled upon that which is now in the yard.—   The mosquitoes are very numerous and troublesome & I suppose we shall hardly be free from them for a year to come.— They deprive us of our evenings, for it is too damp now to stay in the mosquitoes house on the gallery and we are obliged to retire under the bar where we can only read

My *hurry* with sewing is over now, though I see plenty to do, to keep me busy. Week before last I thought I accomplished a wonderful feat for me—as you know I am slow with the needle. I made Dr R——two pr. of nice linen pantaloons all stitched & fixed just as the city tailors make them & a muslin dress for myself besides. I took one of his ready made pr for a model, ripped them up & made mine just like them. He is very much pleased with the fit & make of them and of course *I* am.

My health is quite good now—but my *temper* is *quite bad*— these darkies "do plague me to death" sometimes. Susan goes by fits & starts— good three or four weeks & then so ugly & contrary that an angel could hardly keep mild & pleasant. To-day it has been push, hurry, push, to get the washing any where near done & though it is four o clock she is just hanging out the colored clothes. The white things have only been washed in *one* water & boiled— she has done nothing but wash since six o clock this morning, so you may know how slow she is—only three   Dr R——baby & myself to wash for.

But I must not stop to write more this time   write soon as I am anxious to hear from you now & feel when you do not write that you are in trouble. Give my love to Georgy & Emma & accept much for yourself from Your daughter who is always thinking of you & often wishing to see you—

T. B. Fox.

As soon as anything is decided about Emma. I shall let you know immediately.

T.

My Dear Mother,   Hygiene Aug. 16th 1858.

Your two letters of July 31st & Aug 7th reached me Saturday night. I am always glad to hear from you, though what you write often makes me sad, & unhappy. Probably you never dreamed on the morning of that July 31st, how far away, a mere quarter of a century, would bear your first wee girl, from you & how you would be reduced to such extremities as you are. As I read the letter, and look at my little one sleeping beside me, the *sad* thought comes that perhaps we too may be as widely separated when she has seen as many birthdays. I thought of you all, but felt too lonely & unhappy to write; like all the rest of these long summer days it passed by monotonously and was spent in the common routine of duties. The summer has been one that will never be forgotten, but will never be remembered as a pleasant one. Dr R —— amuses me by calling this parish the penitentiary of the U. S. He thinks our prospects rather gloomy for the coming year; if he cannot make something more than a living here, he will not stay, as he thinks he can at least make a living elsewhere & then we can have the enjoyment of some society. Just think—I have not seen a white woman for *six weeks*! The water is *falling* slowly—commenced the 1st of August & has gone down about *five* inches—not a very fine prospect for dry land   very slow!

Baby is quite well now; Saturday the day she was eleven months old succeeded in creeping across the room for the first time. She is very backward in comparison with other children here, of the same age; *they* have teeth and walk or stand alone, while she has not a sign of a tooth yet

Dr Raymond & myself are quite well; yesterday I felt badly all day and took some quinine fearing a chill. The yellow fever is in New Orleans, there were fifty deaths last Thursday from the fever and the average is about three hundred a week. We do not fear it much down here; this parish has heretofore seemed particularly exempt from it and we hope the same will be the case now.

I am sorry to hear that Emma is disappointed in not coming with me this Fall—Poor Child! she does n't know how unpleasant Trinys home would be for her in many respects. Still I wish she was with me and I would try to make her as contented as possible; she would be company for me & Fannie too. The poor little thing will grow up here by herself and never know what it is to have childish companions and enjoy the sports of playmates. We may not stay here much longer though, and as soon as we feel more settled I shall be urgent about Emma's coming to live with me, unless Le Roy should agree with my plan.

What I wrote in my last has almost slipped from my mind & I have tried in vain to recall what there was to lead you to think that I supposed you extravagant—for I assure you such an idea has not entered my head; I know too well how you must have deprived yourself, to get along with so little for the last two years. Often when giving out dinner or breakfast, I wish to myself, that I could send you the same   I try to be just as economical as I can & yet our grocer's bill alone is over *three* hundred—but then there are seven mouths to be filled and just so much meat must be cooked for these *poor oppressed* darkies every day. I use about two barrels of flour *$16*, one of sugar *$14*, (we give it to the negroes twice a day) a *sac* of coffee (175 lbs) *$16*; 15 dollars worth of rice, $18, of lard and two barrels of pork *$25*, besides hams & shoulders *$25*. Of course we cannot get much fresh meat—none at all now; we have occasionally a chicken or duck or fresh fish whenever we choose to catch them. Then we have to buy corn & fodder which is $250.00 a year & clothing for ourselves & negroes about 200.00 more; then there are extras—a dollar here & a dollar there, so that the expenses swell up to a thousand a year & often over, as every year something has to be done to the house or we need new furniture or fences & so the dimes go. You know *the* physician of any place has to keep up a certain style & it costs twice as much to live here as it does at the North. I keep an accurate list of every thing that is spent & know to a dollar how much we have coming to us, it is very little so far this year, for there has been but little outside practice—all of Dr R——s horseback riding has been for those who employ him by the year & are at liberty to call on him at any time without extra charge. It is not very sickly yet but I dread the time when the water leaves the ground moist & *malarious.*— Father's wife has never recovered from her confinement last March and is still confined to the house with swollen limbs & general debility. Dr Raymond is treating her by letter & has just finished a long one to his Father. She has improved since he commenced prescribing for her. They are very anxious that we should come to Woodburne, but we shall not go this summer— we talk some of visiting them on Christmas, but that is such

a long way ahead that it is *talk,* to me.— You say the Merrills are coming South and you wish you were coming too— so do *I*— would it not
be delightful to have you spend the winter with me?— the very thought
makes me foolish, for I say, why could not I have been *rich,* & then I
could send on for Mother & the children. Give much of my love to
Hannah; if she comes to N. O. Dr Raymond says he will take me up,
purposely to see her— I would like to have her come down & stay
awhile with me and would urge her to do so if there was any society or
anything here to make her visit pleasant.

As to Uncle Brague's people, I can never feel grateful enough to them
for their kindness to you. I thought of writing to them last week & two
or three times tried to commence but was called away; now that you
wish me to, I will certainly do so. Hattie must have received mine before this time for I mailed it three or four weeks ago. I have another
letter to answer to-day; after that is finished if there is time I will write
to Uncle Brague. Perhaps you wonder that I should say—"if there is
time"—when there is only three white folks Dr R——Pet, & myself &
three negroes to wait upon us— but for all that, I find plenty to keep
me busy & am often behindhand in sewing or answering letters. Last
week I finished a fine shirt for Dr. Raymond & commenced another,
made two good coarse ones for Reuben, and altered two dresses for
baby, besides mending. Baby is out-growing all her little chemises &
night-gowns & must have a new supply for Winter—besides thick
dresses.

I am cutting off all her little slips, so that they only come to the floor
& she does look so cunning & pretty when I have finished dressing her
in the morning—with her little white apron & red corals and brown or
blue or pink dresses—white get soiled so soon, I do not put them on
her much. I was so sorry to read about Emma's wanting a new dress for
examination! Tell her—to never mind, but be a smart scholar and the
people will notice her more than if she was dressed in fine clothes. How
I can sympathize with her; do you not remember how I wanted one, the
first term?

EVENING, AFTER DINNER

I have come out on the gallery steps to write for the mosquitoes have
already begun to leave the dark corners & places of the room & whet
their bills for the night. We have dinner very late Mondays & Thurs-

days, as we seldom breakfast until nine or ten. Dr R——goes over to
Fansy plantation riding before daybreak, crossing the river in a skiff &
riding down on the other side on horseback. He is generally gone about
three or four hours & I have breakfast ready by the time he comes back,
besides having the house put in order & the washing commenced.—
Nothing beautiful greets my eye as I look up from my writing— heavy
dark clouds above & an expense of dirty looking water below. The
ducks are *sailing* about in it, here in the yard & yonder in the corner by
the dying orange-tree the calf—now a half grown heifer & pretty too—
stands half way up to her knees in water, looking very disconsolate &
probably wondering if it is not most supper time— We are obliged to
let it suck yet, but feed it some on shucks & corn-meal. The old cow
gives about half her measure of milk yet & we hope will supply us for
some time. I named her Bess when we first bought her. It would give
me great pleasure to send you in a pitcher of milk from her, but as it is
not very convenient   here is a picayune for Georgy to go & buy him
some; and you will give Mother & Emma a share won't you Georgy?
Here comes an old negro man who has caught some fish from the back-
water   "Do you want to buy any fish, Madame"— No, Uncle, I dont
want any to-night," so he walks slowly away regretting the *dime,* which
he would have spent for a drink at the little grocery just below, kept by
an unprincipled Frenchman, who prides himself on selling bad whisky
to the negroes & receiving stolen goods from them in payment, when
they have no cash.

I have tried in vain to remember the Miss Townsend of whom you
write, but cannot recall her face— there was a teacher by that name but
if single yet, she must be a "right old maid". She had red hair; is that the
one. Whoever it is I wish Emma could have come with her. I presume
H. Meade[43] is at Baconham yet; if she had left there, some of the
Woodburne people would have told me.— The needles are very acceptable but you would not wonder that I loath the sight of them should I
give you a list of the sewing I have done since last Spring. It seems as if
I never should finish—am always in a hurry for something. It is hard to
make a complete sewing-machine of myself, when I love to read & write

---

43. Harriet Mead, a Pittsfield resident who also studied at Maplewood Institute, became
    tutor at Baconham once Tryphena married in 1856.

so much— Fortunately Dr Raymond is so kind as to read aloud to me a great deal; otherwise all that I ever learned would be forgotten. At present he is reading *Gel Blas*[44] aloud to me *in French* to accustom me more to the language & I am translating to myself Voltaire's Louis 14th—which promises to be very interesting. I seldom have to look out the meaning of a French word now. As for my music, *it is* all laid aside, excepting my songs.

These I sing over occasionally when alone, & busy with the needle. But this is spun out long enough, both for your *eyes* & patience & the little time left must be devoted to writing to Sister Lucy— you cannot imagine what nice long letters she sends me— if you will remail them, I will send you some of them to read—sometime. Much love to Emma & Georgy & much to yourself From your daughter—

Tryphena F.

Dr Raymond has been called away, but would wish to be remembered if here. Baby has gone to walk—or rather Ann has taken her. I wish you could hear her say bon (bonnet) & by & pa-pa— & then she jabbers a great deal of "Cherokee" besides.— Am *much* obliged for the envelopes.

□ □ □

"BRIGHT & EARLY" SUNDAY MORNING SEPT. 5TH 1858

DEAR MOTHER—

Am I not smart this morning? was up before sunrise; have bathed & dressed, given out breakfast, weighed out fifteen quinine powders, and am now ready to tell you that yours of Aug was received last night. I am much obliged for the needles and also for Le Roy's address. I should like to see him very much; it makes me feel quite happy to hear that he is doing so well. I told Dr Raymond what you wrote and he seemed to be very much gratified to hear he has such a brother-in-law. He has often asked about him & wondered that he did not write to me; I could not tell him much & I feared that he had concluded that he had rather a scape-grace of a brother.

'The Dr' is gone this morning to visit a lady who is very sick with fever— she lives about four miles above; her husband has an interest in the plantation; they are Creoles but of a very excellent family—the Vil-

---

44. *Historie de Gil Blas de Santillane: précédée des jugements et témoinages sur Le Sage et sur Gil Blas*, written by Alain René Le Sage (1668–1747).

lerè's.[45] I am afraid she will not live— she has five young children the oldest not more than seven & the youngest a babe about two months old. Besides her husband is devoted to her, so much so that his life almost depends upon hers— *I never knew a man* to think so *much of his wife* and that is saying a great deal for me. There are a great many cases of fever now—probably caused by the malaria. They are mostly intermittent, yet are very obstinate and difficult to break. Large doses of quinine are required to produce any effect. The Yellow Fever still rages in the city. We had a letter from Lizzie last night. She writes that there is a number of cases in Algiers. I hoped that she would come down and stay with us while the fever raged, but she seems intending to face it & I presume she does 'nt like to leave Seguin to keep house when he has so many patients to attend to.

Here comes "Miss Fannie" from her morning walk and seems very anxious to leave Ann, for mother. She is very healthy now and has cut two teeth without any sickness or ailment.

Week before last Susan and one of her children—her second girl about three years old, had fever which confined them to bed five days and last week Reuben had two hard chills with fever, so that he had to keep in his room & be waited upon most of the time. Friday Ann was complaining but I gave her a dose of salts & she seems better— I do not know what would be done if she should be sick as she is my *mainstay* in the servant's line.

When Susan is sick, she steps willingly into her place and does all of Susan's work & her own, excepting nursing baby, which I do myself then. She is so active that she can do the work of two easily, and instead of having to push her to "move-on" I am obliged to tell her she has done enough for one day. Then when Reuben is sick, she flies around & does his work & her own too— feeds the horses & cow, brings wood & water, saddles the horse, blacks boots & shoes & does it all without being told. Susan would see the horses starve & everything go to ruin before she would do it, unless ordered. She makes a very good servant though & tries to please more than she did at first. The water has fallen about three feet & left our yard almost dry. It presents a very desolate

---

45. It is possible that she refers to Felix Villère, a sugar planter who lived near Hygiene with his wife, Levern. This could also be Cecil Villère and his wife, Marie.

appearance, being entirely stripped of vegetation. We have winter fields & summer skies. The garden will be sufficiently dry to work in, this week. The roads are dry in places, but not so we can take a ride of any length on account of miry spots. Dr R——was going to take me out this evening but he will have to go & see Mrs Villère again & it is not good riding all the way between here & there— The mosquitoes have been very annoying both day & night for the last three weeks. One can sit down scarcely five minutes in any peace.

I have been sewing a little the past week, nursing baby & giving medicines & reading some. Have listened to several essays & lectures on fever in general & yellow fever in particular besides lectures on other medical subjects, read aloud by Dr D. R. Fox, *my professor.* My reading has not amounted to much—mostly "Gil Blas" in French. I commenced it more for improving in French than anything else, but find it really *amusing*— Did you ever read it? The volume I have is a very large one & copiously illustrated— it belongs to Mrs Reggio. Then I catch up a paper now & then when nursing baby, & read *Harper,* as soon as it arrives. I feel under much obligation to Messrs H——for their good company—more appreciated than ever here in a Louisiana swamp.— The insects here keep one busy. Dirt-daubers are constantly making their nests in every nook & corner, spiders take possession of a room for one night & leave it full of cob-webs, & ants crawl into the drawers & dirty clothes basket & make holes for me to mend. Last week I found one of baby's prettiest dresses—a yellow chambray worked around the bottom, almost ruined; it was completely perforated with little ant holes, which one washing converted into large vents.

Dear Mother—   MONDAY SEPT. 20TH.

When I commenced this I thought to finish & send it by the first mail, but two have passed and I have had my hands full of sickness & trouble— I know that you are looking for help from me in every letter & it worries me that I cannot send it now. I will make no promises for they are only broken—but believe me in this. I will send you money when I can, be it little or much. This back-water has put us to about three hundred dollars expense for corn, hay, & fodder & last week Dr. R——had to buy 75 bbs of corn & pay $1.15 cents pr. barrel, when we thought we should have enough to last till Jan. Everything has had to be fed all summer & there has been no grass or forage for stock. As to sickness, some one is down all the time. I thought Susan & her children cured — but one week passed, when all had fevers again. Susan grunted & did nothing all last week. I had to bring her two children into the house & doctor & wait upon them myself, though I could hardly crawl around — threatened, with inflammation of the bowels in pain all night & nursing sick negroes & baby all day. Susan & the children are better this morning & now Reuben is down again with fever — had a hard chill last night.[46] So I have the prospect of another week's nursing to do. It is a thing that cannot be left to any body else excepting Dr R —— & he is so busy that he hardly finds time to eat & tell me what to give. I know pretty well now how to treat these fever & can break one up in two days. They leave the patient very weak & stimulants & nourishment have to be carefully given.

The water — both river & back water — have fallen very much since writing the first page — about 7 feet. The roads are dry & quite passable. The mosquitoes have almost disappeared, finding these cool mornings too stunning for them. The Yellow Fever still prevails in the city, but is decreasing. There have been no cases here in the country. It has appeared in Natchez & Vicksburg causing a regular stampede among the people. Father Fox writes that their house is crowded with company. The Pastor & his family from V—— & some young ladies. His teacher has been very sick; Harriet Mead too has had a severe attack of bilious fever, but was better when he wrote. I had a letter from Sister Lucy last night; her husband is low — his limbs are swelling & he is losing his senses, I should think from what she wrote — I wrote that Dr. R —— was very busy but neglected to tell you, that Mr Doyal had discharged Dr Greenwood & given the practice to Dr R —— again, at least for this year. He may send another physician down the first of Jan. There are a good many negroes sick with fever & Dr R —— is obliged to go nearly every day, & sometimes twice a day to visit them. He has been

---

46. See Todd L. Savitt, *Medicine and Slavery: The Diseases and Health Care of Blacks in Antebellum Virginia* (Urbana: University of Illinois Press, 1978); Martha Carolyn Mitchell, "Health and the Medical Profession in the Lower South, 1845–1860," *JSH* 10 (November 1944): 424–46.

very successful with his patients lately. He cured Mrs Villère, who was so sick; I wrote about her on the first page; & has been as fortunate with a good many others.

—How much I should [like] to see you— I want to talk to you so much & my pen dont write half fast enough. I am improving the time while baby is asleep, for when she is awake, one can do but little else than watch & run after her. She creeps very fast now & tries to stand alone. We took a long ride yesterday evening & I need not tell you that I enjoyed it very much after being so confined all summer. We went seven miles down the road— the appearance of the country is desolate enough. Naked fields, torn down fences, drift wood & the view of the water still within a few acres of the road give the coast a very unculti-vated & uninhabitable look. It is time for me to attend to Reuben— here is the programme—a powder of calomel & rhubarb, followed by hot tea, foot-baths, water-gruel, & when the fever goes down, quinine in three or four doses; then to-morrow, quinine again, bark tea, rice water, toast, &c, &c. low diet all of which mistress sees made & gives herself, so to be sure it is done & well done. But with all my endeavors to be a good housekeeper I tell you Mother, I fall woefully short of the mark. It is a constant struggle with myself to "make things go right"

With much Love to you all I close this in the greatest hurry, as Dr R——is waiting to go to the mail— Good Bye. Believe me affection-ately yours, I will write again soon.

T. B. Fox.

□ □ □

MONDAY, OCT. 25TH ˮ58

To tell the truth, Dear Mother, I am downright lonesome and have been trying hard all the evening to drive away "the blues"— There is enough to be done, to keep me busy, but "the spirit dont move me" to take hold of anything with energy. To spend the last half hour, I have been reading over yours & Lucy's letters received Saturday— they both give me subject for *thought*, but I am tired of thinking. I want *somebody* to visit with, to talk to, *somebody* to spur me on, for it seems as though all pride, ambition, & every other feeling had left me. We just live here & that is all— it is the same unvarying round of eating & sleeping, day after day & month after month. Dr R——has been gone since three o clock this morning— He was summoned to court 24 miles below, in a case that he knows nothing of, but he had to go or pay a fine of $250.00 It will be late before he returns & I know he will be nearly worn out.

As I wrote last week, there is not much news to tell you. Baby has not been very well from teething; she is cutting the upper side teeth, she has *three* above & two below & begins to walk considerably— I wish you could see her toddling about the floor! I am busy making her winter dresses—finished one this morning that was commenced last week & have begun another. — a turkey red calico, which her papa bought for her in town last week. Here is a little piece for Emma. How I wish I could send her some of my things that I do not need; they make me think of her every time I see them. I had a chill Saturday & dont feel well to day.

Tuesday Noon. Nov. 2nd

I was so busy the last part of the week sewing & mending garments for winter, that I found no leisure to finish this & now am too unwell to write. I had a chill Sunday afternoon, fever all night, & another chill in the morning & was very sick all day yesterday, but am dressed & sitting up some to-day.

I send this to enclose the ten dollar bill which you will find & will write more in a few days. Give my love to Georgy & Emma & accept much for yourself from Yours Affectionately

T. B. F.

Kind remembrances from Dr. R——& "Miss Fanny"; she is toddling all about the house now; creeps but very little

□ □ □

Dear Mother,   Hygiene Monday Nov. 15th. 1"58

It seems that all my letters to you must be hurried lately— yours of the 1st was received Saturday and I steal a little time to answer it this afternoon not knowing when I shall find any more to *steal*. Emma's letter pleased me very much; I had no idea she could write and compose so well; tell her she must write to me again next week, and to improve her, I will send her a list of words which were not spelt right so that she can study them and in a few months she will be able with attention, to spell all common words right. Tell her to study her lessons over & over again so that she will not miss the questions when she goes to recite. It would really be a pleasure to me to teach her for I *love* to teach. Every day Fanny learns the name of some new object from my repeating it over & over again to her. She learned [to say] "up "up a few days ago & it has been the burden of her song most of the time to-day, and I am obliged to take her up to satisfy her. You say you are sorry, I have so many chills &c, I dont mind them—for in the interval, my health & appetite are both very good. As for flesh there is not much to spare but you know Fanny is large now & I can hardly expect to be fleshy while nursing. I shall not wean her until Feb. or March unless obliged to do so from ill health. Dr R——is so busy that he hardly finds time to eat. We had breakfast this morning by candle-light—the first time. But the days are so short & he had so many to visit & I had so much to do here that we concluded it was the best way— to-morrow morning he will have to be off by day-break again. We have seen considerable trouble & anxiety since I last wrote. During that week I got quite strong & the Monday after we had workmen come, making *three* more to cook for & wait on; besides, Monday evening the Rev Mr. Russell became our guest to remain until the next evening. Everything went smoothly, but Tuesday morning to my great disappointment & annoyance Susan was taken violently with headache & high fever so that we had to bring her into the house & watch her to save her life; she was very sick all the week; yesterday I had to send her back to her room, as we had put her into our only spare room & it was getting so soiled I feared it would never be passable for a stranger again. Negroes are *so* peculiar—so utterly void of white folk's habits of cleanliness & energy! So with her dangerous sickness, requiring so much watching & doctoring & waiting upon, with Fanny to be nursed, house to be kept in order & the extra men to cook for besides all the last week's washing & ironing, you can imagine there has been enough to keep Ann as busy as she could be with the work & leave but little time for *me* "to stop & think"— It has been *action* from four in the morning until midnight. I am not tired; I believe the excitement does me good. It is so long since I swept a room or set a table that it is a novelty & I do a great many things with baby on my arm. There is no woman we can hire for a week or so; not even to do a day's washing. I do not pretend to take a stitch in the day but sit up at night. Susan is weak to-day, but will be well enough to wait on herself to-morrow if nothing happens, but she will be of no service to me for a week or ten days yet. I dread to have her sick, it is so hard to get her out again. She is naturally lazy & to-day would not have taken her own baby & washed & nursed it if I had not made her! she was waiting for Ann to do it, as she did last week, but it is too much for Ann "to play nigger" to every body & she is anxious to get the washing done & out of the way—an unheard of thing in Susan. I get along pretty well with Fanny by making Adelaide—Susan's oldest, come in & play with her. She is a bright little negress—not very black—& very go[od] features—good natured, quick to learn & tolerable quick motion. I shall take her in the house, New Year's day to make a house-girl of her. I am going to take a great deal of pains to bring her up to be faithful & smart & cleanly in her habits. She thinks there is nobody like "mistress" & is quite delighted when I call her "to go wash her face & hands & come play with Miss Fanny." She amuses Fanny very well & saves me a good many steps in the way of errands, &c. Perhaps you wonder that three men should make so much difference, but two are negroes & one a white man & this is the way our meals come. First Ann prepares breakfast for Dr R——& myself, then makes hot coffee & warms the breakfast for Mr. Bru; when he is done, it is all carried out of the house & served out to the blacks in the kitchen all of which Ann has to do & you know it takes some for three sets to eat. By the time all are through, it is late & as much as Ann can do to get the dishes washed & kitchen cleaned in time to put dinner on. I arrange my own room & keep the house in as good order as I can, but it has taken most of my time to wait on Susan & nurse baby. Dr R——had to cup her & she had to have poultices & emetics & drops & powders & injections & as fast as one pain was cured she had an *ail* some-where else. She is *hysterical* any how. Somebody [Fanny] says up, up" for the twentieth time *to-day*.

EVENING

I suppose you have received my last of Nov. 2— enclosing the ten dollar bill; by this time. It was an unexpected offer on the part of "the Dr"—for it was a part of a debt which he little expected to get & he thought it best to send it to you not knowing when he could send you [money] again. I am afraid not until in Jan. As to the house & lot, you know best what to do & what you *can* do. I would be glad to help you so that you might keep it, for your own sake, *unencumbered*. But I can make no promises because none of the property here is mine, nor do I earn any of it & Dr R——has a great many ways to take all he earns. I do not know how I can help you excepting by taking one of the children, which we will probably do in the course of this coming year. Dr R——says but little about it & I never feel at liberty to broach the subject myself. That he is disposed to help you, you can see by his sending money whenever he can spare it. Our expenses will be heavy this year, for the house has to be painted outside & we have had to build Susan a cabin with a *fireplace* on account of her having young children. She has been living in the ironing room next to the kitchen & using my kitchen fireplace, but I find it is not a good plan to allow her to do that; besides the ironing room was neither large or close enough for health.

We hoped to get along until next fall without repairing the house, but the back-water & moisture of the summer has made it necessary to repair at once— We had no white frost here until the *ninth* of this month. The weather is mild & rainy now, but from the feeling of the rain to night, I shall look for another frost in a day or two. We have no garden for the bugs ate up the vegetables as fast as they came up. I believe this is all "the news," & could you see the *pile* of socks & stockings that are waiting at my elbow to be mended you would not wonder that the pen is laid aside. Good-night— Much Love to yourself & the children. Yours affectionately,

T. B. F.

□ □ □

MONDAY P. M. JUNE 13TH 1859

My Dear Mother—you can hardly imagine how *rich* I deem myself! for a whole afternoon is mine to *write* & I can sit down & talk to you and not feel as though there was something else which ought to be done or attended to. Not but what many things there are to be made & mended & many a little change for the better might be done around the house or yard, but there is nothing really necessary to demand my time & attention. It is a long time since I have written to you; there have been many preventing reasons & many troubles to take away all mood for writing. I am quite happy and relieved, as you will doubtless see by reading my chit-chat.

Both Dr R——& myself are quite well   baby has diarrhea most of the time but as she does not look badly & has a tolerable appetite— I do not feel alarmed about her. You can have no idea how much she talks & how distinctly she pronounces her words— it is really astonishing in a child of her age—not yet two years old. At present we are by ourselves. Seguin & Lizzie left two weeks ago for Woodburne— they stayed with us five weeks. Their stay with us was not as pleasant as I could have wished. Their boy about a year older than Fanny is the worst child without any exception that I ever met & he teased Fanny constantly when allowed to be with her. I was obliged to watch her & keep her as much as possible away from him as he really abused her & what made the matter very aggravating was—Lizzie would not punish him for any of his ugliness. He struck Fanny with a broken bottle one day & made a wound over her eye & down her cheek that did not heal for several days.

Lizzie herself put on a great many airs & acted out "too proud for poor folks" to perfection, & much to Dr R——s & my own amusement. Seguin was very good company & I should have been glad to have him spend the summer with us, but I did not care for Lizzie & the two children— Dr R——says if he had such a wife as Seguin has he would leave for California between two days and when I say "oh! dont talk that way"— he replies "you may be sure I am not joking".— But Susan has become my greatest annoyance. When I needed her most with seven in the family she would do nothing for two weeks because she had a little sore on her finger— the more there was to be done the more she shirked always— the next Monday her master had to punish her & the next Monday after giving me unheard of impudence at which I told her I must tell her master as soon as he came from town; she *ran away* & was gone a week. Her master caught her & has sent her off— she is in the cotton-field at Wood-burne & Dr R——& myself are both agreed that she shall never come back here— her three young children are here & I have the care of them but do not mind it since I know that when I tell Ann to do this or that for them my orders are promptly obeyed. I would rather do my own work did I own forty slaves than be annoyed & vexed from morning till night as I was with Susan. Every thing goes on quietly now. I hire a woman to come & wash one day & iron the next so that Ann has only the cooking, house-cleaning & waiting upon Susan's two young children— Adelaide is old enough to take care of herself & does a great many useful errands around the house. Fanny requires no regular nurse now.

Since Lizzie & Seguin's departure & my riddance of Susan I have been *very* much hurried with sewing but am through my hurry now. Dr R——Fanny & my-self have all clothes sufficient to keep clean & that is about all one wants down here. My house is in pretty good order for the summer & the garden & yard only need a little attention. So you may imagine why I feel better now than I have for the last six weeks— when washing & ironing were far behind, every room in the house unfit to live in, my sewing all behind-hand & not a moments' time for me to read or write.

Dr R's practice is not very urgent now— he did have a good many patients about a month ago, but there is no sickness now to speak of. His farm so far has not realized to him his expectations. We have had a very dry season since April & crops of every description have almost perished for rain. To-day we have had a fine shower— Father wrote from Woodburne that the cotton & corn were suffering for rain so the drought must extend through the country. I suppose he & his wife are on their way North now— they expected to start last week. You don't know what a funny little body interrupts me with Ma-ma "Fanny wants to sew" she has seen Adelaide sewing & nothing will do until *she* has thread & needle. She is just as much attached to Jenny as ever, though the present Jenny is a gutta-percha one, purchased by her Pa-Pa a few weeks ago to fill the place of the "poor baby". Her pa-pa pets her a great deal & she thinks more of him than me now.

Last week I managed to finish "Shirley"[47] commenced soon after my return[48]— it quite charmed me   I think it good for me to read a novel now & then— I am so apt to become desponding & lose all ambition for everything. Shirley Keeldar[49] reminded me of Hannah Merrill. Have they returned from the South yet? I should like to see Hannah so much— I think the school-days I passed with her are the happiest ones I can look back upon. Poor Hattie what you wrote me of her makes me very sad; she is mistaken in thinking I have not written, I sent her a long letter soon after I returned but have not heard one word from her. —

47. Tryphena refers to *Shirley: A Tale by Currer Bell, Author of "Jane Eyre"* (London: Smith, Elder, 1849), written by Charlotte Brontë.
48. Tryphena and Fanny visited Pittsfield during the winter of 1858–1859, when Anna became seriously ill. See TBHF to ARH, December 5, 1858, February 27, 1859, MDAH.
49. Shirley Keeldar, the protagonist in *Shirley*, is young, wealthy, and keenly aware of gender distinctions and roles.

There is a pleasant air-castle in which I sometimes live but I cannot say if it is to be realized, that is your coming to live with me in the fall. The thought of your living as you now do, is the only drawback to my almost perfect enjoyment. I hope I shall hear from you soon & that I can write oftener the rest of the summer. — As yet we have not suffered at all from heat & we are unusually well-protected from mosquitoes by the present arrangement of the parlor. We have put nicely fitting frames with netting stretched across them to every door & window, so we have the draft through the netting while no mosquitoes can get in — My flowers are not looking very well now on account of the drought. The geraniums & hydranges are growing beautifully. But none look as well as your plants. I have some very pretty pink lilies; they grow only a foot high & each stalk bears one blossom. The double poppies & gilly flowers are both in blossom & one or two have appeared on my honeysuckle.

But I have written you quite a long letter & as Lucy ought to hear from Hygiene I must write a letter to her.

Make Emma write to me — here is much love for her & Georgy both. & with much for yourself believe me Your daughter as ever

T. B. Fox.

Have you had green peas & new potatoes & string beans & beans & eggplant, & tomatoes & cucumbers? We have — aplenty of them & every day I have wished that I could send you some. I had such a bread-pudding for dinner to-day as you used to make & you can imagine how it made me think of old times. I made pickles last week; they are very nice for my first ones.

□ □ □

Dear Mother,   THURSDAY NIGHT— Nov. 17. 1859.

I snatch a slight interval between sewing & nursing to answer yours of the 10th rc'vd Sat. night. As usual, my troubles & trials are all I have to write of self, for though only twenty-five, I feel as though I were forty-five & certainly have more cares & responsibilities than many a woman of that age.[50] But to answer your first; you should have had that money sooner were mine the purse to go to — but you must imag-

---

50. Aside from ordinary illnesses in the household, Tryphena was pregnant. Her second child, Edward Randolph, was born January 16, 1860.

ine how it would have been with you & father—(particularly if you had been penniless at marriage—) & you had relied upon him to help with grand-pa's people. Dr R——is willing enough to assist you, but sometimes our debts & expenses accumulate so rapidly that he grows very thoughtful & says *we must* be more economical & says not a word about the ten dollars for you when the month comes round & I can't ask him for it & *so* I have to wait. When he made me the promise, I thought I should have to worry no more about you all, but that you would be well provided for, for the winter if he kept it— as it is I am more anxious than ever. Le Roy's conduct is very strange[51]— he ought at least send money for George's clothes & books. Your visit to Grandpa's I *envy*— I do wish to see them all so much. Hattie writes to me occasionally—I suppose she has another heir by this time. Tell Hannah M——she must "bring her knitting" & spend the day with me.

The paper with the collar did not come with your letter— Dr R——dropped it from his buggy coming home from the P. O. & an overseer found it, opened it & finally a week after sent it to me. The collar is very pretty & I am much obliged to Emma for it; & should like to see that prize shawl; it surprised & pleased me very much to see that she had gained a premium.[52] Georgy is very ingenious with his pencil, his note is very neatly done— he must send me more & learn to write with a pen this winter. The little picture pleased Fanny very much.[53] She remembers him very well & not a day passes that she does not speak of him. She does not seem to remember Emma as well.

Her health has not been good for the last two weeks— she is very fretful—but what is the use of my writing of any one's health for we have all been sick—Dr. R——confined to his *bed* & buggy with chill & fever which he has at last succeeded in breaking up—myself all worn out nursing him, Reuben & the three little negroes. The baby was so low I had to take him into the house & take just the same care of him as

---

51. Le Roy lived and worked in New York. When he became less diligent about writing, his mother and sister began to speculate about his behavior. He married the daughter of Duncan and Bella McFraquhar, Margaret, in November 1858. See TBHF to ARH, January 17, 1858, MDAH; *The Genealogy of the Cleveland and Cleaveland Families*, no. 438, vol. 3, p. 2018, Berkshire Athenaeum, Pittsfield, Massachusetts.
52. Emma apparently entered a local competition and Tryphena saw the award mentioned in the *Pittsfield Sun.*
53. George drew pictures or cut paper designs for inclusion in his letters to Tryphena for Fanny's amusement.

though he was an infant—be up with him nights & dose & nurse him through the day. Then both the others had fever, so that instead of one child I have four. All last week I had a chill every other evening—fever all night & the next day dragged around to attend to house-hold matters & sew what I could on a set of shirts, which Dr. R——needs very much—for he talks of going up to Father's in two or three weeks— My health is so delicate he will be obliged to bring Susan back; *the worst of all evils*— if it were not for her children she should never come—but Ann is getting slack about taking care of them & they need a Mother's care these cold nights & Ann is not going to get up to cover them or dress them in the morning soon enough to prevent them taking cold & having chills. I am obliged to have the youngest brought to my room every night & sometimes I am up with him & Fanny five or six times—so you may know I am nearly worn out. Dr. R——says if Susan frets me much he will hire her out somewhere & hire a woman in her place—but I know how it will be— if once she comes back, I shall have to put up with all sorts of laziness & impudence. Ann is to come in the house to wait on me & act as nurse again. I like her because she took such good care of Fanny. We have intended to keep Susan at Fathers until we could sell her or buy another to fill her place, but our expenses have been too heavy this year for us to buy another now & no one up there wishes to buy her. Father only gives six dollars a month & if we hire a woman to fill her place we have to give $12. so you see, as long as I must have another servant it is *economy*, to let her come back—but with no peace now, what will it be then?

We have had very warm & very cold weather— Night before last there was a white frost, which killed nearly all vegetation & gave everything a truly wintry appearance. Most planters have commenced grinding & new sugar & syrup are plenty— I wish I could send you some of the syrup— it is better than anything that can be bought. It is raining very hard & is dark & late & yet Dr. R——has not returned from a long disagreeable *canoe* visit to one of the plantations back of us. I am afraid it will give him another chill but go he must, sick or well. No one here thinks a Dr——can be sick. I shall be obliged to bid you Good-night & leave him to take supper alone, for I am not at all strong to-day, it being the first one, that no chill shook me by the hand. Tuesday I was confined to bed all day—yesterday sewed a little on the shirts & lay down the rest of the time & to-day have sewed all day— if you only knew the quantity of work that is piled up in the wardrobe & all *needed*—winter clothes for Fanny & the little negroes, you would not wonder that it frets me to be confined to bed or to have all sick around me, so that it is impossible to sit one half hour, without jumping up, to give a dose of medicine or see what is to be done— But enough—. Good Night & Good Bye with much love for you *all* from Yours as ever,

Tryphena B. Fox.

□ □ □

Dear Mother,   HOME, JAN. 1ST 1860. SUNDAY EVE. 9 O CLOCK
Yours of the 22nd was received this morning and I cannot spend the last of New Year's day better, than in answering it and at the same time, wish you all a very Happy New Year— Before this, you have probably received the $10, which Dr. R—enclosed to you, in great haste, while in town Thursday. I had a letter partly written to send by him, but was prevented from finishing it in time & so enclose it in this it will explain my long silence.

All are quite well now— of course I do my share of *grunting* & coughing but manage to "keep moving" in spite of a bad cold, *cramps* & other maladies too numerous to mention.

We are enjoying another cold spell. Dame Nature gives us quite a circle of balmy, then windy   next rainy, again cold windy and lastly clear cold frosty days—completing her circuit every ten or twelve days.

Last Sunday—Christmas—was one of the most lovely Sabbaths I ever spent—warm as many a June day is with you, with that peculiarly delicious hazy atmosphere known only during our Indian Summer. The day passed very happily to me for I spent it, trying to make the others happy— You know the negroes look upon it as their especial holiday and always expect a "Christmas gift" from Master & Mistress. Though I could neither go or send to town this year & was too sick the week before to make anything for them, I managed to please all. Old Reuben was delighted with a whole suit of his master's clothes— (quite good ones which I had been saving all the year for him) from me, a silver dollar, from his master & a dime from "Miss Fanny". I gave Susan a new pr. of shoes—($1.50)—and a paper box, containing needles, thread, tape, hooks & eyes & buttons and a worked linen collar which I made for myself but it did not fit me nicely. That blue basque of Emma's which you gave me & which I packed away last spring just fitted Adelaide & made her walk five times faster than ever I knew her to, when in the greatest haste; and it is really a very pretty little garment for her to wear as "dress up". Maria in one of her Miss Fanny's *yellow* aprons of last summer & Buddy in a bonnet, strutted about the yard all the afternoon not only to their own amusement but very much to Dr. R's & mine.[54] I gave Ann a good muslin dress & checked skirt for next summer with which she was quite delighted.

Although I was very sick I managed to show Ann how to make some cakes & candy the day before & Susan made me 2 fancy pumpkin pies, so that we had a nice dinner and I did so much wish that you & E—— & G——could have been with me. My bill of fare was—Beef Soup, *Roast Duck—Boiled Beef,* Rice, Sweet potatoes, stewed pumpkin, stewed apples, corn bread, light bread, Milk, water, Claret, Pickles, Jelly &c. &c. All this was served on one table, then I set the round side table out as "*Fannys*" & we adjourned to that for our dessert   Here's a picture (as good as I can make it) for Georgy   I just write all this *to you,* of course such nonsense should not go to any one else.

I wrote a short letter to Le Roy, last week and am quite anxious to find whether he will answer it or not— what you have heard is probably true— Maria Gold is in N.O. staying with a friend of hers. I am going to invite her to come down & see me. I had a long letter from Lucy yesterday; she is not very well & is going to Woodburne to spend some time. Emily will be down soon. Aunt Randolph sent me a large bundle by Dr. R——which he lost while coming on the cars, but found waiting for him in town this last week. It contained a *nice cradle spread*—piece work, such as old ladies like to make   a pretty bed-spread—3 linen chemises for myself & a beautiful Valenciennes set—collar, undersleeves, & chemisette. I expect these last belonged to Sister Fanny, but do not know. To Fan, she sent a little fancy bag & star pincushion of Indian work.

For Christmas present, Dr. R——brot me this new portfolio on

---

54. Maria was possibly Tryphena's name for Susan's daughter Margaret. She is not to be confused with the slave Maria purchased in 1860 by Dr. Fox. Buddy is Susan's son, born in February 1858.

a – plates

b – Goblets of milk

c – Glass dishes of preserves – one
quinces, the other, white plum
most beautifully made;
A gallon jar of each was
sent me as a present
from Woodburn.

d – pretty pumpkin pies, with
fancy edge & frosting.

e – Two plates – one filled with
oranges – the other little
fried cakes, in various shapes
rolled in white sugar.

f – Vases of evergreens with a
festoon of moss across them
from one to the other, with
Fanny's Christmas cake
underneath, nicely iced
with a wreath of green
box leaves in the centre.

which I am writing my first letter—nicely gilded & well filled with paper, envelopes &c, &c. and a pretty 8 day clock which cost 7 dollars—an article I have *wanted* & *needed* ever since my marriage. I dont know that it will make any difference with my work, for the servants are just so slow anyhow but it will be company for me. This morning I had them all called at five & it is now after seven & yet Susan has not brot the breakfast in & the washing will be behind-hand all day. But it is freezing cold & I must take it easy. No use trying to get much out of a darkey on a frosty morning— They only know how to hover over the fire.

How much does Emma ask for her shawl— what colors has it & cant we strike a bargain? She must write to me. & in your next I wish you would wind some *working* cotton around the letter not too fine. Am much obliged for the envelopes & note paper. With much love *to all,* from *all,* I remain Yours Aff.

T. B. F.—

I am busy now making the little wardrobe for "somebody"—a little girl again I expect— Never was smart like other people   Good Bye- With love.

T. B. Fox.

Fanny had "Mothers Goose Melodies"— a basket of bananas & apples & a bundle of candy—for her Christmas present

□ □ □

Dear Mother,   THURSDAY MORNING FEB IST 1860

This is the first day I have sat up. It is two weeks yesterday since my poor little baby was born— it struggled along until Tuesday morning the 30th when it breathed its last in my arms. It seemed very well until the ninth day when he began to grow poor & pale & when the nurse dressed it she found a large *boil* under its right jaw halfway between the chin & ear. Dr R——lanced it & about a teaspoon-ful & a half of matter ran out. It continued to discharge until the day before he died. The poor little thing evidently suffered inexpressibly from the abscess & was wasted to skin & bones when it died. I could not have wished it to live under such circumstances, but it was hard for me to give him up. He was a beautiful child & I never, *never loved* anything as I did him. He was my summer's wish & all the dreary sick days of winter I was only consoled with the hope of soon having a boy baby to love & relieve the loneliness of my many solitary hours. But he is come & gone & life will resume the same old routine Friday & only the memory of his fleeting life will remain with its deep love & keen anguish to remind me that the monotony has been broken.

Sister Emily & Father came down the day he was a week old, Jan. 25th, much to our joy & surprise. They supposed me up & well. It was a most fortunate arrival, for the next day I was taken violently ill, which proved in a few hours to be inflammation of the bowels. Dr R —— sent to N. Orleans for Dr Seguin & by prompt treatment by calomel, leeches &c, &c, & the most careful nursing I am to-day sitting propped up in the arm-chair. My strength is entirely gone & I fear it will be some time before I get about again. Father went home Saturday. Sister E —— will stay until Spring   She takes all domestic cares from me & stays in my room all her leisure time, so I do not feel so lonely when Dr. R —— is gone as I should.

I have had the best of nurses, since the Saturday after the Wednesday baby was born, I had a good midwife with me at the time & Dr R —— but she could not stay with me nights. I had to depend on Susan & Ann to wait on me & they handled the baby so roughly for such a little delicate thing, that I could not bear to have them touch him. I might have been spared all the sickness & feebleness if this old Creole mulatress could have been with me from the first for she knew how to nurse the baby & I should not have attempted to sit up so much in bed & lift him about, myself. I thought I was strong enough to do it & it would not hurt me. She is with me yet.

I am too tired to write any more — Give my love to Hattie & let her read this if she wishes in place of one to her. I will write as soon as I can. Dont worry about me, for I have no pain now & am only troubled with a bed-sore & calomel sore mouth — My appetite is excellent. Good Bye with love to all — Write soon. I have yours & Georgy's   Your daughter

T. B. Fox.

I have some of baby's hair & will send you a little next time. He had black eyes & all said very much resembled his father— We were *so proud* of him Mother; I am afraid I loved him too much for I never felt so towards Fanny although I thought I loved her as much as a mother could.

For the present the baby is in Judge Pinckard's[55] tomb on the next plantation. We are going to have one of our own built as soon as possible. To think Mother that Death should so soon have visited our hearth-stones! Although only two weeks old, the loss of my babe is to me as though I had loved & cherished him for years—

□ □ □

Dear Mother,   HYGIENE, MAR. 17TH, 1860.

Yours of Feb 19th & Mar 3rd have just reached me— the first was sent to Washington,[56] but by failure of the mails I did not get it while there. You have probably received the one I wrote to you informing you of my health & visit to Lucy before this. I stayed in W—— two weeks & enjoyed myself very much—more than I have before since the first year after my marriage—no household cares, no servants to look after & no petty annoyances excepting Fanny's worrying for me. Notwithstanding the pleasure of my visit, I was very well contented to get home—for to a wife & *housekeeper* there is or ought to be "no place like home." My journey down the river on one of the most splendid of river palaces the "Charmer" was as pleasant as could be hoped without Dr Raymond. He met me at N. Orleans & the next morning bright & early we returned home. Susan managed to be quite smart the Tuesday after I left— she was to have done all the work for Sister E—— & the Dr during my absence, but concluded she would *have a baby*—a fine mulatto boy. As a negress could not be hired to fill her place Emily had to do all the housework & nursing herself during the whole two weeks of my visit. I not hearing from home at all, knew nothing of it or I should have been very much worried & hurried back. When the child was a week old, Sister went to spend the day with Mrs Borland[57] & Susan neglected the child & it took cold & died from the effect of it the day

55. William M. Pinckard.
56. Tryphena went to Washington, Mississippi, near Natchez, for a one-month visit with Lucy Fox Newman, her sister-in-law.
57. Wife of Dr. E. Borland.

after my return in my arms — I feel badly about its death for it was a pretty baby & I took a fancy to it on account of its being so near the age mine would have been, but for its premature birth. We are getting along just as we can for the present — Maria[58] does pretty well in the kitchen with my showing [her] & I do the housework. I think Maria is going to make me a most excellent servant. She is young & heedless but a little training & teaching will make her all I can want & save me many a step & hour's labor. She is very apt; her great fault is — want of order. Everything is left just where she last used it.

Susan is well enough to do anything, but it is customary to give *four* weeks & I am determined she shall have her month & *then* go to work in downright good earnest. I hope there are better & happier days in store for me — it seems as though there was never any true enjoyment of the present moment here at home; always something to deprive me of rest & peace. But is it not so with everybody?

Dr R —— & Fan & E are all well — the Dr. is very busy gardening at present as there is not much practice. We have lettuce to eat, cabbages, beets, okra, egg-plants, melons &c, &c all out of the ground & peas & strawberries in bloom. My flowers have but little attention & consequently dont flourish as I would like. How delighted I should be if you only lived with me & would take the flower garden as your especial charge. The roses are in full bloom & look beautifully. Sewing does not hurry me much. A set of shirts for Dr R —— are all that are absolutely needed at present. Sister Emily leaves me next week to make a short visit to the Wilkinsons who live below here. She will be gone a few days & then after a short stay here & in N. O. return home by the way of Washington.

No letter has arrived yet from Hattie; how delighted I should be to see her & her little ones. I suppose Hannah Merrill has not been South this winter. Give my love to her & her father & mother & tell them when they do come again, they must certainly make a visit — it would be so pleasant for me if Hannah would come & spend part of next winter with me. I am expecting Sister Lucy down soon & a Miss Hattie Rogers — a cousin of Dr R —— s. She is a New England girl & very good

---

58. The slave Maria was about eighteen years old when Dr. Fox bought her in February, 1860. TBHF to ARH, February 20, 1860, MDAH.

company; we spent the last week of my visit at Sister Lucy's together. Father Fox talks of coming down too this spring, so I shall have quite a round of visitors & visiting.   It grieves me to think how you are situated, but I live in hope that it is not always to be thus; all might have been different now, had not my health been so miserable the last year. Keep up a good heart— we will help you as much as possible— the expense of my trip, was one great objection to my mind, to making such a visit, but since I have returned with so much better health & spirits I am not so sorry though it would have given *me* as much pleasure to have sent that much to you—but it was not my "say so".

Remember me to all at Uncle B——s & Grandpa's with much love. Give *our* love to Georgy & Emma & with much for yourself believe me. Yours as ever.

T. B. Fox.

□ □ □

Dear Mother,   Hygiene Thursday p. m. June 24th ˮ60
Every time I receive a letter from you I think "I will write oftener"— but am so low-spirited most of the time I cannot bear to put my thoughts on paper, much less send them to you. I suppose there is a good reason for my being so at present; I have been in doubt about the matter, as my health was so very excellent & is yet   I have never since my marriage been so well, so notwithstanding my constant sickness & suffering with Fanny & the other little one, I am pretty well convinced that my condition affects my mind this time instead of body; you would be shocked to see how restless & unhappy I am & so ill natured too & yet I cannot help it. Dr Raymond is very kind to me, does every thing in his power to make me happy & the servants are unusually *good*. Susan has turned over quite a new leaf & considering many things I would not wish a better servant. Maria does pretty well, as she ought to do where there is so small a family & so little hard work. The weather has been unusually warm & dry, though we have had a few showers the last few days. There is not much sickness now; the epidemic of dysentery is over; Some cases of yellow fever are reported in N. O. and there have been some cases of scarlet fever in the neighborhood but they were not malignant and it has not spread. Our garden is nearly dried up; we have an abundance of cabbage, tomatoes, & mush-melon & that is about all.

We ought to have plenty of egg-plant, but have none. There is ochra enough to make a "gumbo" once in a while, which is a very nice dish made of ochra fried with any kind of meat and afterwards mixed with a little onion, red peppers, tomatoes, & corn; some make it with the ochra alone, but it is not so rich or *"Frenchy."* It is half way between a stew & soup & is eaten like the latter, with a spoon-ful of rice added to each soup-plate. Shrimp & fresh fish are plentiful now & very easily caught. My spring chickens are large enough to eat so I have quite a variety if we do not live in town, where we can go to the market for fresh meats & fruits.

I have not much to do now; my sewing for the summer is mostly done, so I am spending a little time every day on some *small* extra garments which *I hope* will be needed some day; many of those cut out & commenced last fall & winter were never completed & though it is a sad task to finish them, I am doing it, rather than throw them aside.

Dr R——thinks if my health should be at all affected as it was last year, it will be best for me to go to Woodburne & stay, but I dont like the idea of being so far away from him & shall not go without my *life* depends upon it.

You ought to see Somebody on the floor, playing by herself, poor little thing, she has no companion to play with her & has to amuse herself the best she can. She has the back-gammon board & every now & then looks up to me for approval as she turns the boxes over & moves the men "a la papa." She is *his pet,* & grows every day more attached to him & misses him when absent as much as I do. She grows very fast & is prettier this summer than ever, though very badly tanned. The dry, sunny winds have tanned us both as much as though we had lived in the open air.

I have finished reading Bayard Taylor's "Greece & Russia"[59] & am now reading a geological work "The Testimony of the Rocks," by Hugh Miller.[60] You know he was a Scotchman who rose from the humble rank of stone-cutter, to be a very eminent geologist & finally committed suicide from over-tasking himself which caused a kind of

---

59. Bayard Taylor's *Travels in Greece and Russia, with an Excursion to Crete* (New York: G. P. Putnam, 1859) was fourth in an eighteen-volume travel series.
60. Hugh Miller, *The Testimony of the Rocks* (New York: Hurst, 1857).

insanity. This is his last work   The last of which was sent to the press just the day before he died. It is very interesting & helps me to remember much of my Geology which I had partially forgotten.

Yesterday evening I went to ride with Dr R——& while I was gone Mr & Mrs Guythe with their children came up to see us. They followed on up the road, overtook us & returned. We had a nice ride & a sociable chat of an hour or so. They are good-hearted people, but not very intelligent or refined, so that one does not gain much by visiting them. If we had a few nice families here; it would be all that is necessary to make this as pleasant a neighborhood as one could wish.

SATURDAY AFTERNOON.

Have been quite sick since writing the above; felt badly all that afternoon & at night had a high fever which lasted till morning—have been taking quinine yesterday & to-day & feel pretty well this evening. On reading over the first of this I think I must have been *feverish* or something else when writing it—but you must make allowances & take it as written for I have not time to copy it & omit the *feverish portion*. It is after 3 now & Dr R——says a ride to the Office will do me good so I must seal this & go to dress myself. This dime is to buy one of those little picture books for Fanny about the size of a small envelope so you can send it in your next—one with *pictures* & *verses*. If one costs more let me know & I will send another when I write again.

Write soon— I am getting anxious to hear if you have received the $10. yet but suppose I shall hear from you this evening.

Good Bye— With much love Emma & Georgy & yourself from *all.* Yours affectionately

T. B. Fox.

Dont let *any one* see this.

□ □ □

Dear Mother,   SEPT. 14 1860.

Though not very well, duty prompts me to try to lay aside my headache & languor & write you a few lines. All have been as well as unusual since my last & our home is so free from sickness, that I cannot be thankful enough when I compare our health now with what it was last year at this time.

We are having quite cool nights & mornings now though the greater part of the day is extremely warm & sultry. It is said that there is some yellow fever in town but not enough to hinder summer wanderers from returning. We had intended to go to the city to-morrow but shall delay the visit now, until next Saturday.

Dr. R——has not much besides ordinary practice, so that he has been with me more for the last month, than in a long time before. — To-day is Fanny's birth-day; I made a mistake & thought it was yesterday & invited Mrs Stackhouse's little girl & boy[61] up to take tea with her — made them some ice cream & had some cakes, &c for her supper-table. They looked at picture-books & played with doll-babies & thought they had a nice time. This morning we rode up as far as Mr Johnson's plantation & spent a pleasant hour or two with Mr & Mrs Morse & their three little girls. I have told you about Mrs M——She is excellent company & I am always delighted with my visits there. Mrs Johnson who has spent the summer at the North with her family, is expected home in a few weeks. I hope she will be as sociable as her sister has been. They are the only people whom I care to visit for they have books & music & flowers & all those refinements which one naturally seeks as have there the least cultivation of taste. I am so much isolated here that I crave all those surroundings which a social circle gives, more than if associating with persons of education oftener.

SUNDAY MORNING.

As the Dr. goes to the Office this morning I shall have [to] prepare this for the mail in some haste, though I had all day yesterday to finish it — but Dr. R——was at home & when he is here I jokingly tell him he is my company & feel obliged to entertain him, so we read books & newspapers, talk & play back-gammon & look over accounts & make out lists of wants & expenses. There are so many things needed about the house & clothing & bedding to make the servants comfortable for the winter that I am discouraged; you have no idea what a wasteful, improvident race the negroes are & constant attention on my part cannot save. Good woolen blankets which I gave Susan two years ago are all *torn* not *worn* out. Two mosquito bars—one for herself & one for the children have shared the same fate. Because I was sick & then absent in the Spring their flannels were not put carefully away for this winter, but

---

61. Blanche and Herbert, children of Haywood and Sarah Stackhouse.

thrown & left about, & finally used for scrubbing rags & anything else they happened to want them for. — These are trifling things to write about, but they show you in how many directions my care & attention is needed to save anything. — The morning is quite bright & pleasant after the rain & wind of yesterday   It seems just enough like Sunday to make me feel uncomfortable. There are no church bells, or preparations for service, only the prospect of a long day, when more than usual supervision is necessary on my part — for I insist on having the housework done at an early hour & all the servants dressed clean before dinner — I *almost* wish we were going to spend the day with you — Here comes Fanny with her box of animals & trees, with a house & fence designed to make a miniature farm of. Georgy would fix them nicely for her — she was very much delighted with the "paper doll" & took it to bed with her. She still calls every little boy Georgy though she has probably forgotten *our* Georgy. — You ask if I wrote to Hattie Dewey — she has probably received the answer before this — I sent one by the next mail which I hope she will answer soon for letters give me a great deal of pleasure — they are like company, rousing my energies & ambition & keeping me from complete "stagnation" — Lucy writes me excellent ones & Father Fox now & then sends *me* one as he says, you & Raymond are one. — I wish you or Emma would write to me oftener — it would make me more contented & I should be less anxious. Dr R—— will probably send you the ten dollars by next mail & don't go to the Berkshire if you can help it — or am I wicked in writing so? Good Bye — give much love to Georgy & Emma — tell them to learn all they can at school. Fanny sends love too — Your daughter.

T. B. Fox

□ □ □

SUNDAY A. M. DEC. 16TH, 1860.

Dear Mother, As a ride takes me by the P. O. this morning, I write you a few lines, though no answer has reached me to my last. Neither our Northern papers or letters have been received regularly since Lincoln's election — there has not been *one* number of the "Pittsfield Sun" — I do not think the subscription has run out: can you inquire about it for me? We know nothing of Northern opinions or movements; the Secessionists are strong in number & energetic in action here.

Father Fox, from whom we heard last night, says the same in regard to the Mississippi people & has had no doubt, but we shall soon be involved in a civil war. The banks in N. O have not yet suspended but thirty of the principal cotton houses have, which will cause a good deal of trouble in many families. Money is scarce every where; it is doubtful if Dr R——can collect one third of his dues, for three or four months after the first of Jan.— Our guests will not come as soon as expected. Father cannot leave home until after New Years & Dr R——cannot go for them so they will not be here until about the middle of Jan. I am quite glad, for it will give me time to get rested & feel that everything is finished. We completed the parlor yesterday and it looks very nicely— not very rich but cozy & home like. The dining room will be completed as soon as we can put down the matting & hang the curtain. The bedrooms are all done. I have moved into the lower & back one to be nearer the kitchen and dining-room & avoid so much running through the house as there was when I had the front room. This is a nice little room, the warmest in the house. The paper   curtains & bed spread are all buff & pink & I have covered some little boxes for ottomans with the same paper & made blue cambric cushions for them & my sewing chair. The coal stove which Dr R——bought purposely for the room is small but gives sufficient heat to half *roast* me sometimes.

All the papering & painting is done excepting the outside of the house. Every *piece* of furniture has been washed & varnished excepting the bedstead occupied by the workman, which he will do the last day he stays. There is not much to be done now excepting *pick over* my matrasses; there are four & it will take a week to do it—& hard work at that. They are made of moss & are so full of lumps as to be unfit for use. I shall put Maria & Reuben at it to-morrow probably. My sewing is almost done; so as there is an end to every thing I believe our busy time is *almost* over, but I often think were it not for my own gratification as well as for the comfort of guests all this would be for naught. It may be that all Northerners will hasten home & we shall have no company at all.— It is strange that I do not hear from you— have you received the ten dollars I wrote you about some time ago? I am very anxious about you, what is to be done during the threatened hard times. Shall we hear from one another at all?— We do not consider ourselves in any danger from the negroes *alone*— A Free negro is to be hung at the Court-house of this Parish,[62] this month for attempting to excite insurrection. — There has been nothing of the kind in this vicinity. I send you the Governor's message,[63] that you may have some idea of what is going on here, and I will send you some of the pamphlets which are freely distributed throughout every Southern State. I should like to come home & see you or rather have you come & live with me. Considering all my circumstances — a good & almost luxurious home, a kind husband — an excellent income & plenty of servants, I am not very happy & only *hope* there will be a change for the better. I have a good many every day annoyances, which would not amount to much if written to you yet they wear upon me, as you would soon see, were you here.

Susan is worrying me again, beyond endurance & were it not for the tightness in our money affairs, Dr——would hire me another woman in her place, but as matters now stand we can neither hire or buy & I shall have to put up with many things which would otherwise be intolerable. She is *impudent* & *lazy* & *filthy* & the latter with even my ideas of neatness, I cannot overlook. Perhaps I do not treat her right — probably I do not for I do not like her & never did, & *never shall*; it is not pleasant to live on the same place & in as close proximity as one is obliged to do, with the cook & be all the time at enmity with her & feel angry, whether I say any thing or not. My paper is used up so I can write no more at present. We lost our best & favorite cow yesterday — $60 — strayed away & is probably killed by this time. — She was my pet — & known as "Jingle" because she would run after me & beg for meal if I rattled my store-room keys.

Give much of my love to all — Accept much for yourself & Georgy & Emma & believe me — Your daughter.

T. B. Fox.

---

62. Tryphena refers to the courthouse at Point a la Hache, located south of Jesuit Bend on the opposite side of the Mississippi River.
63. In Governor Thomas Overton Moore's inaugural address of January 23, 1860, he warned the state legislature and visitors of the hostility against southern states by the Republican party, which "threatened the existence of the slaveholding states." See John D. Winters, *The Civil War in Louisiana* (Baton Rouge: Louisiana State University Press, 1963), 4–5.

Portrait (oil on canvas) of George Holder and Le Roy Holder, circa 1835 (courtesy of Mrs. Raymond Birchett, Jackson, Mississippi)

Portrait (oil on canvas) of Anna Rose Holder and Tryphena Blanche Holder, circa 1835 (courtesy of Mrs. Raymond Birchett, Jackson, Mississippi)

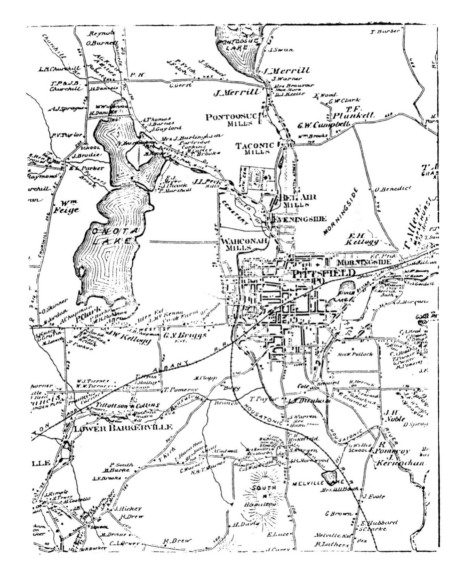

Map of Pittsfield, Massachusetts, and surrounding area (Frederick W. Beers, *County Atlas of Berkshire, Massachusetts*; New York: R. T. White, 1876)

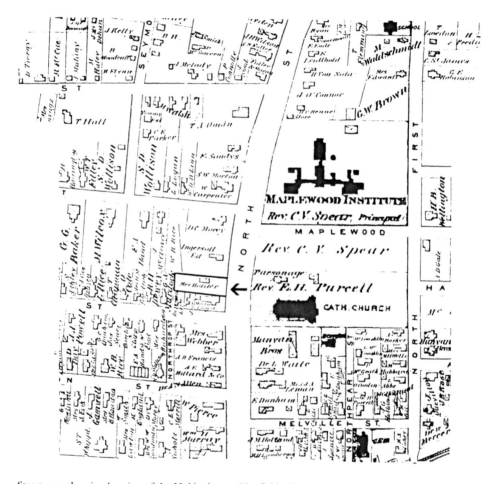

Street map showing location of the Holder home, Pittsfield, Massachusetts (Frederick
W. Beers, *County Atlas of Berkshire, Massachusetts*; New York: R. T. White, 1876)

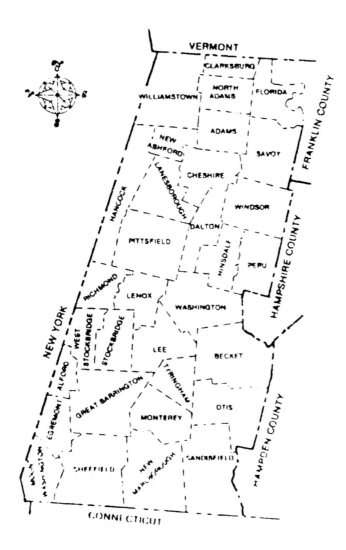

Map of Berkshire County (courtesy of Local History and Genealogy Department,
Berkshire Athenaeum, Pittsfield, Massachusetts)

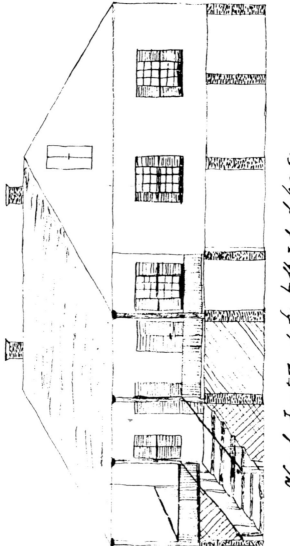

Drawing of Hygiene, winter 1866, by Tryphena Blanche Holder Fox (courtesy of the Mississippi Department of Archives and History, Jackson, Mississippi)

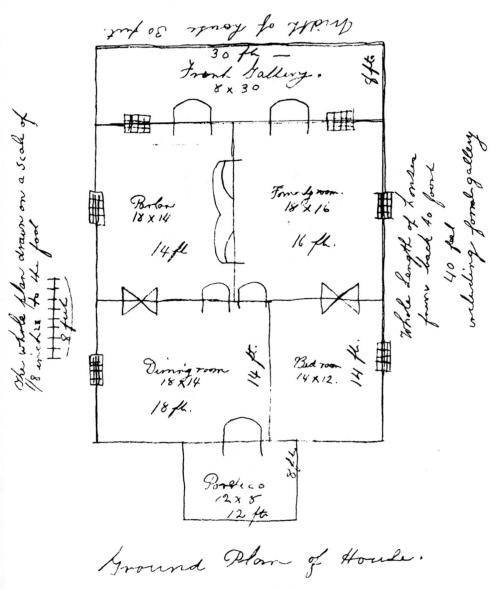

Floor plan of Hygiene, sketched by Tryphena Blanche Holder Fox, winter 1866
(courtesy of the Mississippi Department of Archives and History)

Hygiene, photographed in 1950 (courtesy of Mrs. Raymond Birchett, Jackson, Mississippi)

PART II

The War Years
1861–1865

My Dear Mother,　　　　　　　　　　　　HOME, JAN. 22ND 1861.

As I am in a letter writing mood this morning, you shall have a short account of our visit to Woodburne, though I do not know when it will be mailed. We made a short visit starting from here Monday Morning & returning Saturday night travelling in the cars two nights & spending three nights & two days at Father's—so short a time that I hardly felt paid for going—only I feel more contented & happy since my return & shall probable love my home the better for having been from it for awhile. We saw many, many strange faces while absent & many familiar ones. Pa— has grown old, very fast, since we met, & looks worried   Mother is pretty well & has to be very busy with such a house full to entertain. Emily is the same good-hearted sociable body as ever & talked of coming back with me but finally give it up, as there was some opposition. I like Aunt Ellen & Cousin Mary far more than I expected & I was very much disappointed that the bad weather & Mary's delicate health would not permit them to return with us. They expect to come down in a week or two with Father & Mother.[1] Sometimes I feel as though something would happen to prevent their coming at all, though I hope not, for I should like Aunt Ellen's society so much for a time.

We did not have a very pleasant journey up—after riding in the cars all Monday night, we hoped to reach Father's by Tuesday noon— at Jackson we changed trains for Bovina to ride from there to Father's (6 miles) in a carriage; soon after leaving Jackson, we found the track washed away which it took the workmen an hour to repair— after going on a little farther, there was another place, entirely destroyed & it was some time before we could make up our minds to return to Jackson & from there back home as people said there was no chance of our getting through until Friday morning to Bovina. But Dr. R——after considerable searching in the rain & mud found a private conveyance & we rode from the breakage down to Pa's, a distance of thirteen miles over hills & through mud & arrived there about night—nearly worn out. Friday morning we started for home again, reached N. O. about midnight & went to the City Hotel—the next day took the steamboat for

---

1. Ellen (sister of Sarah Otis Fox, David Raymond Fox's mother) and Dr. Fox's cousin Mary Burton made a subsequent visit to Hygiene in February 1861. TBHF to ARH, February 18, 1861, MDAH.

home, as our carriage was not finished and we had sent the horses home
by Reuben on Monday.

All went remarkably well while we were gone. Mr Vallette the workman stayed & finished a few odd jobs about the house. One of our old
cows died the day after we came back but as she only cost 6 dollars &
her calf will be worth eight if we can keep it until Spring, she is no great
loss.

Much to my surprise, Mrs Messenger & Lui called the second morning after our arrival. She said she had heard so many stories about my
coming that she did n't know which to believe & came to see for herself.
She has not changed much. Lui has grown to be a beautiful young lady.
They both thought me very thin, & much changed — In the afternoon,
Father, Mother, Dr. R——& myself rode down to see Bacon Ham for a
few moments. They have improved both the house & grounds very
much. My old room looked the same & oh! how many many associations were called up, as I stood gazing from the South window once
more. It was difficult to realize that five years & their many changes. It
was "Miss Holder" again for a moment. All the servants greeted me
with smiling faces & I was glad to see them. Mr Messenger looks badly;
it is said that he is dying of consumption & I am half inclined to believe
it. He too seemed very glad to see me. It was perhaps the thought that
I should never see him again which induced me to go — deeming it best,
that the *past* should be forgotten.[2] He told me, he had called on you
two summers ago — but said nothing more about you, only to inquire if
you were well. They talk of coming to N. Orleans, & I have invited
them most cordially to come down & see us, but do not much expect
them. She told me that Harriet Mead, was doing very well in
Alabama — she has a salary of 750. per year & suits & is suited. I saw no
other old acquaintances of the neighborhood excepting a Mr Cameron.
Thursday, we took tea at Uncle Elisha's, with Emily, Daniel, Aunt Lucy
(the hostess), Aunt Randolph & a cousin from the North — a real *Yankee Sailor* — but a good-hearted well meaning one, at that. Daniel's wife
is a nice woman, but has never seen any society — having been born &

---

2. There is nothing in the extant letters to explain what Tryphena refers to here although
   some tension must have existed between Tryphena and the Messengers. Tryphena also
   intimated that an awkward interaction had occurred with Mr. Messenger. See TBHF
   Diary Transcript, December 11, 1865, MDAH.

brought up in *Texas*. They could not get along there & Pa had to send Jimmy with funds, to bring them to Woodburne— They have two children—the baby is only two months old now.

SATURDAY NOON—

I have just time to finish with a few lines before my "gude man" leaves for the Office, and it is so good a time to mail & register you some money I must not let it pass— When the other sheet was written, I intended to finish it, in a day or so with more chit-chat on various subjects, but every day since has found me so miserable that I have done nothing. Fan, too has been quite sick with bad cold & fever & kept me awake nearly every night since our return. I had no idea the journey would tire us so much. The weather too has been very bad— to-day is the first of sunshine that we have had for two weeks & the mud is a foot deep in the yard.

This bill which I send is one of a new issue occasioned by counterfeits on the old pattern. This is a good one—taken by Dr Fox himself from the bank— if you have any trouble let me know— Good Bye— Love to all. Write soon. Yours affectionately

T. B. Fox.

□ □ □

FRIDAY AFTERNOON, MAR. 29TH 1861

Dear Mother— At last both the leisure hours and *inclination* prompt me to write you— it has been a busy time with me of late & when not busy I have been in no mood to write as I wished. It is a lovely Spring, I might say summer, afternoon— the birds sing, flowers are blossomming, the sun shines brightly and unhappy indeed must one be, who cannot enjoy such a day. I am alone, for the gentlemen concluded to spend the evening fishing & went away soon after an early dinner. I must say *gentlemen*, for Dr R——'s half brother, James is domiciled with us for the present, preparing to enter the Medical lectures in N. O— next fall. He is a very pleasant agreeable young man and quite a desirable addition to our little circle. Aunt Ellen & Cousin Mary left me two weeks ago Wednesday. Father & Mother came down the Saturday previous to accompany them home & you can imagine what a busy time I had while they were all here—8 in the family when I had only been accustomed to provide for three.

They seemed to enjoy themselves very much & often said so, so that I had no reason to feel that they were homesick or unhappy while they stayed. We walked, & rode & had boat rides, and read & sewed & talked, so that the six weeks they were here, seemed only like *one*, and is now more like a pleasant dream than any thing else. I went to N. O. with them, the day they left here and had a very pleasant time though I was so very tired for three or four days afterwards that it counted as dear bought enjoyment. While they were here & I was *obliged* to be energetic & active, my health continued very good, but now the excitement has passed, so have my fine health & spirits & I am really *miserable* some days, but there is *good reason* for all my bad feelings.[3] Besides there has been a great number of very sick women this Spring— Dr R— has never before had so many severe & peculiar cases in so short a time. A black woman died last week a month after her *twins* were born, one of which was still-born.

A few nights ago, he was called to a woman who after a terrible ordeal gave birth to a child without any brains or top to its head. It only breathed a few times. Though I try not to think much about these instances, yet I must acknowledge they rouse my fears somewhat, for you know how unfortunate I was before.

Susan, who was confined the Sunday after my guests left had a very fine large boy and both have been remarkably well. She has hardly been out of bed yet, though she is a great, strong, fat thing & her child will be two weeks old Sunday. For my sake I am glad the law allows her a month & hope I shall hardly see her during the time. I have only been into the cabin twice & shall be sorry when my authority must again commence but I shall be pretty well rested by the time her month is up— At present I am having a right easy time, for we hire an excellent negress two days in the week at fifty cents a day & she comes early in the morning, finishes the washing one day & the ironing the next & gives me no more trouble or anxiety about the work being done, than she does you. The new servant Elizabeth (whom we bought about two weeks after Aunt Ellen came to take Maria's place because she took a notion to *run away*) does the cooking and housework and does all so

---

3. Tryphena was pregnant. Her third child, Anna Rose, was born July 12, 1861. See TBHF to ARH, [July 19, 1861], MDAH.

well & quietly & quickly that I know but very little about it any how—so dont you see I am having an easy time? I sit here in my big rocking-chair sewing or reading or writing feeling at least quite happy, if not comfortable & determined to make the best of the time while Susan is laid up & Maria is gone. The latter we shall probably sell as soon as she is found—the great trouble with her being her fondness for *running out nights*; I regret losing my years's training for she had certainly improved in almost every respect, until she suited me very well indeed—as well as any black person I ever expected to find. I had taught her after a great deal of pains & many an hour's hard work on my part, to sweep & dust & arrange a room nicely, to wash & iron fine clothes, particularly shirts, to cook cakes & custards & jellies & cut out & make quite a variety of garments. She was one whom I could depend upon if I were sick or away from home & could feel that she would keep house & attend to everything just as I would myself; that is if she chose to do it   & not run out nights & sleep all day as she was very fond of doing, too fond to suit me when I had a house full of company & was anxious to keep it in decent order & have the work done at a proper time. The Saturday morning that she left I sent her into the parlor to make a fire & arrange the room   She was gone a long time & when I went to see if she was not most done & ready to make a fire in Aunt Ellen's room, not a thing was touched & she lay sprawled out on the hearth-rug *fast asleep.* I punished her for it, & she did tolerably well until night when after supper I ordered her to make haste & wash the supper dishes, she left them until within a few minutes of nine, when we began to talk of retiring & I went to the back door to see if everything was right & in good order for the night, all the buildings shut up & the keys brought in— what should I find but all the dirty dishes standing untouched & she in the kitchen very busy talking to Susan. I disliked to say any thing to her master he whips her so severely, so I punished her again myself— not very severely & she promised to do better for she had troubled me all the week. I thought no more about it but went to bed. She brought the key to the back door & made up her bed in the hall, but the next morning when called she was missing having got out through the Office window, the only place that was left unlocked. Some men helped her out, for we found their tracks under the window in the soft mud. We have had a good many different reports about her, but all attempts to find her have proved failures.

We heard in the summer that she was out almost every night & she looked so tired & jaded that Dr R——said we should have to lock her in, but we have since heard that she went out notwithstanding our locks, through the dining-room window with *Reuben's* help for it is about twenty feet from the ground. So much for her— if there had not been *fifteen*-hundred dollars expended for her, I should not care a picayune, if we never saw her again. It is not pleasant to have such a character around one, though most of these mulatresses are such & it is impossible to make anything different of them.

This woman Elizabeth is about thirty, a good cook, house servant & child's nurse. So far I like her very much. She is black & homely but tries to please me & does her duty without any overlooking on my part, which is certainly a great relief. But enough of servants—you will think I have fallen into that disagreeable *woman* habit, devoting my whole conversation to the subject of servants. So I will spin out my yarn about the rest in my nest.

Fanny has grown very fast this winter & looks more & more like Emma as she grows older excepting her eyes & hair. I wish you could see us all or we you—but what plans do you think are laid for the future? Of course we can only *hope* they may be fulfilled, for many changes may occur before two summers shall have come & gone. Brother James graduates two years from this month, living with us when not attending lectures, & after graduating coming here to attend to Dr R——s practice while *we* take a trip & spend the summer North! It is a long time to look forward to but it will pass quickly & if nothing happens, the plan is a very good one & easily carried out. & Dr R——will help you until then & then you must all come back with us. Aunt Ellen had a good many talks with me about you & she says, you ought to come out & live with me. But she did not know all & I could not tell her. She is a widow herself but is far from being poor. Besides she has four grown sons, three of whom are independent & influential men, while the youngest is studying medicine in Europe. Cousin Mary is very unassuming for one as wealthy as she, & is certainly one of the most amiable & lovable girls I ever knew. I should have been so glad, if she could have remained longer with us; she is just such company as I enjoy, lady-like, refined & well educated. Sometimes I am almost sorry they have been with me, for I feel my loneliness more than ever. Dr. R—— has been unusually busy for this season of the year & has been at home but very little since the first of Feb. Aunt Ellen ranks him as one of her own sons, she says, for he & Daniel are her favorite sisters only surviving children. She seemed to think a great deal of me too & gave me a family relic which showed her feelings towards me. It is a letter written by *Dr Raymonds* mother to another sister a few weeks after his birth—both the sisters are now dead. This letter was given to her a long time ago & she has now given it to me as she says "You are the only one to whom I could bequeath it, it is very precious to me but I shall not live always."

When she left, N. O. the day after I came back home, she sent me by James, two very handsome sauce ladles—heavy & rich to match my soup ladle & Cousin Mary sent me an elegant silver pie-knife—most beautifully chased, with "Blanche" engraved on the handle in the old fashioned English letters. They quite complete my silver set. Emily sent me a pretty glass box made with scarlet ribbon & designed as a mantle ornament in which was the prettiest little baby shirt I ever saw—fine linen cambric trimmed with a row of valenciennes around the neck & sleeves headed with open work on which she had transferred some very fine embroidery.

I owe her a letter thanking her for the pretty gifts, & hoped to write to her to-day but shall not have time. Lucy, too sent me a long letter some time since which yet remains unanswered. I often wish you were here to urge me to my letter writing as you used to do at home. What do you think I was doing this morning after I had finished *No 2* of Fan's little gingham aprons? making Elizabeth a dress-up black silk apron, out of the last good remnant of that old black silk dress you bought me to graduate in— Can you imagine how my thoughts flew from one scene to another, through which I had passed since then—not quite ten years ago. Did I think the first time the dress was worn of its final destiny? & my own surroundings? that I should find a home in Louisiana & be the mistress of slaves & be appropriating a portion of it as a present to one, because she had tried to please? & then to see her *face* when I gave it to her. I could not have been more delighted when you gave me the dress. But I must go & give out supper, for it is six o clock

& my gude man will soon be at home. It will be a "frugal fare" to-night for I did not bestir myself to make a cake this morning as I ought to have done. There will be nice bread & butter, both home-made (& I can make such nice yellow butter that I wish you had some of it, & fresh fish, coffee, milk, cheese & preserves— the latter quite a nice relish, made of *pumpkin*— I cook it in lime-water a few hours then make a thin syrup & boil the fruit in it until tender & clean— then skim the pumpkin out & let the syrup boil until rich & thick, which I pour over the fruit while hot. A little lemon makes it much better, but as I had none, I flavored it with vanilla—then last, but not least on my bill of fare— strawberries & cream!

SATURDAY EVE.

I close in haste for my gude man says I must take a ride to the P. O. with him   So Good Bye   Love to all. I will write again soon   Yours.

T. B. *Fox.*

□ □ □

HOME SUNDAY, MAY. 12TH "61

Dear Mother— I received your two letters May 1st, & May 3rd last night and was very sorry to find that you could not change the money. Dr. Fox is afraid to send you gold by the mail, & will have to go to the city to send it by express. He is busy Mondays, but will try to go on Tuesday—so you may expect to receive the money in a few days after this. Your letter has worried me more than I can tell you—you must not be assisted, in the way you spoke of. Tell Mr West I will pay him whatever he advances until you hear from me again. I live so far from you & so differently & have everything without trouble or *care as* to *where the money comes from,* that I cannot realize your position, till I get one of your letters—then too since the last ten dollars was sent I have felt quite easy about you—little dreaming you could make no use of it. The money is *good* here; it is *at a premium*; it is considered the *best* money in the Southern market   If you buy it there at the North for *fifty cents, do it* (Dr. R——will send you the gold for that purpose) & send the bills to him— he will change them for gold at the bank $1.00 for $1.00, & send back gold to you by express—you will make double—viz. you can write or send to the broker in Albany a $5, gold piece or Northern bank bill telling him you will give it for a $10, bill on any N. O. bank— send the Southern money to me & Dr. R will send you that $10. changed into gold. He will inquire about Northern money when he goes to N. O. & if *it* is below *par* here, & at par there will buy up a quantity on purpose to send to you. — Perhaps some business man there will do the business for you by paying him a certain per. cent. for his trouble, though Dr. R——would not accommodate only those friendly to the South—such as Mr Merrill; you see one could make a great deal of money in a short time by such changing— I get the Pittsfield Sun quite regularly, but if it is not to be relied upon for Northern news, better than *Southern* it is of no use to us here— The "Confederate Loan" was taken up *some time ago*—a company of men raised a large sum in N. O. immediately— I believe *three* million of the *fifteen,* and the rest was taken up by companies & private individuals with the greatest avidity, so that applicants for *shares* were refused, on the grounds that the fifteen million were already taken up. Excitement in regard to the War is as great here, as with you. companies are forming & drilling all the time, the only business almost consists in *war furnishing*[4] & war & its preparations are the constant themes of conversation. The ladies of this neighborhood are busy with a flag to be presented to our Cavalry company the "Plaquemines Rangers"— it is to be a very nice one, costing over a hundred dollars. Though Dr. R——is one of the prominent members of the company, I do not take much interest in the matter— suppose I shall probably be called upon to assist in making it this coming week. The colors will be blue & silver grey to correspond with the uniforms.[5]

TUESDAY MORNING 4 O CLOCK

Dr Fox is off for the city, this morning, so I close this— I was very much pleased with George's letter & will try to keep my resolution of answering it.

Write as soon as you receive this. With much love for all   believe me-

Yours aff—

T. B. Fox.

---

4. Members of the Plaquemines [Louisiana] Rangers, under the command of Captain C. J. Villère, received a double barreled shotgun, a Colt revolver, and a cavalry saber. See *Confederate States of America Service Records for Louisiana,* November 26, 1861, NA.
5. See Drew Gilpin Faust, "Alters of Sacrifice: Confederate Women and the Narratives of War," *JAH* 76 (March 1990): 1200–1228.

Dr. R——intends sending you to-day *by Express* $20.00 in gold, so it ought to reach you with this.

□ □ □

Dear Mother— Although I heard nearly a month ago that the mails were stopped, I find it is not so, by your letters still reaching me; all mailed in May, however. I shall probably not get any dated after the first of June. It was a mistake about the gold-piece; I did not enclose any. I wrote that letter expecting it to be sent a few days sooner than the one with the draft would be & you would have a little change to help you until the draft could reach you but Dr Fox, went to town, to send the draft the next day so I did not put in the gold. He did not know what I had written or he would have added a line in explanation.— I shall miss your letters very much, but if we cannot send by mail, I suppose we can by express now & then.— Am I lazy, or what is the trouble? I do not feel like writing & have not, for a long time; if you were here I could talk & talk, until you would be tired; sometimes you would doubt if you were with *me* or some one else—half the time I hardly know myself; my disposition is so different from what it used to be, & not only my disposition but my appearance—dark as a *mulatress*, cross & ugly. But this has been a trying day; it rained hard all the morning and it seemed as if each one tried [to see] how much mud & dirt they could bring into the house; then the flies which have been *very* troublesome for the last month, just swarmed into the rooms, out of the rain, and filled every light crack & crevice. Dinner has stood upon the table, under covers & in the chafing dish since two o clock and it is now six & of course it has called in an extra swarm, although I have tried to brush them out & keep the room quite dark. Although it is Sunday, I have not felt that quiet that I love & which rests me so much.

Trifles worry me and I cannot help it— Little Fan, has been unusually good however & that has been one comfort. I generally keep her with me Sundays, talking to her & showing her pictures but to-day I let her have Adelaide to play with her, set table & dress doll-babies & though they have enjoyed it, my conscience rather reproaches *me*. Dr

---

6. This letter appears to have been written early in June but not mailed until June 28, 1861, according to the postmark.

R——was at home all the morning, but went away at noon expecting to be back by two & has not come yet—was probably called for farther down. It has been tolerably healthy, the last month, but the sickly season commences now soon & he will be busy all the time. You cannot imagine how I dread my confinement; as the time approaches, I suffer more & more. Lucy will come to stay with me, if nothing happens.[7] I expect her week after next. It will save me much care & anxiety to have some white person to keep house & take charge of matters. I do not care for myself, but Dr Raymond gets so worried with house hold matters & the servants when I am sick, particularly if he has a good many right sick patients on hand. There is a prospect of bad weather for the next month or six weeks— we have had a long drought until this last-week, when it commenced raining & there has been but little sunshine since.

My pet is calling for supper;—what do you think it is? a young mocking-bird, which Dr R——brought home to me nearly three weeks ago. I immediately commenced calling him Jimmy and he knows it very well now; has learned to catch flies & drink out of his little cup & is as tame as one could wish. He has grown very much since I have had him & is quite a pet with us all. Some negroes had caught it, from the yard at our lower place & as they had no business there, & we do not like to have the mocking birds disturbed, Dr R——took it away from them. Bird-dealers in town, buy them from the negroes giving them from .25 to 50 cts apiece. They feed them entirely on boiled Irish potatoes & the yolk of hard boiled eggs carefully mashed together. Mine has never missed a fresh meal daily, until to-day when there was not an egg to be found on the place, so I have given him crumbs & fresh beef chopped very fine & let him out of the cage to catch flies off the window glass. It is so funny to see him hop out of the cage & fly to my work stand among the spools, when I call him. Yesterday he sat down very composedly as if he was much interested in my sewing & watched me a long time. Fan says Oh Ma! see Jimmy is going to make an egg now! but he soon flew to the top of the bed & only came down when hungry. He loves to be out of the cage. I have thought of you so often since I have had him; if I could only raise him & then send him to you!

---

7. Lucy had arranged to be at Hygiene for Tryphena's confinement.

It is getting quite late & my gude man does n't come yet — the mosquitoes are swarming in, in myriads & I cannot write much longer. — I shall keep adding to this, until some chance of sending by express, if we can do that so you will have a long one, all at one time.

You would be surprised, were I to tell you how many times I have jumped up since commencing this. To send Reuben for the cows & calves, to give Fan a "drink of water", to feed Jimmy, then to call Susan & tell her to have boiling water, to make a cup of coffee when her master comes, then to light the chaffing-dish lamp again, then Fan another drink &c, &c — All easier to do, myself, than to call any one to do it for me, & I have let them all go this evening, and enjoy themselves *gabbing* in the kitchen. It is time they were in, doing up the work for the night, but you may be sure they would n't start till dark if it was midnight, unless called. If a wish could transport me to you, I should leave all & spend the evening with you — though I have no such longings for home as I used to have. Dr Raymond is perfectly disgusted with every Northern movement & I don't believe will ever care to go North again. You ask if our ports are all blockaded — most certainly they are, & there was a little skirmish between the troops at one of them not far from here not long ago. No one killed. It is too dark for me to see & little Fan. will want ma-ma, to sing her to sleep — a habit I cannot break up — it never annoys me, only when there is company & that, we don't have very often. Two gentlemen dropped in last Friday, just as supper was coming in & as ill luck would have it, I had ordered nothing but batter-cakes & coffee just for the Dr. & myself & there was not a morsel of cake in the house or light bread either. But I soon found them a tolerable good supper without either; Susan is much faster than she used to be & makes nice soda biscuits & egg corn-bread in almost no time & I always have butter & plenty of milk & cream & *clabber*, at all times — the latter is very nice with sweet cream & sugar & we eat it morning, noon & night.

SUNDAY, JUNE 16TH. 1861.

As I wrote last Sunday I will keep adding to this, until there is a chance of sending it to you. There is nothing particular to write, excepting about ourselves and our own affairs. All continue as well as usual and as yet do not suffer from the heat, although this is usually our warmest month. It is cloudy this morning and would be very sultry, but for the Southern breeze from the sea, which is very cool & pleasant. Dr R——has gone up the road, 5 miles, to see a negro boy who has been sick a week or more with whopping cough & fever He has a very sick patient, 3 miles below, that he has been to visit twice a day for the last ten days. It has fever with inflammation of the bowels & was sick eight days before he saw it; there is but little hope of its recovery; the mother is obstinate & persists in giving the child, things to eat & drink, which are very injurious—*sour wine* &c. The Dr. is very much worried; I believe he feels worse when a patient dies than any other physician & half the friends; he thinks that so many persons die, who would recover, if the nurses were more careful & followed the Doctor's prescriptions exactly. We took a delightful ride last night to the P. Office; it was just before a most brilliant sunset & with the beautiful, green cane-fields on one side & the old river, so grand & yet so calm, with its silvery surface, & here & there a white, gliding, sail, on the other   it seemed as if the road had never been one half so picturesque & charming before. I love this country very much & should never forget many a beautiful scene I have witnessed in my many rides, were we to live elsewhere. Lack of society, is the great drawback to life, but perhaps if we had that, we should not be happier. The cane is now two & three feet high & there were never finer crops.

Flowers of every description are in full bloom and give a beautiful appearance to the various yards, otherwise shaded with ever greens. One of my oleanders is twelve feet high & covered with buds. I found one full bloom on it this morning, which I could not resist picking & its two beautiful rich rose-like flowers help to fill the vase with pink lilies, honeysuckle & green box.[8] The bouquet is the prettiest ornament in the room, & I should like very much to send it to you or better, have you here, to see how pleasant my room is, for I have moved from the back one where we stayed during the winter, to my old front room, with its fine views upon the river & plantations.

We had letters from all the Dr's family last night. Pa, had been quite sick; he is very much worried with Bob, the youngest son but one; he neither go to school, as all are anxious for him to do, or go into any business & insists upon joining the army, which Pa declares he shall not

---

8. Perhaps Tryphena refers to boxwood plants.

do, being a mere boy.[9] Mother is tolerable & expects to be confined in July—so does Lizzie (Seguin's wife) I cannot help but laugh at the increase of Foxes this year & wonder what is to become of *geese*. I hope we may all be spared & the little ones be all our hearts could wish. It seems to be natural for a Mother to have so many fears. Lucy wrote that she would be down on Thursday; you don't know how relieved I am, to know that she is coming. I feel that if anything happens to me, *she*, alone, is the one who could fill my place for a time, & she would take little Fan, who is very dear to her, both as her favorite brother's child & her pet sister's namesake. — Jimmy also wrote to me; he talks of coming back to study here & has given up going North, for the present. We do not get our papers very regularly, so know but little that is going on & are just as well off, in our ignorance.

4 O CLOCK. THURS. MORNING

Dr. R. goes to town this morning, to meet Lucy who comes on the boat to-day, so I have risen to finish this, in a perfect cloud of mosquitoes. Shall have a long day here by myself & they may not come from the city to-night. Do not feel very well—but shall not confine myself any more for the present to my sewing. Have made four new fine shirts & 2 pr. linen pants for Dr. Raymond in the last two weeks, besides altering & making some garments for myself. Besides have superintended a good deal of extra housekeeping. Finished cleaning to-day & then am ready & shall expect our little *stranger* in the course of a week or so. The mosquitoes sting so, that I cannot write. You shall hear from me again soon; if I cannot write, Lucy will. I hope this will find you well & may He who preserves the lives of all, keep us, to meet again. Good Bye— Love to George. Emma & yourself   From Your Aff. Daughter.

T. B. Fox.

I wish you would send this letter to Grandma— I have had it a good while.

---

9. When Reverend Fox failed to dissuade the sixteen-year-old Robert from joining the Confederacy, he locked the boy's clothing away to keep him from leaving. This proved futile; therefore, Fox wrote directly to Jefferson Davis, who owned a cotton plantation in Warren County, Mississippi, asking him to return the boy because of his age. See "Claim of James A. Fox," no. 10,663, Southern Claims Commission, NA.

Dear Mother,   Saturday, July 6th 1861

I received your letter of June 27th by express to-night — & suppose you must have mine by this time; it was sent three or four weeks ago; I did not mail any gold in that previous letter; there was a mistake on my part about it. Do not go in debt at Mr W——s more than you can help for I did not ask Dr. R——about it & thought it would help you until you received the thirty dollars & then you could pay him; I do not know when he can send you anything more, for cash is not over plentiful here & he has only about enough to get through the year on & help you again after a while. Be assured it shall not be from any extravagances on my part, if we cannot help you now. Our expenses threaten to be so much heavier than we expected that I do not know how matters will turn out. I have seen "hard times," for the past three weeks. Susan has been very sick indeed; we did not expect her to live from one hour to another a week ago, but she is somewhat better now; though very weak & confined to her bed & needing almost constant nursing. Brother James & Sister Lucy came about two weeks ago adding two to my household & no one to help me in cooking, nursing & extra housework but Elizabeth & though she is faithful, she is very slow so that the heaviest burden falls on me. I am expecting to be confined every day — was so much in danger of a miscarriage last week after two days fatigue & worry that Dr R——sent for my old nurse being almost sure my baby would be born before morning. Susan not only needs nursing & doctoring, in both of which brother James has kindly helped me but her youngest child now three months old has had to be fed & cared for as if it were my own baby & it has been no slight task for me to lift it about when I am so unaccustomed to any such exertion. Was I used to making beds & sweeping rooms & running up & down to the kitchen & cabin it would not hurt me, but I have found it necessary to do but very little until this sickness of Susans —

I enclose this scrap of a letter written before my illness as it will give you some insight into my occupations at the time. It was hard for me to give up at such a time & throw all on Sister Lucy but you know its one of those things that cannot be helped or put off & the little stranger sleeps & eats her present life away, quite unconscious of all the trouble & sickness around her. I sincerely hope Sister Lucy will not "overdo" or

take the fever though we do not consider it contagious. The weather is
very warm & sultry, & every one suffers more than usual from the heat.

□ □ □

My Dear Mother,   [JULY 19TH 1861][10]

Your little granddaughter is now seven days old— she was born Friday the 12th   We are both quite well; she was a very *large*, plump baby
at birth and continues so; I am very proud of her & not a bit disappointed that she is a girl. Fanny is quite delighted at the prospect of a
little sister who can help her dress dolls & make beds, & is very devoted
in her attentions. Dr Raymond eyes the little baby girl with a good deal
of fatherly pride, but has never condescended to take her up yet.

I suffered more & was sick longer at her birth than ever before &
look rather delicate but hope to pick up soon, if I do not have an attack
of fever; I was up most of the day yesterday & have not rested well dining the night   "Rachel"—the old nurse says I have some fever this
morning— you do not know how I dread the idea of being confined
here any longer, for all the servants are sick excepting Reuben. Had it
not been for Sister Lucy I do not know what would have become of all.
Susan, is better but not able to walk yet or help herself at all. Adelaide
the little house-girl, was taken with fever three or four days before my
confinement "Buddy" a few days after & Margaret, last night; so all
three of them lay stretched on a pallet in the Office, needing Sister
Lucy's hourly attention, when Dr Raymond is not here.

Elizabeth has been very faithful up night & day, until she is nearly
worn out & had two or three attacks of vomiting yesterday. Besides,
Brother James has been so sick this last week that for two or three days
we thought he would not live. He had bilious fever with some disease
of the kidneys; so that Dr. R——had to cup him twice & afterwards
leech him. Generally I have been able to hire a woman to come & do the
washing but "Cely" has had something the matter with her foot &
could not come & all that has been done for the whole house-hold,
white & black, for the last three weeks has been what little Elizabeth
could do at odd times & she is very slow at it so every out of the way
corner is filled with dirty clothes— you don't know how tired I am of

10. This letter was postmarked "Sunday July 21st 1861," but as the first section was writ-
    ten the preceding Friday the date has been changed accordingly.

thinking what is to be done? — Of course Rachel has washed all my bed & night clothes & the baby things, so I have not been worried about them.

JULY 21 SUNDAY NOON

I commenced this [letter] Friday morning long before day thinking Dr R—— was going to town, but he gave it up the children were so sick   They are no better; Susan cannot walk yet; Brother James is able to have his clothes on & sit up a part of the time. I was very ill from over-exertion all day Friday & had to take a large quantity of opium to ease a severe pain in my back & head which came in about six o clock & lasted until ten, prostrating me very much. I am sitting up a little to-day— Baby is very well— we think of calling her *Rose, after you* —for one name— her papa will not say what he likes yet so the matter is not decided yet. I think he would like her names Rose Blanche— you know that is what he has always called me, but I should like Rose *Ellen*, after you & Aunt Ellen— she was so kind to me & seemed to think so much of me. I shall write again after a while— All is quiet *here* as to *war* excitement.

The blockade is still at the mouth of the river & no more tow-boats or steam ships pass up or down, making our home more quiet than ever. My letters to you cost 41 cents. Give my love to *all* our people & regards to any inquiring friends. Much Love to yourself & the children. Sister Lucy will stay another week and perhaps longer if the sick are no better. I hope to have a washer-woman in the morning—a stranger. We hear nothing of Maria yet. Dr Seguin came down last night from N. O. not knowing we were sick— he goes back to-day so I send my letter by him.

Dr R——send love with *mine* & the little *girls*, — Your daughter,

T. B. Fox

□ □ □

HYGIENE THURSDAY AUG. 8TH 1861.

Dear Mother, You have probably received my last by this time & been relieved of any anxiety you may have had on my account. Baby will be four weeks old to-morrow and is still very healthy; baby-like she does nothing but eat & sleep. I am quite well, but not as strong as I hoped to be by this time; have not been out yet excepting the store-room &

kitchen; my back is so weak, that it even tires me to go that short distance. The servants have all recovered; Susan is well enough to do her
usual work, but Adelaide & "Buddy" still look weak & puny & are taking tonics. Sister Lucy & James left us two weeks ago next Saturday.
James looked badly & felt badly too that he could not stay & study medicine, but the climate does not agree with him at all. He talks of going
on to Virginia if he is well enough. I have not heard from them since
they left & am almost afraid Lucy is sick— she had a great deal imposed
upon her here & not being accustomed to too much work, must have
been nearly tired out though she would not own it. It seems as if something always happens, when any of our friends stay with us, to make
their visit unpleasant. — As soon as they are gone, everything goes on in
the old routine & we live peaceably & I have a great deal of time when
I could sit & visit with them—if no sick darkies to nurse then, nor their
place to fill in the housekeeping. — Here comes little Fan, with a needle
broken off under her thumb-nail— what is to be done? wait, I suppose,
until pa-pa comes. Do you know Mother I am getting to be right foolish in regard to my children? With the addition of every one, my feelings towards them, change more than I can tell you & a kind of dread
haunts me that I may lose one or both of these. I never thought a child
could be so dear.

There has been a very severe epidemic of diphtheria on one of the
plantations on the other side; only one case has died, so far, but they
have required his daily attention and I am so afraid the children may
have it, not only mine, but the four black children. I shall have all the
nursing of the latter to do, for you have no idea of how worthless a
nurse Susan is, for her own children & Elizabeth knows nothing about
waiting upon the sick. She is a good servant, but so very slow, that
sometimes I get completely out of patience. this morning is an example
of many. it is nearly eleven o clock & she has not washed the breakfast
dishes yet—is just going about it— you wonder what she has done: before I got up, she made her master a cup of coffee (for he had to be off
by five) then churned a little cream & made a little butter, & dressed
Fan; by that time I was up, so she brought me baby's bath, put my
room & her master's in order, held baby while I breakfasted, then has
spent the rest of her time eating her own breakfast & sweeping & dust-
ing the dining room. You ought to see her walk around a bed & pick &

look & *fuss* when she is making it! it would be a treat for any Yankee
woman who was in the habit of seeing people do their work quickly. I
find fault with her sometimes & cannot help it, for with all her slow
ways, she is not very neat & it would shock you sometimes to see how
out of order & dirty everything is in the back part of the house. After
five years experience in housekeeping with black people I have found
that I must give up my notions of a very nice & orderly house or scold
& watch & oversee all the time, not only ruining my own mind & temper but making the servants really dissatisfied & the more careless from
being looked after. It seems so trivial too for a woman to be always on
the lookout for a dirty dish or a dusty mantle piece. So [if] the house is
passably decent I am going to let it go. You have no idea how little
knowledge is now at my command, that I gained while at school; history, the natural sciences, biography, & even what little poetry I could
once readily recall, are now all submerged beneath a chaos of brooms,
dusters, & dish-cloths, chickens, eggs & darkies with or without clean
hands, faces & aprons. —

NEARLY 9 O CLOCK.

Dont these babies occupy one's time? Since writing the above I have
been able to do nothing but nurse baby & do a little mending — the fact
is, I have done nothing so far, since her birth, & to see me with her &
Fan, you would be reminded of an overgrown girl with two doll-babies
to play with. Sewing does not press me much now. I am making me a
purple muslin which will probably be finished, *for winter* & I have two
dresses to finish for baby; one a blue chambray, nearly done & the other
a fine white nansook to be made with inserting & tucks up the front
breadth. I would not make a handsome one before her birth, fearing she
might not live.

— Fan's papa bought her a very pretty doll & it has taken some of my
spare moments to dress that; the suit is nearly completed & she is perfectly delighted with it. The dress is a dotted white Swiss muslin *tucked*,
over a blue cambric skirt. I have promised to make it some black mo-
rocco shoes & a pretty black silk cape — If Emma was here I should
give her that job. We were speaking of you to-day & Dr R —— said I had
better enclose a dollar anyhow, as it would not be known. I think he
will send you more money soon, though he did not say so. Times are
hard here, but not as they are at the North. We do not hear any thing,

of the war more than you, & that only through the papers & do not consider either New Orleans or the people of the country in any immediate danger. Like every one else, we were terribly shocked with the accounts from Manassas[11] — I wonder if one of those men; Lincolnites, — could tell what he was fighting for? it is so dreadful to think of such a waste of life & such desolation in so many homes & hearts & all for what? The Southerners can *never* be conquered; they may all be killed, but conquered, never.

If you suffer very much, can you not go & stay with Grandma, until we see what can be done. I am very anxious that you should come & live with me not only for your sake but to be *honest*, for my own too. I feel as though it would be better for both of us; at present it cannot be done, but there may be some change for the better both in national & individual affairs in the fall or winter & then you might come. Mr. West need not be afraid of Dr R's not helping you — he shall not lose what you have had there — We have not heard from Pa, for some time; I suppose that before this, there is an addition to his family. Robert, the youngest son but one, has gone to Virginia, but we do not think he was at the battle.

Give my love to all of Mr. Merrill's people & to all of our friends. Tell Hattie I have not forgotten her, & will try to write & tell her about my new baby. Much love to yourself Georgy & Emma from all — Dr R——Fanny, little *Rose*, & daughter,

T. B. Fox.

□ □ □

Dear Mother,   HYGIENE DEC 27TH 1861.

The pen, ink, paper, & your last letter all lay here on the table so conveniently, that I cannot resist the plea that they seem to urge though I am terribly lazy & would be glad of some excuse to any exertion. I say lazy, but that means "worn out," with tooth-ache. The filling came out of one of my back teeth, some time ago & for the last two weeks, I have suffered with it, half the time not only during the day, but at night. Dr R——has promised to take it out, so I am waiting his leisure. He is absent now, & will probably be gone all night, over to a Mr Davis' plan-

---

11. The First Battle of Manassas (or the First Battle of Bull Run) occurred July 21, 1861.

tation on the bayou. All the morning he was absent & until three this afternoon, when he brought Mr Warren home to dine with him. He has a patient—a boy about eight years old, who shot off his own shoulder, accidentally, about a month ago. He had been out hunting when, on returning & quite near home, he placed his gun on one of the lower rails of the fence, crawled through himself & in trying to pull the gun after him, it went off & shot away the top of the shoulder. The arm is saved but he will not have much use of it as there is no socket or top to the ball, to keep it in place; only the flesh which has grown over the wound. The boy's father is very much delighted with Dr Fox's treatment; the other physicians wished to take the arm off, immediately, while Dr. F——opposed & said it ought to be saved if possible & he would attempt it. At about twelve, all the gentlemen of the neighborhood met at "the store" to complete the formation of the cavalry company lately started. They are all strong secessionists. I suppose you have received the "Gov.s message" which I sent you & which will give you some idea of the earnestness of the Southern people.— You speak of danger from the negroes; nothing has occurred yet to alarm any one in this vicinity, still every one acknowledges that it is far better & wiser, to be on our guard, than to rest in perfect sloth & tranquility until the negroes have every possible means of meeting, forming, & putting into execution the most terrible plans for murder & blood-shed.

All the gentlemen of the parish are forming into companies to keep the different portions of the parish under the strictest watch. I do not fear one half now, that I did three weeks ago, though there they may be just as much danger. I am alone to-night not another white person excepting the workman—who is a little, cowardly Frenchman—is within a quarter of a mile, yet I shall not be at all afraid. All the alarm & anxiety I feel now is for you & for all of the people of the North who depend upon their daily wages for a living. What is to become of them? I never sit down to the table, but I think of the many, to whom a small portion, even of our abundance would be so acceptable. The Abolitionists talk about "the poor negro"—I dare say not one white person in ten throughout the whole North had such a dinner for Christmas as did mine yesterday & probably all the others throughout Southland, & many & many a white person would have been glad of their every day dinner of to-day, though it was nothing more than nice pickled pork, with turnips & turnip greens, sweet potatoes, corn bread & sweet milk, and as much of each kind as all the *seven* could eat. It is a beautiful moonlight night, though some-what cold. It gives me a lonely, home-sick feeling to look out, for the Christmas days, now, call up those of old. and they are too truly pleasant in memory not to be regretted. Did I tell you in my last that I had been reading "Jane Eyre" again? You have no idea how much pleasure it give me: somehow all the scenes call you so constantly to mind that I seem to be living with you: not because you or your life are like hers, but I suppose because you are so much an ad-mirer of the work. We are reading Dickens' new Novel—"Great Expectations"— which comes in Chapters in Harper's Weekly.[12] It promises to be a very good story. Dr R——has promised me Godey for this coming year, which will be a pleasant monthly companion stepping in to give one advice on various subjects & keep me somewhere near *"the fashion".* I have not had or made but one garment this season & that was a new calico dress to wear while the papering & painting was going on, so to keep my French Calico out of paste & paint

JAN 4TH, 1862

Have been quite sick & confined to my bed with fever, occasioned by the tooth-ache I wrote about. Dr. R——tried to pull the tooth & it broke off & since then I have suffered terribly with it as I have had a kind of neuralgia in my head besides. Dr R—— was to go to Wood-burne next week on a flying trip & I was to stay & take care of things, but he has concluded to take me & Fan along too; he thinks I need change of air & of course he has proposed it I don't object & am per-fectly delighted at the prospect of going— We only stay a few days & bring our friends back with us. The house is almost finished, only the office remains to be papered & the medicines brought up & arranged. I want to leave everything in good order, so not to be worried on my return. I have not much to do, to get ready—a dress to make for myself, some sheets to finish, a couple of dresses for Fanny & one for Maria.[13] We stay so short a time I shall not need much, but what I do have will be noticed   "Raymond's wife" you know; he is the oracle of the family.

---

12. Charles Dickens's *Great Expectations* began appearing in *Harper's Weekly Magazine,* November 24, 1860, and ran to August 3, 1861.
13. The dress was for Susan's daughter, not the runaway slave Maria.

All the rest have very good health & the neighborhood is remarkably healthy; it is the most suitable time for Dr. R——to leave & I do hope nothing will happen to prevent. We start a week from Tuesday. I will try to write again & may send you some money. Mrs Dr. Borland returned from Virginia just before Christmas. She sent Fanny a box of toys, a raw silk dress   a tippet & some candy, & to me a collar & pr. of mitts. Dr. R——gave me a gold bracelet for a New Year's gift. The bracelet part is made of his watch-chain—a beautiful thing which I always coveted & he took it to town & had a $4. dollar clasp put on it, as a surprise to me. But I must not sit here any longer gossiping— My old tooth will begin to ache, by the time I am ready to go to work. Good Bye—give much love to all our people—Grandma especially & with much love to yourself—believe me Yours truly.

T. B. Fox

□ □ □

[JAN. 29TH ˮ62]

Dear Mother— You can hardly imagine how glad I am of the opportunity to write you even one page. I have been very anxious about you, these past six months, and now hope I may hear from you in return— Direct your letters as you used to do & then add "Via Norfolk & Flag of Truce", as I have done. — We are all very well— all the servants who were so sick in the summer, recovered. Dr. Fox is as busy as ever & as much from home. His practice last year amounted to more than that of any previous year. Fanny is both growing & learning very fast— Your little namesake is as bright and pretty as you could desire; she looks as Semantha did; has very dark hair & eyes with long, dark eyelashes. My health is better this winter than usual; and as secluded as ever— Have been to the city quite often & enjoyed the trips very much. Maria returned in August & has proved an excellent nurse for both F—— & Rose.[14] All the others have done well too, so that our domestic life glides along quite smoothly. The neighborhood has been unusually

---

14. Tryphena recorded Maria's return in her diary. She wrote: "Saturday Dr. R found Maria in Mr Stackhouse's quarters. It will be six months the 17th of this, since she ran away. Their carriage driver has harbored her most of the time. She has been severely whipped, and has come back evidently resolved to do her best that she can; as to her being a run-away, we have forgiven and shall forget. As Dr. R says she is a negro and now that she has been punished, it is enough." See TBHF Diary Transcript, August 12, 1861, MDAH.

healthy & the whole winter *extremely mild*; we have had *no killing frost*. I am limited to one page; Give my love to *all* our friends—Grandma in particular— Write if possible. Dr R——sends much love with mine & the children's   Your daughter—

T. B. Fox.

□ □ □

WOODBURNE PLANTATION JULY 3RD. 63.[15]

My Dear Mother— I write again fearing that you might not have received my last, of June— All are still well, but living in a state of terrible suspense, not knowing what moment this dreadful fight between Johnson's & Grant's forces may commence. Pa's plantation is immediately on the line—2 miles you know from Big Black. Pickets are stationed at several points around the house & troops of soldiers have been camped in the yard the last few days. Pa has grown old & rapidly during the past 6 weeks & looks anxious & care-worn; he is in his 70th year & cannot bear up under such severe trials now; there are *four* families of us here now, besides 3 who are no relations. Dr Raymond is staying with me & Fanny, merely to help Pa as much as he can—for there are no negro men left to do any thing now. Daniel's wife & three children were with Mrs M[essenger]— She "has been burned out of house & home" & Angelina was forced to come here. Lizzie & her three little ones have been with us, since last September. Seguin is in Vicksburg & she of course hears nothing from him. Daniel is on Deer Creek. James & Robert—we know not where— As yet we have drawn no rations from the Northern army but we shall be obliged to do so, soon— Many of the negroes have left, the corn & meat were taken the 1st week the Yankees came in here & they are driving off cattle & sheep & killing the hogs every day. The garden is a perfect waste & nothing is left but a few green apples & the flowers & weeds. We are not allowed to pass outside the pickets to gather berries. The cows are yet left us, but may be taken any day & I cannot but shudder to think—how are these nine children to be fed then— they are all under six years of age. Older people can get along with a piece of dry corn bread, but the little

---

15. This letter was written one day before the fall of Vicksburg. (Far to the north, the battle of Gettysburg was in its second day.) The area around Woodburne had been occupied by Union troops following the battle of Big Black River on May 17.

ones will soon suffer from diarrhea & dysentery. Oh! Mother! you northern people know nothing of the horrors of war & may you be spared what I have suffered during the last year. I have tried to say & to feel—*"Thy will be done"*—but the many trials have been severe notwithstanding my resignation. You will learn from my last probably, how little Fanny lay three months with a violent attack of scarlet fever & how she is at last recovered, though even now a mere skeleton with a large scar upon her neck & that my other little darling, my pet; my Rose bud, lies in the grave yard, taken suddenly from me, with the same fearful disease.[16] Our home is gone—everything there destroyed[17] & Reuben, Maria & Elizabeth all free— Susan & her children are with us yet, *But I would rather have my home.* We own nothing now but our clothing & but very little of that—but I do not write these things to distress you for Dr. Raymond has still a stout heart & I rejoice that he is a professional man & not a planter. I must write no more, as this is liable to scrutiny & it will not be sent if too *long.* Remember me with much love to Grandma & all there, to Georgy & Emma & to all old friends—and with much love to yourself Dear Mother   I am as of old—Your devoted daughter.

T. B. Fox

□ □ □

Dear Mother,   [DE KALB. KEMPER CO. MISS. JAN 18TH 1864.]

It is a long, long time since I have had an opportunity of sending to you; now I have so much to tell you, hardly know what to write: for my letter must be left open for inspection & must be shorter than I wish. You will be glad to learn that we are all able to attend to daily duties, but Dr. R——is not well. I try to shut my eyes—not see the terrible truth that is ever before me. The last twelve months have deprived me of one my darlings, of my home & home comforts, of servants, & everything but a little clothing, but all of these are nothing when compared with what the next year may take from me. He has been very ill with some affection of the lungs but is better now, but has still the same hacking cough & thin, pale face. At present we are pleasantly situated,

---

16. Anna Rose died April 2, 1863. See TBHF Diary Transcript, April 2, 1861, MDAH.
17. Tryphena's household furnishings and other material possessions were scattered, but Hygiene was not destroyed. After the war, she succeeded in recovering most of her furnishings.

boarding at Dr McLanahan's in the center of the town. It is a small place—the county seat of Kemper Co. Dr Raymond is President of the Medical Board for examining Conscripts & has a very easy time. His salary which would be ample in ordinary times is just sufficient to clothe & feed us at the present high prices of every thing. Mrs McLanahan is an exceedingly kind & intelligent lady & treats me more like a daughter than a stranger; we have been here since the tenth of Nov. & shall probably remain for several months yet. The Yankees have never been here yet but all the people seem to realize our condition & show us much sympathy. You have no idea, Mother, how many homeless wanderers this war has caused—wanderers who have been accustomed to every comfort, how deprived of everything & now, know not where to lay their heads.[18] The Northern people know nothing of this war— there would be peace if they did; peace & consent to let us alone; how do they hope to conquer a people who will give up every thing even to life rather than be conquered? My husband could have saved our home & property just by taking the oath of allegiance to the United States— do they think that such men as he will take it now? But I must not write in this strain or they will not let me send it. My room has two additions—a cradle & a spinning wheel. The cradle for our boy—a fine little fellow about five months old—whom we have named "George Edward Randolph". The first for my side, the last two after Dr R——s twin brother & Aunt Randolph. He is perfectly healthy but very frail looking, with a little pale face & large black eyes—papa's pet & mother's pride. Fanny has quite recovered from her terrible attack of scarlet fever & is growing very fast. I am more fleshy than ever before since my marriage. I suppose owing to the change of climate as it has been extremely cold ever since I came here & there has been much snow & ice. Besides I have no cares now & take but little thought for the morrow. Have a good woman to nurse the baby & do my washing & ironing; she is an excellent servant of about forty—very faithful & trusty. We have to give a high price for her & board & clothe her—her clothing she is to spin herself while baby is quiet or asleep, hence the spinning wheel in my room. She has not accomplished much yet for I have a

---

18. See Daniel E. Sutherland, "Looking for a Home: Louisiana Emigrants during the Civil War and Reconstruction," *LaH* 21 (Fall 1980): 431–59.

great deal of company & much visiting to do. There are several officers & [a] good many soldiers stationed here, & we have a very sociable time— There have been several parties & dinings. I have been to most of them & enjoyed them very much. Clothing & food are very dear, but I do not need much of the former—am reduced to a *homespun* dress & unbleached domestic underclothes, but I am contented; have learned to realize that if one is warm & neatly dressed it is all sufficient; we shall probably be more happy hereafter; when my darling was taken from me, I learned to place my hopes above & not on things below. I should like to know how you are, & how you & Georgy & Emma are getting along this cold weather. Please write & direct it to Rev. J. A. Fox, Vicksburg with the one inside to me & ask him to "Please Forward"— put those words on both & I may be able to get it. Write only of family matters—about all of you whom I love & would be so happy to see— Grandma & brother & Uncle B——& Aunt M & M——& C——& *all*.[19] Also Hattie Dewey— Give much love to them all. Accept much for yourself & the children— May God grant that this terrible war may soon close & that we may meet again. Your daughter

T. B. Fox.

□ □ □

Dear Mother,   JULY 26TH 1864. ABERDEEN, MONROE CO. MISS.

Yours[20] of June 18th reached me July 23rd & you can imagine my joy on learning that you were well; I have so many anxious hours about you that even a sight of your handwriting is a relief to me for then I know you are alive & well enough to hold a pen— Why did not Harriet Dewey enclose a few words, as I see the envelope is directed by her— I should be glad to hear from her, for the sake of by-gone days. It grieves me that you still have so hard a trial to gain even a pittance, but it grieves me too that I can no longer assist you— My only hope is that

---

19. Tryphena refers to her mother's sisters: Mahala Cleveland Brague (b. 1814), Mary Eliza Cleveland (b. 1819), and Catherine Waldo Cleveland (b. 1822).

20. In Anna's letter dated July 18, 1863, rather than June 18, 1863, she offered her condolence: "I received your letter of July 3 yesterday with the awfull news of your suffering and privations and the death of my poor grandchild and namesake . . . I feel that Death has taken another of my dear ones. Le Roy I know nothing of he enlisted in the Navy last fall and has not been heard from since." Le Roy died December 27, 1864, after completing the one year enlistment that ended February 12, 1864. See ARH to TBHF, July 18, 1863, MDAH; Muster Rolls of the U.S.S. *Sassacus*, 1863–65, U.S.S. *Satellite*, 1863, U.S.S. *Saugus*, 1864–1865, April 1864, NA.

this war will soon be over & it may be I shall be so situated as to help you again—I hope more than I did before. Le Roy acts very strangely— I am sorry for Emma & really wish I could have her with me, but it would be an impossibility now.[21] I am sometimes very homesick thinking of you & grandma & the few there whom I love, but I don't think I shall ever care to visit the north again. I believe I have written to you once since we came to Aberdeen. We have rented a house, hired a servant, borrowed some furniture & are getting along tolerably—though it is only camping out to what our former life used to be. One room answers for parlor, dining-room & bed-room & the furniture is coarse & rough but I prefer it to boarding. Dr. R——has his own rations & buys those of three other officers & we get along pretty well on them. The Gov. is very much in arrears to him now which makes things rather hard for us, but we hope to be paid off soon. Had he not found kind friends almost everywhere, I do not know what would have become of us. His health has improved very much since the warm weather. He has no cough now & looks like a different man from what he was last winter. I think anxiety affects him very much. I try to keep him cheered up & tell him we shall not starve if we have lost every thing. It may seem a *glorious* thing to those Yankees, for them to come on here & turn us from our homes & confiscate our property & take our furniture & clothing for themselves, but it would not seem so if we were to do the same to them. I learn that they sold my new piano which was a present from Dr. R——& cost $500 for *three dollars* & sent it on to some of the *Northern Sisters!* & may she ever hear mingled with the melody, the low, mournful wails of a houseless mother & beggar children![22]

You say you would like to see my babe! would that I might lay him on your lap— He is a beautiful boy—but too frail—too unearthly. I fear he is not given me for a long sojourn. There is so much expression in his little face & large black eyes. Every one praises him & calls him a very handsome child & I cannot help but see that he is not a common baby— even had I not a mother's pride. He is not well now—as he is

21. Emma had taken a job at Pontoosuc woolen mill.
22. The piano had unusual importance to Tryphena, and it was removed from Hygiene before she had any opportunities to play or enjoy it. Fox bought it while she was at Woodburne before the fall of Vicksburg and they did not return to Hygiene until after the war. It was removed from Hygiene, but it had not been sold.

teething & has cut two—one upper & one lower on the left side. The gums are much swollen on the other side [. . .] and I hope he will be better as soon as they come through. I have not many clothes for him & do not know what I shall do for him when winter comes. There is no imported flannel in the country & only enough made at home for those who make it— But its of no use to borrow trouble. I have learned that "God will Provide". Every thing has turned out right so far. I believe that if we have Faith & Resignation we have the true secrets for true happiness here on earth.

Dr. R. had a very nice suit of grey *homespun* jeans given him about a month ago— It is very pretty cloth— you would hardly believe it home-made. The Southern ladies have certainly carried the art of making cloth by hand far beyond their expectations at first. The same lady has given me bleached domestic enough to make two suits of underclothes & Fanny some. I little thought three years ago that I should be wearing *coarse unbleached* now. I have found it uncomfortably warm, but the past few mornings have been cool & I did not mind it; it is just such as I used to give my servants 3 suits of every year. Who do you suppose will give it to them now? and all the nice calico & linsey I used to give them besides for dresses & joseys. I have heard that Susan went to Memphis & one of her children is dead—they needed "Mistress nursing & care"—& that Maria was still in Vicksburg faring badly— I am sorry for her & believe she would gladly come back to me if she could. But if I could have them I should not wish it— I am happier now than ever before since my marriage— no one can tell the trouble that four or five around the house can give one, until they have tried it.

I nurse my own baby with Fanny's help (& she amuses him a great many times when I am busy) and find my time pretty well occupied when he is quiet, sewing & writing— Have but very little house-keeping to attend to as the servant I have is a good one & attends to almost everything—or rather what little we have.

Fanny is growing strong & healthy again— the first time she has been well since we left our home: she had a very severe attack of Pneumonia in May.

I must say Good Bye. I will write again soon. Send your letter to me in an envelope directed to Mrs D. Raymond Fox, Aberdeen, Miss——

& put that in another one directed as Sister Lucy will tell you.[23]— Give much of my love to *Grandma* & Aunts C & M & much to Uncle & Aunt Brague— I am sorry to hear that she is so low. Give much to George & Emma— tell Emma to write to me. With much to yourself & many prayers that your life henceforth may not be *all* care & anxiety I remain as ever— Your Affectionate Daughter.

T. B. Fox.

□ □ □

My Dear Mother,   ABERDEEN, MISS. OCT. 14TH, '64

THIS IS MY HUSBAND'S 41ST BIRTHDAY

It is a long time since I have heard anything from you. I wrote in answer to that letter directed by Hattie Dewey in the summer & sent it to Sister Lucy— she had it mailed & told you how to direct to her but I presume you have never received it or maybe there is an answer in Natchez for me. The authorities are very strict now & will allow no communication if they can help it. I feel very anxious about you as the cold weather comes on, but I am like one with his hands tied—can do nothing for you— only pray for you nightly that God will provide for you & make your old age more easy than the past years have been.

We are all tolerable well now—but have been very sickly— All of us had chills & fever more or less ever since the last of Aug. The baby is very puny—has chills & ear-ache a great deal & is just cutting his eye teeth, does not walk yet—hardly stands alone & is very poor. The bishop was with us last Aug. & christened him, which has taken a great weight from my mind— I so feared he might be taken from me before he could be baptized. Dr. R—— looks very badly but as he has been having chills very often I hope he will be better now that we are having frosts & there will not be so much malaria. He has no cough this fall, so I am not so uneasy about him as I was last winter. My health is very delicate, but it is only from nursing Georgy, I suppose and I have had a great deal of my own cooking & other work to do lately as our servant was laid up some days at two different times with chills. But with all draw-backs I try to be cheerful & contented— I am thankful that we have a warm chimney corner, plenty to eat & enough to wear to keep us

---

23. Lucy Fox Newman forwarded mail to Tryphena after Dr. Fox joined the army and moved to Northern Mississippi with his family.

warm even though we do not *look* as nicely as we used to. I have no flannels or woolen goods for the children & cannot get any but I expect they will get along somehow. It takes all of Dr. R——'s monthly salary to furnish us with the actual necessaries of life & it would hardly be sufficient did we not have a great deal given us & he gets some outside practice— He has already quite a reputation here as physician & surgeon— He cured a lady's sore eyes, for which he received $200. & helped take a cancer from another lady's breast which brought him another $200— it is the *third* time he has performed that operation since we came here. The other lady was a Dr's wife so he would charge nothing but she made him a beautiful piece of gray homespun jeans. it is as fine & pretty as boughten goods & makes him a nice warm coat & pr. of pants. I made the pants & trimmed them with a side strip of black velvet & he hired the coat made— I am very proud of the suit for him— for his other was all "tattered & torn"— Now he looks quite genteel as well as Confederate. I am wearing an old brown calico that I had three years ago & a black cloth apron, intended for a coat lining. My dress has about 40 patches on it, but does very well when starched & ironed. I need another dark calico but as I cannot get one for less than $90.. shall go without a good while yet. My new winter shoes cost $39.. they are the only new thing I shall get for this winter.

As to provisions, we have plenty—fresh beef, flour & corn-meal— lard is scarce & very high— My friends here are kind & supply me with a good deal of butter, sweet potatoes & *syrup* made from the sorghum— There is plenty to eat through the country— Northern people must not think we are most starved out or naked—every body almost is making homespun. I have just heard the *sad* news of Mrs *Messenger's death*— she was sick about three weeks—had several diseases— All are quite well at Pa's excepting Sister Emily— I am afraid she will grieve herself to death— her betrothed died from wounds in the summer; she was with him. I could write much more but must not— Give my love to Grandma & Aunts C——& M & Uncle & Aunt B——& with much love for yourself & the children & with many prayers for your welfare & hopes that this war may soon be over & we may meet again I am, as ever Your Aff. daughter.

                                                          T. B. Fox

[Apparently Lucy Fox Newman wrote the following directions on a separate piece of paper to enclose in the letter.]

Do not direct your letter to Blanche at all—but simply to Mrs. Lucy A. Newman, Care of Samuel Wood, Esq.—Natchez.

□ □ □

Dear Mother,   [ABERDEEN, MISS. JUNE 12TH 1865]

When I became convinced of our great humiliation, and it was long after the first reports reached here, there was only one gleam through all the darkness, one pleasure with so much pain & that was the thought— I can write & hear from mother again, often. This is the first opportunity I have had, but one; then I did not think that I might send to you, until it was too late. It was when Dr R——went to N. O. three weeks ago. He started rather suddenly & I had much to do & much to think of. Since then the mails have been stopped & I have not been able to hear from him—expected him back last week & am getting anxious about him.

Self & children are tolerable well— George is rather puny from teeth-ing & indigestion— Fanny grows very rapidly & *you* would know her among strangers from her resemblance to our Mary. She is a quick good child, but rather given to babyish ways, which I notice more, now that she is thrown among play mates. She gives me great pleasure in one respect— She is truly conscientious & never tells a falsehood or deceives me. George is as pretty as ever— I wish you could see him. He does not look like any of my family—is a true *Fox*. He says a great many words but no sentences yet, although almost two years old. You doubtless wonder what we are going to do—& so do we. Dr. R——went to our old home to see if he could recover any of his property or collect any debts— if the practice is still a good one & we can have our places back we shall return there, if not, probably settle here. He is well known here & has a pretty good reputation, but there are so many doctors that all cannot stand a good chance—besides the practice would be very labo-rious for him, as he would be obliged to ride on horse-back one half the time. The climate too is against both of us— the latter part of winter I suffered very much from rheumatism & the children were sick more than two thirds of the time. I would like best to return to N. Orleans, but of course would not give up a good practice for an inclination, for we have our daily bread to earn now— there is hardly a farthing left us. Our horse (a faithful old fellow worth about 200..), a cow & calf & few chickens & few articles of household furniture are all that is left us. None of us have clothes hardly fit to be seen in & you would be shocked to see the hat Fanny wears—poor child, it mortifies her very much, for she goes in good society & the little girls are well dressed. I would have been willing to have worn sack cloth could we have achieved our Independence, but now all the sacrifices we have made, seem of double weight.

I am afraid it will be a long time before I can hear from you—but as soon as you receive this write & direct to Mrs. D. R. Fox— Care of J. Eckford Esq Memphis, Tenn. & he will send it through to this place though I may not be here then. I will write again as soon as I can hear from Dr.—

At present I am living in the house rented by Dr R—— for the year, with plenty of flour, meat, lard & sugar & molasses for a month or six weeks— Have the same negro man & woman to wait upon me, with a good garden to gather vegetables from—so you see I am quite comfortable as to outward circumstances, but with all— I am very anxious & unhappy— what would become of me, if anything should happen to Dr R——is ever uppermost in my thoughts—alone here a stranger in a strange land— But I must not trouble you— he will doubtless be with me, by the time this is with you—if not I shall go to N. O. myself— I can be supported there as well as here.— Give my love to all of the family—Grandma particularly if she is alive— I hope to see her yet—& you & Emma & George. Good Bye— & believe me as ever Your devoted daughter

T. B. Fox.

I have no envelopes & no money to buy one with, so I send you a confederate one.

Government has just paid Dr R——when the crash came & left us 2000 poorer than we ought to have been, for we might have bought some clothing had it come a little sooner—

Mother—do you notice how hard & cold this letter seems—well—it is just as my face looks now. You would not know me were you to see me— If ever there was one lovable & desirable feature or expression on it, it is gone now—ten years has changed me completely.

Dear Mother,   HOME.[24] SAT. JULY 15TH 1865

Your last of June 28th has reached me— I am very glad to hear from you— it is one of my *chief pleasures* now that the war is over. Write as often as you can, even if I do not write, for I am very, very busy now trying to restore my old home to its former condition as far as our means will allow— You never saw a house so *stripped* of everything— even the paper was torn from the office wall, so they might get the cloth upon which it was pasted for *sheets.* I have much sewing to do— Dr. R. hired sheets & mosquito bars made before I came, but there are curtains & towels & spreads & pillow cases to make besides clothing for every one of us. I only keep one servant & of course attend to some of the housekeeping myself, besides watching Georgy & hearing Fan's lessons—so you see I have my hands full— & often wish you were here with me, not only for your company, but to be candid, because I know you would help me in many little ways & it would be so pleasant for me— I do not know that you would like living here— it is a lonesome place for one accustomed to town life & the mosquitoes are a terrible pest— Dr R——can do nothing about sending you money to come on, for the present, & so *he says nothing,* but I hope that it may so be, that you can come in the winter— Emma can keep house for George & it will be pleasant for all. He has not collected as much as he expected by one half & what has been collected has been spent immediately in beds, bedding, crockery, groceries, horse-feed, &c— &c— we have had to commence fresh as young people do when going to house-keeping— even a new stove $30.   What grieves me is—that I am obliged to have coarse, common things when I had such nice ones—my beautiful white china is all gone & we have been obliged to replace it with *common stone china*—and at a greater expense too, for everything is very dear.

All those nice linen sheets &c, that you sent me are stolen & I have to buy common unbleached— I went to town on Wed—to see the "Authorities" & try to get an order for my furniture, but only had a *promise* of one— it is to be sent on the boat to-day—*perhaps*— The agent made it an excuse not to give me an order then, because it was a few moments after office hours & he did not wish to impose upon his employees! &

---

24. Tryphena and her family returned to Hygiene June 25, 1865.
    See TBHF to ARH, June 30, 1865, MDAH.

there stood the clerk, pen in hand, ready & willing to make out the order, but I *must wait* just for *that Yankee* to show his power & authority. "Come in to-morrow morning at 9 o clock & you can have it"— "Why Mr. Conway,"[25] said I, "I have come from the country, rode fifteen miles in a buggy, have been in before & you were not here & must return home tonight"—"Cant help it Madam, cannot give you the order to-night"—was not he a gentleman?

I am trying to make some money— There was a nigger school upon the place when I came, which I determined to get rid of immediately[26]— they had converted my servants rooms into the schoolroom—but when I learned that the teacher[27] was very anxious to board here & would give me twenty-five dollars per *month* & not much trouble & 8 dollars a month rent for the rooms, I determined to put up with the annoyance of the little darkey school & take the money to help refurnish my empty house & clothe my half-naked children— it amounts to 33. dollars per month.

The teacher is a young girl about 17—rather rough & coarse & a foreigner— her mother is a very poor woman living in town. She rather helps than troubles me—& behaves very well, what I have seen of her is very neat & quiet & is fond of the children—took good care of them & the house while I was gone to town & I felt much easier than I would have done to have left them with the servant. The servant Alice, is a young active girl & does nearly as much as three of mine used to do. I give her 10. pr. month & hire the woman to come & wash one day every week for .50 pr. day. I have had no trouble with servants since mine were taken from me—take life a great deal more easy & really enjoy it, which I did not before— You know that I often wrote you that

25. Thomas W. Conway, former army chaplain, local assistant commissioner of the Bureau of Refugees, Freedmen, and Abandoned Land for Louisiana and South Carolina. See Ira Berlin, Thavolia Glymph, Steven F. Miller, Joseph P. Reidy, Leslie S. Rowland, Julie Saville, eds., *Freedom: A Documentary History of Emancipation, 1861–1867*, ser. 1, vol. 3, *The Wartime Genesis of Free Labor: The Lower South* (New York: Cambridge University Press, 1990), 370–71; Eric Foner, *Reconstruction: America's Unfinished Revolution, 1863–1877* (New York: Harper & Row, 1988), 143.

26. The Freedmen's Bureau established a school in the former slave quarters on the Fox property. See "Report of the First Superintendent State of Louisiana," Bureau of Refugees, Freedmen, and Abandoned Lands, Record Group 105, NA (hereafter cited as Freedmen's Bureau).

27. Emma Puschcareff, whom Tryphena refers to as "Miss Emma," boarded at Hygiene until October, 1865. See below.

they were like so many children to be clothed & nursed & fed & were constantly to be looked after—whether *they* are any happier *now*, I cannot say, I only know this, that *I* am happier & should be ten years younger, in looks & feelings had there never been such a thing as *slaves*. You speak of my coming to you—I could not did I wish it—the fare now is 80. dollars from here to N. York first class passage & 40. second & it would cost me over three hundred to go there & back with the children & I dont know when we can call that much money our own again. *If* there can be anything raised for travelling expenses between now & Dec—I want to send it to you & either you or Emma have the benefit of it—

I had brother's miniature with me, but it has become much injured, have you one like *that* he sent me? if so, I should like a copy after a while—I have no money now to pay for one.— Give much love to Emma— tell her, I say she *must write*—& Georgy too. When is Hat going to send me that long promised letter—telling me all about herself & babies, how many has she? My kindest regards to Mr Merrill's people. Where is Hannah now.— Dont show my letter to any-one— If you have any of my old letters—please keep them, I want to look them over, *some day*. All my books, music, old letters— journals—our diplomas & everything of the kind is gone— I am going to ride down to the plantation where many of them are this evening & see if I cannot have them, if they do not send the order from town. The negroes in the neighborhood have many of my things & I hope they can be persuaded to give them up. Do you remember the pretty tufted work on canvass which the fair gave me a silver butter-knife for? I converted it into a sofa cushion & it was a beautiful thing. I can hear nothing of it & am afraid some honest Yankee boxed it up & sent it to his lady-love. My piano I have no hopes of getting though it was said to be in N. O. Somebodys *mistress* has it. I could write many a page but must stop now, for Georgy is fretting & it is time to see about dinner— I wish you was to dine with me— my bill of fare is succotash, rice, irish potatoes, fish with egg sauce, & boiled meat & cabbage—a plain country dinner you see but we *poor* folks, can afford nothing more now. Good Bye again & with much love I am Your daughter.

T. B. Fox.

[Aug. 21st 1865]

Dear Mother— As I go to town again to-morrow, I write a few lines, to put into the Office. I hope you have received my last & the answer is on its way back before this. Fearing it may not have reached you, I write about the quilts again[28]   I wish 7 comforters & 2 double blankets,— I have $50. laid aside for them. Could they be sent to me by Express for $5, if so I wish you would buy materials there, & make them up for me— can you do so & save ten out of the fifty for yourself—to pay for your trouble? Old dress skirts or damaged cambric or calico would do—any thing to make good substantial comforters about like those you gave me. Select me good sized blankets—not too fine—as I cannot have *nice* things now as I used to do. There was $1.25 enclosed in my last to pay your expenses to Grand-ma's. You spoke of the taxes to be paid— Dr R——says he dont care what I do with the money paid by the gov. for the school—on the first of Sept. there will be 25. due me—as soon as I am paid I will send it to you, to pay the taxes with & Dr R——thinks you had better make some inquiry about that land in N. Y. State—if worth redeeming he will pay the expenses of redeeming it.—

We do not yet know whether we can get our land back or not. I have just copied the Drs application or rather petition for its release & return, which is to be sent on with testimonials. This we have taken peaceable possession of and as it is not on the list of abandoned property, I suppose we shall have no trouble about it— You ought to have been *eye-witness* to a little scene that occurred here on Sat. Eve. An impudent *Yankee*—(an *Irish* one) rode into the yard, inquired if Dr Fox was at home—was told 'no', then asked for Mrs Fox. Alice showed him into the Office where I was sitting— he remarked that he wished to see the owner on business—& hauled out a large, official envelope— Seeing him dressed in the Yankee uniform I supposed he had come for taxes or something of that kind & so lead the way into the parlor, as the secretary was there— He did not take the seat I offered, but remarked that he would brush off some of the dust first—walked through the back door, ordered the negro man to unsaddle & feed his horse, pulled

28. Tryphena had asked Anna for help in replacing the bedding destroyed during the war. See TBHF to ARH, August 9, 1865, MDAH.

off his coat & told Alice to bring him a basin of water & towels &c   A-
lice came & told me, what he had said & I began to think to myself well
I am mistress *here* that's certain, so I too walked to the back door—
"Did you wish to remain here all night Sir"— "Yes ma'am, I am going
to stay all night"—but said I, it is impossible for me to accommodate
you— it is but a short time since I returned to my home—which I
found empty, & I have not sufficient bedding for myself & children—
none for strangers"   there is a grocery just below where you can stay.
He hesitated—asked several questions about troops having been in the
house, the distance to the grocery &c. &c. He then went towards the
negro man to question him I suppose—when I happened to think that
perhaps he supposed this Gov. property so I remarked "perhaps you are
mistaken— this place don't belong to the Gov. it belongs to me".
"Why"! said he, "is not this the plantation"; "no"! said I, "it is not"—
the plantation is below— oh! Said he, "madam I beg your pardon   I
am mistaken" but I did n't wait to hear his excuses & you ought to have
heard the *tone* in which I *ordered* that saddle put on his horse & the bowl
& towels taken back to the house—& you ought to have seen him *skulk-
ing* out— I felt like breaking his head— it proved all a lie— he wanted
nothing of Dr Fox, has not been near him—went to the other place &
stayed over Sunday with the *negroes, where he belonged.* If he thought he
was going to find Yankees here he was mistaken—& his uniform & his
spurs did n't frighten me— I have seen too much of the blue in my
camp life to be afraid of it now—& that same uniform shall never rest
under my roof—if I can help it. You ought to hear Georgy say "I'm a
rebby & I'm a docty just like my pa-pa" "I'm a rebby—being his first
sentence— he has always gone by the name "the little rebel" ever since
his birth— He is a smart chap & amuses him self a greater part of the
time—has a great passion for the hatchet or hammer & you can imagine
my *consternation*—on going into the Office to-day & finding him
seated on the floor, in the midst of a good assortment of vials, which he
had taken from a drawer, smashing away with his hatchet! fortunately
he had not broken but two when I found him. All of us are well excepting the teacher— she has chills & fever yet—all have been afflicted with
them excepting George— he has been very well all the time   As soon as

cool enough we will take him to the City & send you his Photograph—
Good Bye   write often—Yours in haste

T. B. Fox.

☐ ☐ ☐

CITY HOTEL— [NEW ORLEANS, LOUISIANA] AUG 22ND 1865.
My Dear Brother George— You can hardly imagine the *pleasure* your
letter gave me— its direction to Dr Raymond somewhat *surprised* me &
I wondered what gentleman's handwriting that could be, from
Pittsfield— I hope now that you have commenced the correspondence
you will keep it up—and don't wait for me should I not answer immediately, for I have much to occupy me & find but few spare hours for
writing, while you can step to the desk & drop me a line almost at any
time. It gratifies me, more than I can tell you, that you have proved a
good son, to a widowed mother, and I am very glad too, to learn that you
have such kind patrons as the Messrs. Friend & hope that you will continue to please them and they, you.[29] So many young men are out of
employment now, particularly here at the South, that it is a great relief
to hear that you have so good a place, and my dear brother you dont
know what a load of anxiety it takes from *me,* to feel that I have such a
brother & that he can & does assist Mother. I have been so anxious
about you all since leaving my home & wondered so often *how* you
were all getting along, that I feel really blessed, when I realize "that
brighter days are come upon you. But you shall not have all to do, I will
try to keep up my share as long as health is spared me & will send on a
5. or 10. or 20 as often as I can. May God shield & protect & keep you
ever from temptation! & may you be one of the pure & wise young men
of our land—brighter ornaments and of more priceless value now, than
ever before, because so seldom found.

Ought I not to be a proud & happy woman? with a husband &
brother both sober, industrious, and gentlemen? Dr R——never
smokes, or chews, seldom takes a drink although it is so much the fashion here, & is devoted to his family & profession & would be a rich man

---

29. George worked as a clerk at G. and F. Friend, merchants located at 97 North Street,
Pittsfield, Massachusetts. In 1863 he earned $1.50 per week. See ARH to TBHF, June
18, 1863, MDAH.

now, had not losses from every side & in every way kept him poor. May you be more & more like him & my little George like you both.

When I first wrote to Mother about coming South, I supposed that Dr R——s old patrons would all pay up & there would be a $100. or $200. that could be spared after our house was refurnished, to send for mother with. But many are still owing & one planter utterly refuses to pay just a bill of $100.. the other day, which we were sure would be paid. Several of the richest still owe & it is doubtful if we get them, and every thing is so much dearer than I expected that it keeps our purse low to furnish provisions & buy necessary things for the house. I am very much disappointed for I hoped to have mother with me, this winter. We are obliged to pay very high prices for everything here in the city & then the freight down on the boats is another expense & we are obliged to hire a negro man & woman & pay them & feed them & all of us had to be supplied with new clothes, for we came back from the Confederacy in rags & so the money goes. Dr R——is getting a very good practice, but none or not much of that is paid for until the end of the year. Still with a little money on hand, we are better off than many—& I am very, very thankful for all the blessings I have.

Dr R——came in to-day to make some arrangements about getting back his land— some friends advised him to write directly to President Johnson with the approval of Gov. Wells & Mayor Kenedy & as both are friends he hopes to have some notice taken of the matter. As I had some shopping to do I came in with him & am now waiting here at the City Hotel for him— We often stop here — it is not the first hotel in N. O. (as I suppose you know) the St. Charles *standing first,* but the charges of this one suit us better. Sometimes when we come in, we do not go to any Hotel, but that makes the day's journey most too fatiguing for me. There are a great many strangers here to-day — people are still coming in from the late Confederacy on their way back to their own homes in Texas, western Louisiana &c, &c. You who have never had to leave your homes & seen nothing of camp life & armies & soldiers, & marauders, know nothing of war—can never realize the great Civil Strife of 61, 2. 3 & 4. I am glad you are too young to mingle in it—& should there ever be another—my dear brother—remain as you are & what you are [a] quiet, peaceable citizen; never allow yourself to be drawn aside for either party—you will never cease to regret it if you take up arms against fellow country men. — We have regained much of our furniture by *borrowing* it & I suppose no one will ever take it from us. I went twice to the sub-treasury agent & begged him to release it from the Gov. books, as Mr Weed[30] was perfectly willing that I should have it & went with me to tell Mr Conway so, but I could not get any order for its release; so I went down to the plantation about 5 miles away, where we found it & *borrowed* it — the lessees of the place feeling well assured that it was ours & we ought to have it.

My piano, I fear I cannot get, though I have offers of assistance from several influential planters, Dr Fox's firm friends.

If, after receiving pardon & restoration of property from the President, Dr Fox is not able to obtain it he will sue Mr Weed, for it or for its value. I grieve very much for it — a piano now, would be so much company for me, for I am as fond of music as ever & besides Fanny is now old enough to take lessons. & seems to have a natural talent for music. Though, I think Georgy will be more talented in that respect. Although the little fellow is not two years old, he carries portions of several tunes quite well & you ought to hear him burst out, every now & then while busy at his hammering or playing, "Our flag is there," our flag is there" or Little Bo-Peep, has lost her sheep" — the former of which he has learned from the negroes in the school — the school-room is just in the back of the yard & the negroes sing every day & he hears them very plainly. —

It is said that there is some yellow fever in town — if so we shall not come in again very soon. I have not much to buy now, that is really needed, excepting winter clothing & bedding. I wrote to mother that I would pay the taxes & will send the money as soon a I can. If it is going to give her *much trouble*, tell her not to do any thing about the comforters. If she can do it, let me know & I will send on the money to buy the materials with. I may not have answered all of your letter — for Dr R. has it in his pocket; If you only knew how much it pleased me you would *write often   Direct to me & not to Dr R* — Good Bye — I am so

---

30. Possibly Charles A. Weed, a northerner responsible for harvesting sugar on abandoned plantations in southern Louisiana for the U.S. government; his sister and brother-in-law leased the Star plantation, which was near Hygiene. See Berlin, *Freedom: A Documentary History*, 352.

proud & happy to realize that I have such a brother— With love for Emma & Mother, & yourself, I am Your aff. sister—

T. B. F.

Tell Emma—many thanks for her letter & the pretty crochet lace & I will answer soon.

T. B. F.

□ □ □

"City Hotel"—Aug. 22nd 1865.

Dear Sister Emma— As I am sitting here, doing nothing, I think I may as well write to you now, for thears no telling when I shall have leisure after reaching home. Mother's, yours', & George's letters were all handed me since I came into town by Cousin John & you can hardly imagine how glad I was to receive them, although some portions of them pained me very much. I am glad you have so independent a spirit & care not for the opinion of those who slight you, because you are doing your duty. You are a true woman—if you do the best you can & do what is right. I used to care for the opinion of people & if I could not do as I would, was much mortified, but all that false pride has left me now— there is not much needed to make us happy, truly happy here—; a *consciousness* that we are doing our duty to God & man, will give us more real happiness than all else together.— I very much wish that you could be with me, but I suppose I must not think of that— I would not much like to have you teach a negro school although such high wages is paid— you would find it too laborious for you— it is no easy task to keep 40 negro children in order for six hours every day, & *beat* something in the way of learning into their empty heads besides. If there was any white school in the neighborhood I would try to get it for you, but there are none— only *negroes* are worth being taught now-a-days & the little white children must get their education as best they may.

If there were enough white children in our neighborhood we might get up a school at home & you could teach Fanny with the others, but there are but few other children near us. Fanny says lessons to me every day & is getting along quite well, though her lessons are not as regular as I could wish.

At home. Thursday A. M. Aug 24th

Did not have time to finish your letter in town the other day, so will add a few lines this morning and send it off, promising to do better next time. Am too busy to write much for there's a single mosquito bar to be made to-day and I ought to finish a dress for Georgy, which I have had on hand a good while & which I was too tired to finish last night— It took the better part of the day yesterday to put "things to right" & clean our clothes & fold & put them away for we dont wear "town fixings," much down here in the country & my black silk was tolerably dirty & so were the Doctor's dress ups. (A No 1's as Mr Crossman[31] used to say)—

Does mother ever hear from him now, or from any of our old friends—? Georgy is very fretful—cried nearly all day yesterday & I had to stop to nurse him often, so though I did n't do much, I was busy all day.— The crochet edge is very pretty— I enclose a fifty & wish you would buy material & crochet a watch-case for Dr R—— a birthday present—not too large a one as you could not send it by letter— his birth-day is on the 14th of Oct.— I am sorry you are obliged to work at the Hotel[32]—still it is no disgrace—better that than live in idleness and poverty. Tell mother I will write to her as soon as I can. & Fanny is writing you a letter which she will send in mine to mother.— You must be sure to write again— I am glad to hear that Kate Brague is doing so well and sorry for her too— it astonished me & pained me very much to hear about Aunt Mahala. I always looked upon her as so near a perfect woman—that I cannot realize that it is her of whom you write. I hope Mother has received my two last and will be able to go & see Grandma for me. Your dresses are pretty, I have only had one new one, as I needed so many other things— I send a little scrap also pieces of Fanny's two.— Good Bye—accept much love from all particularly— from Your Aff. Sister

T. B. Fox.

---

31. Apparently a Pittsfield resident familiar to the Holder children.
32. Emma had taken a job at the Berkshire Hotel, located in downtown Pittsfield.

Tell Mother Mr Messenger and Sister Emily were married about the 1st of Aug— & have gone North to visit his Mother— They may give her a call. I dont know.

□ □ □

HOME. MONDAY. SEPT 10TH 1865

Dear Mother— As I made a resolution to write to you as soon as I had put the house in order, I will now undertake to keep that resolution. With Fanny's & Tempe's help everything is "put to rights," though I suppose that if one of you nice Northern housekeepers were to come in, you would not think any of the rooms even *decent*— you would see cob-webs in various places, would think the parlor floor needed scrubbing & the mirror a good polishing & some of the grease spots coaxed from the dining-room floor & the once white walls of the back passage, thoroughly washed—but you would soon find that if you undertook to keep the whole house in perfect order all the time, it would be a hard matter—with only one servant. Spiders, dirt-daubers, a muddy country & a gude-man like Dr R——all combined, would soon overcome your nice notions & make you contented to have things, passable. I don't wish you to think that I am finding fault with *my* doctor," for I suppose he is like all the rest of the lords of creation only, *more so* & can beat them all, in throwing things about, tracking in & out when it is very muddy, occupying every room in the house from the parlor to the Office & having that *rare* faculty of leaving each one in fine disorder. Having the bump of order naturally well developed myself, you can imagine I am kept somewhat busy—for though it is a little house & a little family & we have now a man & maid servant, yet I find but little time to read or write. This morning as I said before I made out a little memoranda for the week & am determined to follow it as much as possible. Having no cultivated society, which calls for my education, I find to my regret, that much is forgotten of what I once knew. In the Confederacy we were deprived of books in a great measure & were often so situated that we could not borrow, so that my reading was very limited— In fact, I sometimes feel as though we had been imprisoned for the last three years so little do we know of what has been transpiring in the great world around us. — I tried to write to you yesterday, but Dr

R——came in & my attention was called off & besides it has been my practice not to write on Sunday, since the death of my darling— I am glad to learn that you have a new minister & that you & Emma go to Church— I want you to go for yourselves & *me too*— I have no chance here— never *mind* the clothes or the people— you ought to have seen me—as I went in Aberdeen—with my old, dowdy bonnet & grey woolen shawl, which served the family as wrap *overcoat* for Dr R, cloak for Georgy, & *bed-blanket* & and an old red woolen de laine dress that Sister Em gave me which I had washed & made over & trimmed with split-black velvet which a clergyman's wife gave me on an old black silk mantilla. I had been taught by a terrible blow that we must not care for the things of this world—must look beyond for true happiness. I would give a great deal for the privilege of attending service regularly—for I experienced while at Pa's & in Aberdeen, how much good it does one. As Dr R——has a span of horses now & had a double harness given him recently, we shall try to go to church in N. O. sometimes, but it is almost too far to attempt to go often. Besides it is too far to take the children & I should be afraid to leave them with a servant very often, for fear she would get tired of them & neglect them. Dr R——will try here, the rest of this year— if he finds he cannot make over two thousand a year he will go elsewhere. There is no use of our living here without friends or society unless we can make enough in a few years to support us in a town or city, when we can have those advantages. He can command Sufficient practice to make a *living* any where & if he could not, I could help him by teaching— I hope we may not have to move as I like living here, with those exceptions, better than any where else & we are near enough to N. O. to go there for society & its advantages provided we can make enough here to *afford* it. My old carriage has been terribly abused, but we hope to be able to fix it up ourselves so that it will do to ride in for a year or two, until we can afford to buy another. I sent in my bill for the rent of the school-room, but they would not pay it to Miss Emma, so I'm going in to collect it myself & will send it to you, as soon as the roads are dry enough. Am waiting to get an answer from you about the comforters before doing any thing. I would be willing to have second hand ones, so that they are not too much worn & are clean & that would save you the trouble of making them.

None of us have any winter clothes—& I hardly know what to get for out side wrappings for myself & Fanny. When Maria left me, she was so kind as to take with her, my old brown mantle (which I wore North) & my bay-State shawl. Fanny has entirely out-grown her cloak. What do you think will be worn this winter & how much would some kind of a nice cloak or wrap cost me there? Ask Hat about it— she will probably know, as I suppose she keeps up with the fashions even with her three boys. There is one gentleman who owes Dr R—— $117.. & which Dr R——says I may have if I can get it & which will clothe us all well so you may be sure I am going to try my *powers* of word & wit upon him & see if I cannot collect it— Dr R. thinks the gentleman will entirely refuse to pay anyone for he says "Mr F——" has no Soul any way & as I cannot *force* him to pay it now, he will not do it, although in justice due & hard-earned at that!! As we were not here to collect it 3 years ago, it is outlawed. I hope he will pay me a part anyhow— if he doesn't I shall have to go without any thing new & wear my old dirty shawl another winter. & Fanny will have to stay at home for the need of something to wrap in. I suppose Georgy will have to go into pants, he is getting to be such a *man*— & as I never dressed a little boy & have no patterns & no one to show me how to make any thing of the kind, shall make a poor out at making him look as he ought. Perhaps Hat, has some pretty little patterns for boys—if so, tell her I wish she would send me out some & give me some hints on the subject. I dont believe I shall be able to get a word from her in any other way for I have waited for *that letter*, more than two months.

Should you have an opportunity of getting a *church paper* send me one occasionally— get acquainted with Mr Wells— he will no doubt have something of the kind— tell him I feel as if I belonged to his flock, although I am so far away— Dont show any of my letters outside the family or tell what I write you. The one great fault of my life now is my *ingrafted* hatred of anything that has on a Yankee uniform, but I am going to try to overcome that & render good for evil— If I could only see you & tell you how I came to have so strong a prejudice, you would not wonder. We have all like thousands of others here in the South, suffered terribly—have been cold & hungry & almost naked & homeless, for *the victor* & it is hard to forgive. Good Bye— I must write to Aunt Randolph. She is next to you & my husband.

Enclosed you will find a *piece of string* & a leaf—both from the lemon tree in front of the gallery— the string is a portion of a *spider's web* which is spun in large quantities by a large, yellow & black spider— *one* can find the web on almost every shrub in this region & some enterprising Yankee might make his fortune by turning it to some purpose— it is not very strong and capable of being drawn into a delicate thread but it is very glossy.— The tree is one that was *planted* about five years ago by Fanny & Adelaide while they were out playing one day with lemon seeds— it is now more than twenty feet high, and has borne fruit—from neglect, has none this year. I sat on the gallery & picked the leaf without moving from my chair as the branches have forced their way through the bannisters. I never go out to look at my roses, but I think how they would flourish under your skillful *florist's* hands. the poor things are pale and sickly enough now, but I hope soon to have them attended to. I am not strong & it makes me sick every time I undertake to hoe around them. The orange trees look badly too & only two of them have fruit this year; though nearly all, are old enough to be well loaded.

[unsigned]

[Tryphena enclosed the letter below in the same envelope with the September 10, 1865, letter above.]

Dear Mother— As I need rest & want to write to you too, I am going to pencil you a few lines, for I can write so flat on my back. It is Sunday just after dinner— the sun is very hot but there is a cool breeze. Dr R——has been gone since breakfast to visit a sick man across the river. Fan has been a good girl—learned her Sunday lesson well & read her Bible Story & Hymn with much interest & is now down in Miss Emma's room, telling her all about Job & his troubles & rewards although she is not quite 8 yet, she says the Catechism perfectly & understandingly as far as the Q about the Sacraments. She is thoughtful, far beyond her years, & extremely conscientious, but not remarkably quick or bright. She is a great comfort & help to me in many ways, but particularly in the *natural* watchfulness she seems to have over her little brother— she thinks there is nothing like him & has him with her more than half the time without any wish for her, to do so, from me. She is not pretty either in face or form unless I except her small, well-shaped hands & feet. Mr Messenger (you know he is my brother-in-law

now —) says, her eyes are just like her Mother's, otherwise she looks like
Dr R — George having eaten a hearty dinner is fast asleep much to my
relief, for he is like a butterfly & its hard to keep up with him. He likes
the woman I have now better than Alice, who left me one night about
a week ago, because I reproved her for *taking* (stealing) my coffee &
made her bring it back.[33] The next morning the rain was pouring in
torrents — Dr. R — called her — no answer — so I had the pleasure of
going over to the kitchen (across the yard) & cooking my own breakfast
& bringing it out to the house myself & doing what work was necessary
for the day — not much you may be sure; there was no one here but
ourselves — the teacher having gone to town for a few days — It rained
so hard all that day, that Dr R — could not go out to find another, but
cleared up about sunset; fortunately for me for a gentleman from below
came to take supper & stay all night. — & I could send for the woman
who does my washing. The next day this one came — she is terribly slow
& stupid but good-natured & I shall try to get along with her for a
while — Alice was impulsive & I am told did want to come back, but
will not now. She was a very good servant & I am sorry that it has happened so. There are plenty of free negroes to be hired but there are so
many objections to most of them & they all put on so many airs, that it
is difficult to find a good one. We are going to try & find a white man
with a wife & no children who will come & live with us & do the
work — some Irishman or Dutchman. Give my love to Emma &
Georgy. Good Bye again. — Your Aff. Daughter

T. B. Fox.

□ □ □

Dear Mother,   Plaquemines Parish, La. Oct. 10th. 1865.
    As I go to New Orleans to-morrow, I write you a few lines to-night
& send them with the enclosed $10.00;[34] would send more but do not
like to risk too much at once; will send more as soon as I hear that you
have this: if you can spare five out of it please hand it to Messrs Friends
on the bill: the teacher only paid me $25.. instead of 50.. which was due
me up to the 1st of Oct — when she pays me the rest, I will save it to

---

33. There is no record as to when Alice, obviously a hired servant, began to work for the
    Fox family.
34. Tryphena originally wrote "the enclosed $15.00" but struck through the amount and
    inserted "$10.00" instead.

send to you. It has been a very painful task to me to-day to tell her, that she must find a home elsewhere— we cannot keep her— I cannot tell you the *unenviable* light in which *all* these negro school-mistresses stand— no matter how innocent, they may be, they are looked upon as public characters. I braved public opinion & took this girl to board— have watched her closely; her conduct has been modest & ladylike in my sight, but Dr R. in his many visits about the neighborhood has from time to time heard much scandal—this morning he was told of her conduct while on the boat coming down from the city, & we have decided that she must go— I am sorry for the poor thing & do not believe her really guilty yet—& there is no place to go to except a little grocery about two acres below here.

All of us are tolerable now; Fanny has had fever for three days but is better— Georgy is still very peevish, but gaining strength— I am obliged to go to the city to-morrow to get them winter clothes. *All* the things you sent me, are just what I needed & wanted. I told Dr R——as I showed him the various articles one by one, that it seemed as if you had been at the key-hole listening to my wishes, uttered aloud at various times. One morning I was combing his hair & all at once I broke out with the wish— Oh! if I only had a nice Balmoral—well said he, perhaps after a while you can get one. Oh no! said I there are too many other things needed! & so the matter rested— I was so pleased that I immediately sat down & went to work upon it, although it was late Sat. night. And to whom & how much I am indebted for the nice, pretty shawl?— just what I needed—shall not think about a cloak now My shoes fit nicely. Fan's are too small— we can change them. Tell Emma I know those Ai-dy's must be her handiwork & I'll not forget about them. But—Mother—the thought has obtruded itself a hundred times— you have *deprived yourself* in sending me so much bedding, have you not? & the table-cloth & napkins too— I am afraid you will want them more than I.

The dresses are very pretty & what I needed, only I did not think I could afford them, but if I am paid the 32.. which is due me, for the rent of the school-room I can pay the Messrs F——*all* by the 1st of Dec. The superintendent has promised to pay me in a few days.[35]

---

35. The assistant superintendent of education for the Freedmen's Bureau delayed the payment pending the arrival of a Mr. Pollock, who for unexplained reasons said the

Give my love to Emma & George   tell them I have had no chance to write—having been kept busy nursing the children & trying to do a little sewing for winter— Good Bye— With love. Let me know as soon as you receive this. Your Daughter

T. B. Fox.

[marginalia] Will send more soon—had no other G. B——s—all city money—

□ □ □

HYGIENE NOV. 19TH 1865.

Dear Mother, This morning, I hoped to write you a long letter during the day, but it is now almost sundown & but little time is left me. George has had fever all day & would hardly be put down for a moment. Milly,[36] having finished the necessary cooking & cleaning for the day has him for a while. Dr R——has been absent since before daybreak—went to attend my only & nearest neighbor just opposite; it is her first child & he is gone so long I am very anxious about her. I was sick all last week with daily fevers which at last confined me to my bed—Friday & Saturday & I am weak yet. Some of us are sick all the time & I cannot account for it— the children are dressed in flannel undergarments & have good wholesome food & plenty of air such as it is— Dr R—— thinks it extremely malarious from the fact of there being so much land left uncultivated around us & not properly ditched & drained as it used to be. He is in very poor health & looks poorer & paler than I ever knew him to before although he was very low, one winter in the Confederacy. He thinks of taking a short trip to the sea shore, hoping the salt water, fish & oysters will restore him.— I have a *glad* piece of news to tell you—Dr R—— has found *my piano* at last, & here it stands safely ensconced in its home again & you can imagine how happy I am, for I deemed it lost— It was in one of the Quarter-Masters Offices in N. O— has been there since taken from Mr. Weed by the Provost Marshal at the instigation of some of Dr R——'s friends. The reason we could not find it, was because it was not on the Gov.

---

payment to Tryphena was questionable. See B. F. Burnham to Captain W. R. Pease, October 17, 1865, Narrative Reports Received, June 1865–September 1866, Subordinate School Officials, Louisiana, Roll no. 3, Freedmen's Bureau, RG 105, NA.

36. A hired servant who joined the Fox household in November 1865.

registry & the Capt. Cozzens[37] to whom it was delivered had gone North. On his return, Dr R——applied to him & greatly to our surprise (as we had heard that Cozzens was a great rascal) he was told where the piano was & to whom to apply to get it—so it was sent down to me on the boat on Saturday by Cousin John; I wish you could see my parlor, for it looks pleasant & homelike, even now, though it has no carpet & no ornaments— they are gone—

WEDNESDAY—BEFORE DAY.

Dr R——leaves for town in a few moments so I will close hastily. George is still quite unwell— we were out all day yesterday *searching*, with a police officer & search warrant for our lost things—ransacked two *white folks* houses & 2 quarters; found in one of the first *one* of my nice blankets—much used & dirty—hauled it off the old woman's bed— she made no resistance & said Oui Madame when I called it mine. we then found the little rocking chair you gave me,[38] a nursery chair, some of my *china* plates, a wardrobe, some chairs, a damask table cover & two tables and *my clock*—brought it home & it stands in its old place ticking away just as it used to do— Sister Emily & Mr Messenger are in the city and I expect them down to-day on the boat. I will write again as soon as I can—shall probably be very busy while they are here— Love to Emma & George & yourself. Your Aff. daughter.

T. B. Fox.

Did you get the $25. I sent last

□ □ □

HYGIENE NOV. 30TH ”65

Dear Mother, Is not this a strange world? and do we human beings not realize changes more seemingly fantastic than those of the kaleidoscope?— Since last Saturday, Sister Emily and Mr Messenger (now my brother) have been with me as guests—! they may remain all winter: Sister Emily is very well & looking better than ever & ten years younger. Mr Messenger is very feeble & has the appearance of one in the last stage of consumption; his throat is very sore from ulcers near the windpipe so that he strangles at every attempt to swallow. Dr Ray-

---

37. S. W. Cozzens, Captain, U.S. Army, Superintendent of Plantations, Department of the Gulf. Berlin, *Freedom: A Documentary History*, 366.
38. The chair was a gift for Fanny when she and Tryphena visited Pittsfield in 1858. TBHF to ARH, February 27, 1858, MDAH.

mond is treating his throat & we hope he will soon be much better. They left all at Pa's quite well. Bob (the next to the youngest son who was in all the hardest battles & received *five* wounds) will plant on a portion of Mr Messenger's land on the Big Black. Daniel *rents* a portion of Deer Creek plantation. Brother Jimmy will both practice & plant in Ala, while brother Seguin will probably return to Lake Washington & resume his old practice; so you see, notwithstanding the Yankees served Pa so badly & destroyed all he had excepting his land, his five *rebel* sons have been spared to him & have fine prospects. Eliza is at home but will perhaps come to stay with us for a while. Lucy (the widow near Natchez) having been cheated out of the *interest* of a good principal during the war, has seen hard times, but her father & brothers are now able to help her until the lawsuit is decided, which will restore her loss. For some time after receiving your letter about Emma & her prospects, I could not make up my mind to tell Dr R——but as it has made me very low-spirited, it seems best that he should know the reason. As soon as I told him, he seemed much shocked & said I had better have her come here & live with me—that if he could not raise the money he would borrow it to pay her expenses out here. I had *not* told him that she had been at the Berkshire during the summer. I knew it would worry him & he could not then raise the money to send for her. But I do not like to leave you so alone there— what do you say to her coming? We all know that it is no disgrace to work, but perhaps if she were to come here I might be able to get her a school after a while & it would not be so hard for her & who knows but she might find a good home & husband, unless she already has a sweet-heart there. If you do not think it would be best for her to come, I will help you all, all that I can there. If you do think you can spare her, *let me know* & *Dr—— R—— will make some arrangements for sending for her* & in the meantime tell Sister Emma to fix up her clothes, if she has any spare moments & have them ready to start on short notice. I do not mean to buy anything new, for she will not need much down here with me, only a plain substantial suit for travelling— She would find some plain linen collars & cuffs very convenient & she can easily stitch them evenings. Dr R——thinks she had better come on a Steam-ship if she comes.

Fanny is still very sickly—has chills & fever at all times & there's no telling when to give her quinine. Georgy is quite well again & stays with his pa-pa, constantly when he is at home— They are both out busy gardening to-day, for it is as warm as summer— we have green peas nearly large enough to cook, & have beets, carrots, onions & turnips under fine headway. Nov. has been a delightful month so far & we have had no frost yet. Most of the planters have commenced grinding & I have already had two gallons of nice syrup sent me. There will not be much sugar made in La. this year, consequently it will be very dear.[39] I suppose that Dr R——will have to pay 15 cts, at the sugar-house for that which we used to buy for .7 & the planters let him have it cheaper than others.

I wish I was with you so that I could talk to you a little while— probably the first thing you would hear would be, "I am so tired" & yet have done nothing particular to make me so. Rose very early, helped Milly clean all the back part of the house, dressed the children nicely, then put my room & self in order, & helped Sister wait upon Mr M——, attended to the breakfast things & was getting tired & thinking I would have to iron myself & let Milly cook dinner, when in came old "Aunt Lucy" & offered her services—so I gave her the dinner & Milly the ironing & have n't done much of anything since only wait upon Georgy & all the rest— Have not done a stitch of sewing since they came excepting to hem a part of a ruffle— I am not much pressed for sewing now—have Dr. R——s coat to make yet & my dresses. I have done but little writing lately—all of my letters have been short & far between to everyone. My piano is a very fine-toned 7 octave Gaveau— almost equal to a Pleyel, but I have not practised much yet. Do you remember the lamp-mat I worked—a wreath of bright flowers on a square of black broadcloth? & *Richards* took it off in his pocket & kept it some time? There are many many associations connected with it & I prized [it] for the memories of other days that were interwoven in it rather than for its intrinsic value. We made another search in the negro cabins above, the other day & you can imagine my joy & surprise on finding it packed away in a negro woman's trunk— What has become of Richards & do you ever hear anything of Mr Cropman—? dont forget to tell me. If

---

39. See Berlin, *Freedom: A Documentary History*, 600–602, 608–9, for testimony to the Smith-Brady Commission relevant to the condition of southern Louisiana's sugar culture in 1865.

Richards is about tell him he must name his *seventh* daughter after me & I will name my *seventeenth* son after him. By the way Mother I dont believe I am to have any more & won't little Georgy have a lonesome time of it, down here in the country by himself. I often pity Fanny & think how much company her little brother would have been had he lived or even little Rose although she was four years younger. Fanny goes about by herself & gets along very well, but still would be much happier with a playmate near her own age.

    To-day is Thanksgiving day with you all is it not   I never thought of it until this moment. What a long distance separates us & I am afraid we shall never all meet again—even the few that are left. Give my love to Grandma & Aunt Mary & Uncle Brague & Cousin Kate & tell Hat, I am still waiting for that letter— Write as often as you can if it is only a few lines. Much love to Emma & Georgy & yourself— Your Affection-ate daughter.

T. B. Fox.

Dec 7th—

I had no chance of sending the letter. Emily and Mr M——are still with us & he has improved but little.

□   □   □

Friday Eve. Dec. 22nd.

Dear Mother— I came down to my room, after bidding Brother Rob-ert, "Good Night", with the intention of going to bed, but as there is a good fire, in my little stove & pen, ink & paper are handy, I think it would be more pleasant to sit & write to you awhile; it was a great dis-appointment to me to-night on going to open the door, to greet my husband after nearly a fortnight's absence, to find brother Robert there, instead. He took the horses & buggy to town yesterday to meet Dr R——who was to have returned from Vicksburg, while *brother* Rob-ert was to have gone on up the river, but after waiting in N. O. all day yesterday & to-day was obliged to return himself—my gude man being, I suppose, still at Mr Messenger's—probably detained by Mr M's death & funeral.[40] I do not know when to send for him now & fear we

---

40. In December 1865, Dr. Fox accompanied Messenger, who was gravely ill, to Bacon-ham. Messenger survived the trip, but died in February 1866. TBHF to ARH, De-cember 13, 1865, February 20, 1866, MDAH.

shall have to spend Christmas without him—the first since our marriage. Brother R——brought me yours' of Dec. 4th— you say you have been to the Post Master about the letter & *money*— *it was not* sent through the Post Office but by Express—perhaps the letter may be at that Office now waiting for you— I hope so, for it worries me exceedingly— Tell the Messrs Friends "that they shall not lose any thing, & I am very sorry that they have been kept waiting for the money so long." Brother R——took the rc'pt to N. O. with him to-day to the Express Office & the agent there promised to attend to it immediately.

I had an anxious night, last night, for we commenced looking for Dr. R——about 6 o clock & so sure was I that he would come for he is very punctual, that I had a large bright fire in the dining room, the supper table set there, & an egg-nogg & nice supper prepared for him. At first, the children kept watch with me, but finally, Georgy forgot about his pa-pa & went to Sleep & then Fan, gave up his coming, ate her supper & went off to bed too, leaving me quite alone— At eight I told Milly she could bring me part of the supper & I would keep it warm & she could lock the kitchen & go to bed & at nine, I was beginning to be very uneasy. Still I occasionally replenished the fires & raised the window to listen, hoping yet that he would come & so I waited & watched until eleven when I gave up his coming for that night & went to bed partially undressed to dream of Steam-boats blowing up or laying awake thinking that perhaps he was at Pa's too sick to come home as he was not well when he left but— I hoped the trip & change of air would do him good. You say "what would become of you & the children if he were taken away"— do you not think the same kind heavenly Father, who watched over us & kept us, through the terrible vicissitudes of the war, would still watch over & provide for the widow & fatherless— should He in his mercy see fit to make us such? The time has been, more than once, during the last three years, when we did not know in the morning where we could lay our heads at night, or from where the next morsel would come & yet we have *never* been without food & shelter, though sometimes the fare was very coarse & the shelter rude & rough.

The farm is paid for entirely & brings in a yearly rent of *three hundred* dollars clean. There are two good gardens on this place in which we could raise vegetables sufficient for our family & there is a good stock of poultry so that I shall probably raise more than we shall want & I could get up a school in a month which would pay tolerably well, so you see if Dr R——were to have his profession taken from him to-morrow, we could manage to live. Besides were we so reduced as to render it necessary, the empty cabins (two of which are now used as the negro school-room & bring 8 dollars a month) could be rented for $16. pr month payable monthly. I use one now as a kitchen, & Milly has the other, but were it *necessary,* I could take this room for a kitchen & give Milly the Office & I should have four rooms left—a dining-room, parlor & two bed-rooms. So you see I can cheer you up, as I often do Dr R——when he is low-spirited & desponding— it is never good for us to look on the dark side you know, every cloud has its silver lining and though we cannot always see it, yet we must remember it is there. Do not be anxious about me— you have already had care & anxiety enough & my nightly prayer is that you may be spared from suffering any more & that your coming years may be calm & peaceful ones.— I was sorry to learn that Emma had been sick— I wish she were with me & hope she may be some day, if she feels as though she could leave you & you, that you could spare her. I begin to realize what a *daughter* is, to a mother, for my little Fanny grows dearer & dearer to me every day. Her lessons have been very much interrupted of late but I hope now to be able to go on with them in earnest. I am afraid she has not much musical talent, but I am going to begin her lessons in music & do the best I can for her. I have had but very little time to practice yet, but I am astonished to find how *readily* the old pieces are recalled & how well I can play them.— My Piano is like an old schoolmate & companion coming to live with me & Dr R——sits & listens as if he really enjoyed the old songs & tunes, though I sometimes wonder if he does not do it just out of compliment, for he says he has n't a particle of musical talent. Nearly ten—& the fire is all out & my fingers are getting stiff so I must fix for bed but first have my *entry* of *sales* to make, for you must know I have turned Doctress since my gude man left & all the ailing negroes in the neighborhood have been to me for Prescriptions & medicines & even the jew at the grocery has been to see me twice & ask me what to do for his wife. The Dr would have charged them all $1.00 (one dollar) a piece for advice but I suppose mine must go for nothing as I have no license out: the Dr. has to pay *$20.* for his.

CHRISTMAS MORNING. DEC 25TH 65

Brother Robert starts off to town again for my gude man & I spend Christmas alone— How I wish I could spend it with you & G. & E. Were not my bonnet so soiled, I might go to church in N. O. to-day but I am afraid I could not be good, with a dirty bonnet & feel that it was too conspicuous. Besides it would be rather risky to leave the house & every thing to the servants on such a free negro, *whisky* holiday. Write soon—all of you & with much love　believe me　Your Affectionate Daughter.

T. B. Fox.

I send Brother Robert's photograph—is he not a good looking young man & as *good* as he looks—has not a single bad habit. & has spent the last three years in the army too. He has always been a pet of mine.

We are going to have the children's taken soon & send them to you— I hope you will get the money without delay.

PART III

After the War
1866–1876

Dear Mother—   [? FEBRUARY 17, 1866]

After waiting so long to hear from me, I wish I had something to gladden you, but I have only bad news for you— But you need not worry or be anxious about us for we are quite comfortable & none of us are hurt. (*Thursday Feb 2ND*) about twelve o clock in the day our house burned to the ground! The roof was all on fire before we knew anything about it & in half an hour the house was in ashes— the nearest neighbors ran to our assistance but could not give much as the flames had spread so rapidly. I succeeded in saving my new trunk, which had some valuable clothing in it, *all* the bed clothing and one mosquito bar, also some clothes from a wardrobe in the front room— The Dr saved the *piano* and a portion of the parlor furniture while the neighbors saved the furniture except the bedstead in our room & the mattrasses in the other rooms. No one thought of my silver & every piece was lost—or rather melted— we have succeeded in finding some of it— The Drs gold watch—a large handsome one— was *stolen*— who ever took the bureau from our room stole the watch as all the other things which were beside it—a tumbler, a cologne bottle—a little box of jewelry & a little fancy basket were all carefully taken out. The Dr had taken off his watch & placed it near the cologne bottle not 15 minutes before as he was going in the garden to plant some seed & was afraid he might injure it— he was more careful than usual of it, as he paid a bill of $20.. *the week previous for repairing it*— we know who took the bureau out & hope to regain the watch. The wind fortunately blew toward the North East—had it been in the opposite direction as it is generally, we should have lost everything—stables, kitchen, cabins, fences, corn[,] hay & *all*   as it was, we lost the house alone—& *that* you know what it was to me & we had spent all the *money* that we had collected & all the Dr made from last June in buying furniture & necessaries to make the house & ourselves comfortable— The Dr had spent over $2000. You will wonder what we spent it for— I can hardly tell you—the crockery—a full set—alone—cost over $56. the *sheeting*, mosquito bars & toweling, table cloths, napkins &c over &100.. the blankets $45— besides what you sent me—fortunately I saved every thing which you sent, excepting one lindy & my new brown dress—that dark one which I had just finished & wore to town the week before. I do not mean to say that he spent all that two thousand just for the house, because some was spent for his drugs & medicines—there were $200. worth, every grain & drop of which was lost—also his new saddle bags which were $60— you know everything is so dear here now that it takes a fortune to buy a little. His new horse, buggy & harness were $400 & he spent about $300, for corn, hay & provisions. I fortunately thought of my store-room before it was too late & everything was saved in that—& we have a good supply for six months— Had not the flames spread so rapidly & had not the people been so afraid we might have had all our furniture saved—as it is, we have only a little besides what Dr R——a Mr John—the overseer on the next place—& myself took out— My strength began to fail me when I stripped the last bed & I dont remember what I did— if I could have had presence of mind a little longer I could have saved the side-board drawer which had all the silver in it, excepting a handsome pie-knife which was a present from Cousin Molly & which I prized very highly aside from its value—about $10.— it was locked up in a bureau drawer in the middle room that bureau was lost& everything in it—a drawer for each of us—in which I kept the underclothes & two little drawers above with little valuables & keepsakes—

I prized my silver highly, as you know it was a gift from Dr R——when we were first married & I had carried it on my person or in my hands carefully done up in a box, every where we went, through the war— we saved it from the Yankees, while at Pa's by burying it— There was a large soup ladle, 12 silver forks, 9 silver spoons—(4 large & 5 desert—the others were stolen by Reuben before the war) 2 handsome sauce spoons which Aunt Ellen gave me & a silver butter knife, a parting gift from Brother George (Mr Messenger) & which I prized more than I can tell, since his death— I could not buy the same silver now for three hundred in green-backs. The Drs new overcoat—a garment which he has needed all winter and which had just been given him—was burned— it was in the wardrobe with my brown dress & a poplin, which was old but would have done for the Spring— On counting over the value of things, the Dr estimates that we lost two thirds of the furniture and one third of our clothing Milly—poor thing—was so frightened, that she was perfectly useless to me She caught up a few things which she had ironed & rushed out & *sat down*—had she carried out things as fast as I did we should not have lost much clothing. All of our dining-room furniture was lost excepting the round dining-table & that was not worth much— As I told you no one thought of saving anything in the Office which was the farthest from the fire & every thing might have been carried out without the least danger from flames or falling timbers— We are now camping out in the cabin which the Gov. fitted up for a negro schoolroom— it has a good fire-place in it & is quite comfortable for this climate— the floor & sides are rather open & unfortunately we are having a cold spell just now. But it will soon pass over & it is not probable that we shall have more than one more before *our* winter will be gone. The day that the house burned it was so bright & spring-like that we had all the doors & windows open & need not have had a fire—only there was ironing to be done & as the irons did not heat well on the little cooking stove with the trashy river wood I had Milly iron in the dining room where she could make a larger fire in the fire-place. We have kept a fire there all winter & it is the greatest wonder to us that we have not been burned out before for the fire orig- inated in the *attic*, which we never used or went into & into which there was no communication, excepting by a ladder placed upon the ground and reaching to a window in the cone of the house about 25 feet from the ground— Since our return we had neglected to provide a ladder long enough to reach the window. The mortar had fallen out between the bricks in this attic in several places & probably a spark found its way out through some crevice & fell upon cob-webbs or some loose plank & probably the fire had been burning an hour when we found out— The Dr & myself were standing in our room   the back one with a little stove, when I heard a curious sound over the ceiling between my room & the next or middle room— it sounded as if a bird were cracking something & dropping it upon the ceiling— what is that noise said I—for it was a very curious one for that place— we listened a moment more— it is fire, said the Dr & ran out— it was too true— the smoke was pouring from the roof in every direction and the flames burst out in a few moments. You may know what a trying moment it was to us when we realized that no efforts would save our home & all we could do was carry out things as fast as possible. There were not more than three minutes from the time when I first heard the dropping overhead before we were hard at work carrying out what we could.

The piano was the most valuable thing we had & it was not hurt—
we can sell it for five hundred dollars—if necessary. The Dr has been
around among his old patrons to see what patronage they will give him
for the coming year & so far all promise quite well—so I suppose he
will rebuild & we shall be ready to make another start by July— But it
seems hard that it should have to happen after our three years struggle.
As I said before we just began to feel at home, like old times, & to feel
easy. The Dr had just paid off his *old* & his last years debts and hoped
with what money & provisions we had on hand to live comfortably for
six months, even if he did not get much practice. My press of sewing
was over. I had been hard at work with my needle ever since my return
& had just finished the last garment, so that we all had enough clothing
and with five new linen shirts which had just been given the Dr, I
would not have much sewing to do for several months. I had hoped to
have some time to spend in my flower garden, & with my shrubbery &
with my music. But I was too happy— I shall never forget the feeling of
satisfaction & contentment which I had, that morning, after the house
was all in good order & myself & children neatly dressed & I walked
back & forth from the parlor where I was helping Fanny with her lessons to my room where I was mending & amusing Georgy   showing
Milly a little now & then as I passed by her— you know she knew nothing about ironing when she came here, but has learned quite well—
that—as well as every thing else— still I always managed to be
Somewhere near when she was ironing the Drs fine shirts— She has
been a faithful good servant & seems sorry that she did not save more
for me.

I hope she will stay with me all the year— We give her eight dollars a
month & hire most of the washing done besides, but it is cheap for this
country— other ladies are giving 12 a month & wonder how I can get
along with one who charges only 8.—Of course I helped her a great
deal when we had six rooms to keep in order— now that there is only
this one & the kitchen joining there is not much for either of us to do—
but I feel unsettled yet & can only look after the Dr & the children—
Fanny has taken a very bad cold— yesterday I left them on a *curious*
errand— I will try to tell you about it— A Mr Wm Stackhouse, who owns
the plantation next to us & two other large ones & is very wealthy   once
treated Dr R—— very shamefully in regard to the fences between

them, so that they did not *speak* to one another—cordial *dislike* on both sides. While we were gone Mr Stackhouse bought another plantation five miles away & moved to it, thus taking $200. dollars pr year from D<small>R</small>—as the former owners had paid him that. Since our return & Mrs Stackhouse expressed much sympathy for me in the loss of my furniture & clothing (She is a perfect lady) I have been anxious that the quarrel should be forgotten as I know that through her influence, Dr R——might get the practice of Mr S——three plantations which amounts to $500 pr year—200 for "Belle Chasse", 200, for "Live Oak" & 100 for New Hope—adjoining us— Yesterday morning he was a little desponding—said he wished he had some friend who would go around among the planters & make good bargains for him— particularly he wished someone would see Stackhouse & see what he would be willing to do. Well said I after thinking a moment— I will go & see Mrs Stackhouse, so I put on what I could find to look decent & rode five miles with the cold north wind driving in my face to use my influence for him. Asked her after other conversation what she thought Mr S——would be willing to give that 500, were Dr Fox terms & I hoped under the circumstances he would be willing to give that— She was very, very kind & in an hour after my returning home, wrote me a friendly little letter, stating that she had spoken to Mr S——and if the Dr *would call*, "she was confident they would be able to settle terms as desired." If Mr S——pays that for his   other planters will be willing to pay in he same proportion & Dr R——will probable have his old income of between three & four thousand a year. But we spend money— dollars like dimes—not carelessly or extravagantly, but everything is so dear & one hundred dollars will buy nothing in comparison to what it used to do. We are obliged to keep two horses & two servants & it costs something to feed all— I could do all the work if things were handy as they are to the North— and if I had been more used to it— The first hard work I ever did was when at Pa's in "62—just before Georgy was born—and there were 20 in the family & much to be done & not many to do it—

I have written hurriedly for I thought I should not have much time before the Dr left for town, but he will not go until to-morrow— I will try to write again soon— Good Bye   My love to all of *our* people.— The Express man said he would certainly send that money in three weeks from the time we went to see him about it Jan. 27TH — if he does not Dr R——will sue him & get the money & send it in some other way.

Tell the Messrs Friends if they say anything more that we will try to pay it & let the suit come afterwards— Just now the Dr is in so much trouble that he cannot advance any more. Good Bye again. Your Daughter

                                                            T. B. Fox. —

                                    □   □   □

Dear Brother,   HYGIENE, FEB. 19TH ˮ66
    I have been thinking of writing to you for some time past, but there seemed to be no leisure for me to do so, now, I am going to *take* the leisure, although I ought to be sewing.

The papers you have been sending have come regularly & I am much obliged to you for them—while reading them, it seems almost as if I were back in old Berkshire again. Had we gone to the city as we intended, two weeks ago I would have sent you some N. O. papers, but we have not been yet— we are summoned to appear there before the Commissioner of wills for Miss, to give our affidavits as the witnesses of Mr Messenger's will— he made it here the afternoon before he left Sister Emily wrote while he dictated & his signature to the will was the last time he took a pen in his hand. He could hardly write his name he was so feeble. We go in a day or so if the weather continues fair— Ever since the burning of the house (which misfortune I suppose you & Mother have heard before this, through my last letter) the weather has been very inclement—sometimes bitter cold—sometimes warm with violent rains, then a hail-storm then cold winds;—this afternoon is the first pleasant time we have had— All last week—while it was raining & bitter cold, the workmen were here ceiling & tightening the floor of our cabin to make it *inhabitable*, it is quite comfortable now— we hovered over the stove in the kitchen [last] week, with corn sacks for a carpet & the wind & rain driving about us as in every direction— You know our Southern kitchens are built very open—much like a barn— The cabin now is quite a white folks room— there is a good fire-place at one end & at the other the childrens bed & ours—made up of six mattrasses piled one upon another— our bedsteads were all burned— a

large calico curtain extends from one side of the room to the other &
from ceiling to floor, dividing our sleeping room from this— this is our
parlor, dining-room, sitting-room & the Drs office! a convenient apart-
ment is it not? Would you like a glimpse of the furniture?[1] My piano—a
very handsome one—& which we could not buy now for less than 800.
is opposite the door—on the other side—a common bureau (which the
Dr bought before we were married & which the Yankees *lugged* off
down to the Star plantation & banged about & broke out the mirror—
my nice one was not saved) between, in the middle of the room a
round dining table with three dining chairs—around the fire place Dr
R's big arm-chair, my rocking-chair & those of G & F—over my
head—against the wall, 4 shelves, with Dr R's— new stock of medicines cupping-classes &c &c— this corner is the office & where I am
writing is the secretary part of the book-case, which Dr R——had presence of mind enough to save as it contained most of his valuable papers,
accounts &c. &c. we have ensconced it upon a pine shelf & it answers
the purpose of a secretary very well. Upon the mantle (of unpainted
wood) rests my large mirror, which reflects the room & makes it *appear
large* by which illusion we flatter ourselves that the room *is not so close.*
There is an opening through to the kitchen on the other side of the fire-
place, where the dishes & meals are passed back and forth & the two
small closets at the upper end of the room which serve very well as
wardrobes— After all we don't need so many things in this world to
enable us to live as many of us at times imagine— I do not think that we
miss the many comforts & even luxuries even of our last home as we
would have done, had we not been "through the war" & "camped out"
& "boarded out" & lived 'all sorts' of ways. I feel the *loss* of it, as *my
home,* more *however,* for I had learned to love it during my absence & it
was doubly dear to me after my return— Perhaps I thought too much
of it & so it was taken from me— The Dr will try to rebuild on nearly

---

1. This letter contains two drawings. The caption on one reads: "interior of our room—a
rough sketch—I dont know as you can make it out." Tryphena added, "all the furniture that was saved you can see." The sketch shows space allocations for the kitchen,
Tryphena's family, and Milly, and the placement of furniture in Tryphena's room,
which abutted the servant's room. The other sketch shows the exterior of the cabin
with the caption: "A view of my present home with the *darkeys.*" The postscript reads:
"I have handed this over to the Dr for inspection—he wishes me to add that the cabin
does not *lean*—it stands plumb.—He thinks Fanny would have done better! you
ought to hear us laughing over it!"

the same plan as soon a possible— He is now making yearly engage-
ments & thinks he will be able to raise sufficient means to commence
bargaining with workmen & for the necessary lumber &c &c in a short
time— He says he will not go in debt, which resolution I most heartily
approve of. I would rather live here in this cabin the rest of my days
than to be any more in debt & all we owe now is that bill to the Messrs
Friend and about one hundred dollars for groceries & medicines, which
he can pay in a month or two. That bill to the F——s I hope to be able
to settle when we go to town— the Gov. owes me $56.. for the rent of
this room & I think the money is ready for me—so I will again send on
the amount & not wait for the Express company any longer— I am
afraid we shall lose that 2s. entirely— I believe mails are safer than ex-
presses. I was glad to learn through Mother that your salary had been
raised— I think you are in a fair way now to realize before many years
an *independence* if not a fortune. I can almost imagine you as you may be
ten years from now—a partner, relied upon by the other members of
the firm, steady upright & holding an enviable position among the
Sons of Berkshire.— Give much Love to Mother & Emma— tell them
I will write as often as I can but I have a great deal of sewing to do &
sometimes hardly know what to make first— Last week—notwithstanding the bad weather & the confusion—tell Mother I made 1 pr
drawers & 2 underbodies for F——hemmed three large hkfs for Dr
R—— & made the large curtains & the window curtain to this room,
besides doing some writing for Dr R—— & nursing Georgy a part of
one day— was I not busy? — Good Bye— May God shield you from
temptation & make you one of his true servants is ever the prayer of
your affectionate Sister—

T.—

My letters are only for you & E & Mother— dont leave them about
so that others can read them.

Wed.—in N.O. I mail Mother a letter to-day with 20. in it   Let me
know as soon as it arrives—

I'll send more   The Ex——Office has *sold* out & I reckon we are *sold*
too. for .25.

T. B. F

Dear Mother,   HOME MAR 28TH 66

As the morning was spent in cooking & housework, I may as well *use* up the leisure of this evening by writing to you & others—though Fan's apron lies unfinished & a variety of garments need mending. I have had a busy time lately—in fact ever since the house burned, more particularly the last two weeks as no one was to be had to fill Milly's place—so I have played housemaid & cook and sewed & kept the accounts when there was leisure. The Drs new spring suit is finished & off my hands; it fits him nicely & I am quite proud of it—. Don't give me too much credit though, for I hired a girl to help me sew on it one day, which I was sorry for—as she sewed on the coat collar wrong side up & drew the stitches of the seams so tight I would have ripped them all out had not the Dr needed the suit immediately. I do deserve credit for one thing though— all my patterns were ruined & I cut both coat & pants by laying, & fitting paper to his last winters suit & then cutting from that trying the cloth on him & making what alterations were necessary afterwards.— Milly is getting quite well again— she has had a very serious time—had an internal uterine abscess which broke last week. Three different women who were hired at different times, worked two or three days each & then left. Lucy & Fan were sick— Tempe was lazy I suppose, or too much of a lady to work, now that her husband has returned from the army— anyhow she promised me on Saturday night that she would come back last Monday Morning & then did not come— Ann is an old negro woman—as nice & particular as a white woman— She and her husband were brought away from their old home near Baton Rouge I believe, by the Federals in "62— She tells me she had a most excellent master—a Judge Ackland—who owned a large plantation had a splendid house & furnished all his servants with houses as good as need be." & everything for their comfort— Now the plantation is destroyed— the negroes all scattered— this poor old couple off here by themselves with no one to care whether they live or die. She was very anxious to please me so that I would hire her & trotted all day long doing something. It made me tired to see her & although I tried to get her to sit down & rest it was of no use— the moment my back was turned she was off sweeping the yard or scrubbing something— Saturday morning I saw she was not well & Sat. Eve. she had to go home— she was very anxious to make enough to buy her a pr. of shoes & a head hkf. Her old man had all of his last month's wages stolen from him— I have heard nothing from her since & am going down to see if she is very sick.

Our house does not progress much— it is much more difficult to haul the trees from the swamp than was anticipated & I should not wonder if Dr R——had to buy more than 2/3 of the lumber in N. O. yet. Rough lumber there is $35. pr. thousand flooring $60 & ceiling $55. I will try & draw a plan of the house with the number of feet of lumber needed & the first time Uncle Brague comes show it to him & ask him how much such a house as that would cost at the North. Sometimes I have thought that if Dr R——or myself could go to N. Y. we might buy the whole house ready to put together, charter a vessel & bring it here cheaper than it can be bought in N. O. & brought here. Freight from the city down is *enormous*—$10 pr. thousand feet of lumber & pr. thousand brick. Sometimes I almost lose hope & fear that it is going to cost so much to build that I would be about as well contented where we are—for our little cabin is quite pleasant & very comfortable & many a family have passed their lives in a worse house than this. We are so much by ourselves here that it makes but little difference whether we have room for guests or not. You know I never visit these common French people below us— Mrs H. Stackhouse I have never called on since her husband & Dr Fox's disagreement— Mrs. Hoyt on the Star is a good woman but Dr R——dont like Yankees (his better half either) & Mrs Dr Wilkinson is twelve miles away— Mrs Hally who lived just opposite has moved ten miles away— Mrs Reggio never goes out & the other two—Mrs Reaud & Mrs Fezzan are French ladies & strangers yet— So you see I have no neighbors & need n't worry myself about "company"—

COUSIN JOHN'S STORE FRIDAY MORNING.
Having found yours of Mar. 19th here I add a few lines & send this off— We came in tis morning & had a cold ride. It was so warm & pleasant yesterday that I did not think I should need anything more than the shawl & almost suffered with the cold— My hands were so numb I could hardly hook my dress or comb my hair. I came up to attend Service as it is Good Friday. Dr R will go with me— I have never

been to church here yet, have not been in any since I left Aberdeen. It is a doubly sad day to me— three years ago to-day my darling was buried Her grave is at Woodburne. You know she was named after you Anna Rose— She was a beautiful child—had a head that was the admiration of all who saw her it was of such symmetry & beauty—dark curly hair & her father's soft hazel eyes—a child of lovely disposition— too pure for earth.

It cannot be that you are so old—almost *sixty* I thought of you all the way this morning—thinking how much you could have enjoyed the ride & the scenes we passed— everything is bright & green now—the gardens everywhere in fine order & the planters under full headway with their crops. We pass splendid plantations on one side—have the broad river on the other—come through the forest at the cut off with its tall trees & thick tangled undergrowth reminding one of tropical scenes & then as you approach the city there are innumerable little huts & shanties, with old clothes & chickens & children strewn about in every direction they are the homes of that *recently imported* & very valuable & praiseworthy portion of our community known as *freedmen*. Live principally by smoking & keeping their hands well guarded in their pockets. Nearer town there are beautiful residences buried in rich looking shrubbery—orange trees— Japan plums &c surrounded by pretty hedges. I am writing hurriedly for Dr R——has gone to the Barber's & will be in for me in a moment. Have letters from Pa & Emily (Mrs M) & Jimmy—all well E——sent the thousand dollars[2]— I had intended my next letter should be to Emma but if she will overlook my not writing this time— she shall certainly have one next— It is not because I do not think of her— she has been on my mind ever since your last & I so often wish that you were all out here with me. I am so comfortable & have so much that I do not feel as if I had any right to it when you & she & Georgy have to work so hard—I did not have time to finish the plan— will send it in my next—I mail a letter from Fanny to her Uncle G. it is all her own work— I only told her how to spell *been* & *littuce*.

---

2. Emily lent her brother one thousand dollars to help offset the cost of rebuilding Hygiene. James Fox made the proceeds from the sale of a bale of cotton available for the same purpose. TBHF to ARH, March 20, 1866, MDAH.

She & G——stayed at home— You ought to have seen the Dr & myself coming in this morning—for I tell you Dick & Rebel[3] have to travel when we start for town & they seem to *enjoy* it. I suppose you have the children's pictures— This one of the Dr is pretty good—only too *staring*— he has others which I hope will be better & I will send Emma one of those— they are not finished yet. I am glad that you *will* not work out—if you can help it—*yet*—I have heard of such a thing as poverty & pride & *I* am too proud to have my Mother work out unless life depended upon it— Here comes the Dr   Good Bye— Love to all-
   Your daughter—

T. B. Fox.

□ □ □

[HYGIENE—APR. 9TH 1866.]
Dear Mother— I send the plan of the house as Dr R——expects to build it, drawn to the best of my ability & I hope you & Uncle Brague will understand it. The sills are to be— 3 of them   40 ft. long—8 inches by *ten*; — & 4 of them, 30 ft. long 8 x 10; the *plates*   3— 40 ft. long   4 x 6 & 4—30 ft long 4 x 6. the rooms are 12 ft. high— the whole house & portico to be raised 8 ft from the ground on brick pillars. The doors are represented thus—[sketch of doors] They are 4 x 9 for outside & 3 x 9 for inside doors. Those opening upon the gallery & portico to be double & 2/3 glass— There is a fireplace   X   in every room. After the house is built & finished & furnished & *paid for*— the Dr proposes finishing off 2 basement rooms (a kitchen & dining-room) & two bed rooms in the attic. I shall occupy the room marked "family room" for mine as bedroom &c, &c. there is to be a folding door between it and the parlor.
   The finishing of the rooms is to be, *ceiling* overhead & lathe & plaster at the sides. We prefer ceiling above as the moisture here is so constant

---

3. Fox owned the light bay named "Dick" at the time of his marriage. He paid $300 for the horse "Yankee" in 1866 and promptly changed his name to "Rebel." He traveled on horseback to and from the nearby plantations to visit patients. According to George R. Fox, his father expected his "very old" horse, probably Dick, to die during the winter of 18-7. TBHF to George Holder (hereafter cited as GH), May 22, 1866, George R. Fox to GH, October 29, 1877, MDAH.

as to render it almost impossible to make the plaster firm; it is always tumbling off.

Dr R——estimates that the house as I send it to you—without finishing the basement & attic rooms will cost $2000.00—not counting the *sills* & framework— these he hopes to procure from the swamp adjoining & the St. Ann plantation. The sills & plates are already hewn & partly hauled from the swamp. The first load of joists was hauled here on Wed. the 4th of April so you see there is some prospect of *starting* the house— I suppose the workmen will commence this week— I give you some of the cost items

Brick 6000 @ & 16. pr thousand in N. O	$ 96.00
Transportation on same from N. O. $10. pr 1000	60.00
12 bbls of lime @ $3 pr. bbl.	36.00
Transportation $1. pr bbl.	12.00
Masons work $3. pr. day (2 for self & 1 for assistant) 18 days	54.00
Flooring 1500 ft @ $60. pr 1000.	90.00
Ceiling " " " 55 " "	82.00
Freight on 3000 ft. of lumber $12. pr 1000	36.00
Shingles 14000 @ $6. pr 1000	84.00
Freight on same $2. pr 1000	28.00
6 Windows with Venetian blinds $19— pr window	114.00
3 Doors with V— blinds $20. pr. door	60.00
3 inside doors— $10 " "	30.00
Freight	10.00
Dressed Weatherboarding 2500 ft @ $50. pr 1000	125.00
Freight & Portage	30.00
Lathes—probably $25. 3 bbls of sand & freight. $10	35.00
Locks—Hinges—fixtures $25 & Nails 400 lbs at 10	65.00
Transportation on same	10.00
Work Carpenter	380.00
Extra work	20.00
	$ 1457.50 CTS
Glass & glassing	60.00
	$ 1517.50
	275.50
	$ 1792.50

Paints	$100.00
Oils	60.00
Varnish & c	40.00
Painter	75.00
	$200.00

We estimate that it will take 2 common carpenters who
are living here, near us & (whom we can hire for
$2.00 pr. day) 70 days each—to do the rough work $280.00
Then we shall probably have to give a *finishing
carpenter*   100.00

- -

You will perceive that the whole amounts to $1792.50 — & the prices
are at the lowest estimates—the other $200. will come out in *odds &
ends*—for everything always costs more here or takes longer time than
we think—even allowing good prices & plenty of time.

I have not time to write any more as Emma comes in for her share of
my leisure this time. With love—from All— Your Aff. Daughter—

T. B. Fox.

I am very anxious to procure a *copy* of my diploma   I wish you would
see Hat (Mrs Dewey) and ask her if she thinks it possible. Mine had the
same signatures as hers— Is not Mr Spear at the school yet—? Dr
R——would pay any expense which might be incurred in procuring
one— I am sure Dr Todd would give me his again— of course I could
not have Mr Tylers—but his could be *copied*— Mine was burned in the
house— I prized it so highly that I regret its loss very much.

Love

T.

□ □ □

Dear Sister Emma,   HOME, APR. 17TH 1866.

I have long wanted to write to you, but there has been so much to
occupy my time this Spring, that I have not felt as thought there was
much time for me to spend in writing— particularly long and friendly
letters such as I like to send to those I love—so I have written when
there was leisure, to Mother & hoped that you & Georgy would take
them as "all in the family"   Could I write when I feel like it & when

thinking of you, you would be flooded with letters—for you are constantly in my thoughts— there is nothing which I enjoy that I do not wish that you too might share it.

You know I have long hoped to have Mother & you with me and when the house was burning the keenest grief I felt was, from the thought— "now I cannot have Mother & Emma with me, for I have no home to ask them to." It grieve me more than I can tell you that your lot has fallen just as it has—but still I know it is all for the best. Often I find myself making plans to place you in a different Sphere, but they remain "only plans"—for I am powerless to carry them out. I would give much to have you with or near me— I often find myself wondering who your companions and what your tastes are—if you ever have any time for reading and if so, what books you like best.— And Dear Sister, Do not think it *cant* in me—for I am very anxious to know— have you ever been confirmed yet?— if not, I wish you would think about it— I would not have you *forced* or *led* or *prejudiced in any way*— but simply to investigate the rite of confirmation and its consequences & when you see how important it is & how essential to your welfare—go forward & be confirmed. Probably Mrs. Merrill has some good books upon the subject which she will lend you or perhaps she will talk to you & guide you— Write to me what you think about it— Religion—or love of, & duty to God is not such a disagreeable thing as many would make it & you do not know how much happier it makes one, to try & be— one of God's children— I will not write any more on this subject now for I do not want you to think me officious but I do want to know what your views are & hope you will write them to me. Perhaps you have already been confirmed if so I shall be glad to hear it.— We have no Sabbaths *here* as far as public observance of it is concerned— Most of the people are Catholics and make Sunday a holiday. Had we not been so unfortunate in losing our property, we might have been able to spend our Sundays in N. O & go to church but we cannot afford that now— It costs a great deal to stay at a Hotel in the city over night— I shall try to sometimes returning the same day if we are not entirely *barred* from the city this summer. There is at present a *crevasse* between here and N. O, which workmen have been busy at, for three weeks past & as yet have not stopped yet— Some think they will not be able to do it but the manager is quite sanguine of success, so we dont trouble ourselves much about it. It runs directly across the road about ten miles from here. Dr R——who is obliged to go to the city to-day to purchase building materials has to take the Steamboat thus leaving myself—Dick & Rebel (his usual companions)—at home. It is said that there is another crevasse above the city, which will ruin all the crops in this vicinity— I hope it is not true if so, it will not probably inundate us—yet it may— you know I have lived here through one summer when everything was covered with water and have good reason to dread another such summer.

Our new house is at last under headway— one carpenter commenced day before yesterday & I suppose there will be another in a day or two. As soon as they have the rough work finished Dr R—— will hire a finisher & perhaps in the course of three months we may have a roof over our heads. As far as I am concerned I am quite as happy here as I could be elsewhere. My time passes away very swiftly—nursing & teaching my little ones & sewing & helping the Dr as much as I can with his duties.— You ought to see the crowd of chickens that follow me every time I step out— there are 54 little fellows besides 30 grown ones—the latter furnish me 8 & 10 eggs a day & I often wish I could send a basket full to you home folks. beside the chickens there is Dick & Rebel to be petted & all the pigs & Old Bet their mother who expect, to be noticed & each receive something extra every day. As to sewing—there is still plenty of it to be done & I am very tired of the business but have to stick to it.

Fanny interests me considerably— she is a very good scholar & will make a fine performer. Georgy is our "laughing-gas" for not an hour passes that he does not say or do something funny.

I have not made my new dress yet that Mother sent but am going to try to commence it next week— I wish you had one like it & I send you a two *dollar* bill to help buy you a nice one, as Mother wrote that you needed one. Write soon all about yourself, if you cannot write much at a time have your paper & pencil near & jot down a line or two at a time. Give much love to Georgy & Mother though I send Mother the plan I wrote about   Good Bye & with love believe me   Your Affectionate sister

T. B. Fox.

Cabin. Monday Morning. 11 O clock. [June 12, 1866]
Dear Mother, I think if you could see me just now, you would call
me "disturbed"— every thing is in the middle of the floor—my four
mattrasses for a centre-piece, the chair & piano for the surroundings—
The children, with no less than 5 cats hanging around are seated on one
corner of a mattrass eating lunch—the corner of another serving for table; a chicken has come in & stands upon the top-most corner
cackling— the floor is all mud; there is a pool of water, where the mattrass ought to be & the yard is a *pond*— the clouds are still hanging
black & threatening over us & when are my mattrasses to be dried? the
rain beat in upon us last night during a terrific storm & I had them put
out to catch a streak of sunshine & before I could turn round here came
another storm My feet are wet, my dress soiled & draggled &, for
once, my spirits are *low*— The Dr is gone & will not be back until *three*
& I am tempted to have a good cry— if I thought all traces of the *storm*
would be gone before his return, I would indulge in one, but he might
return unexpectedly & I would not have him find me disheartened for
the whole house— It is I who keep *him* up though you may think me
boasting to say it. I am more worried than I can tell you— I dont mind
the rain or the wet beds, but there seems to be a constant call for my
interference The Dr unintentionally made Mr Gebbs[4] angry on Saturday,
I had to act as mediator & put Mr Gebbs into good humor again—
Then this morning he comes—"Well Madam, I believe I go away, I
work no more"— "I can do *nothing* right"—(the Dr had complained of
the windows) there is nothing more for me to do"— Oh yes! said I, Mr
Gebbs there are the front steps to be made yet— I would be glad to
have you put those up for *me*" & you know whatever *I* want, is all right
with the Dr—."very well Madam—then I stay & make the front
steps"— so I sailed out in the rain to give him the dimensions & show
him what plank we wanted used. You must not think I do this contrary
in the least to Dr Fox's wishes—*anything I do,* is always right with him
and as I have had so much to do with the ordering & planning of the
house he leaves all entirely as I say or wish. But it worries me & it seems
as if the carpenters were so slow now that they have come to the finishing part— we are paying $8. per day & some days I cannot see what

---

4. One of the carpenters hired to rebuild Hygiene.

they have done. Another thing too, to keep back—the mason promised to be here on Friday   he has not come yet. Mantlepieces & lathing cannot be arranged until his work commences so do you wonder I look pale & Ann says "*Sick* aint ye"? *She* is *another* responsiility. She is the same old negress I wrote about before— last week her husband was turned off from Smithes & both ordered off—so she came to me— who is to take care of these old homeless ones if we Southerners do not? the Yankees who freed them that is took them from good homes & judicious owners are not going to care for them. Ann says she will try to earn her board & *two* dollars a month, but I doubt if she can do it— The fact is there is not much for her to do now, until we move into the new house— then she says she will keep that clean for me—may be so, we shall see.

It is no slight thing to take an old body like her into one's family— She may be taken sick to-morrow & have to be nursed & doctored— You have no idea of the suffering & *lack* of proper nursing that is everywhere to be found among the negroes here. They will not nurse & watch with one another & who is going to do it now as the former master & mistress did? I, as a physician's wife, know more of it & have more call for sympathy than almost anyone else— The Doctor comes home nearly every day with some sad story—a negro man lying very low—no wife—no friend—he needs poultices & chicken broth & some one to stay by him & give his medicine—the next day perhaps of a woman dying & 7 or 8 young children hanging around half naked & half starved for want of attention. Some one [is needed] to administer medicines & do the nursing. They are dying out very fast   It is a well founded fact that negro-mothers have but little maternal affection—and thousands of children die *now*, who would have been cared for by *mistress*, in old times. Lucy the woman who washes for me) lost a little boy of four last week from *neglect* & she pretends to be one of the most enlightened of her *clan*. But enough off this— I know you will think that I have the blues & am croaking, but I have not—

Yours of May 22nd came through quickly; I was sorry to hear that George had been sick & that Emma was not well and wished they could be under my gude man's treatment for awhile. When I read that part of your letter about the house needing so many repairs, Dr says, well she'll have to thank the Yankees for that for if they had let us alone; we could have supported her handsomely, repaired the house nicely & spent this summer with her— You know it is the *tenth* [year] of our marriage & we had looked forward to it as our holiday— The Dr used to say that in ten years he would be worth 30.000 & then we would go North & perhaps Europe—but instead of that here we are in *a cabin*—quite a contrast is it not?

Yesterday being the tenth anniversary of our marriage I could not help thinking of our wedding & the many changes since then. Four of the few then present are now dead—Sister Fanny, Aunt Lucy—Mr & Mrs Messenger. Mr Messenger was not present but it was almost the same thing— Baconham is now entirely changed & Sister Emily its mistress. As for *ourselves* we have been very happy; it was a change for the better for both of us— he has *always* been to me a kind & tender husband. I have tried to be a good wife but some defects, in my character, which have been partially obliterated by misfortune, have sometimes caused me to fail my duty. Through all the ten years I can truly say he has never spoken a *cross word to me*—never found fault with me. But with all this kindness & tenderness on his part & wish to be, on mine, we have been very unhappy at times—from misfortunes & petty annoyances from without. Sometimes there have been so many that I have thought well *perhaps* we have more than any other family & it would not have been so had each one of us married differently. But I cannot write so as to explain myself to you, without being too lengthy, so I must wait with the hope of seeing you some day & *telling* you. I often wish that I could write like Fredrika Bremer; I am sure I could give you some *family scenes,* as interesting as were some of hers. I think you would have been amused on Saturday to hear us *quarreling* about taking a ride— *he* insisting that I must go, & *I,* that "it was impossible"— "There was too much to be done." Oh pshaw, said he, Milly can do all that must be done; besides you promised me you would go— He went off to give some orders to the workmen & I thought the matter settled, when after a little here he came—"you almost ready"? No! said I, you must excuse me, I cant very well go this morning without joking   But he kept on, when I interrupted "Oh fie! who ever heard of such a thing as a man married ten years & must have his wife go with him every time he rides out"— why anybody would think you were a lover or a widower with his *new* second wife to hear you— He went off laughing & I came in, almost sorry I didn't go notwithstanding the scrubbing & the pies & cakes & coffee to parch for Sunday. all of which Milly could have done by herself, but I was afraid she might try to do too much before dinner & make the dinner late & workmen dont like late dinners— I let her go away on Sat. and she has not returned yet—but Ann fills her place *tolerable* well— I say tolerable because not knowing my ways exactly our breakfast was quite a failure—steak cooked too much, coffee very *weak* & eggs all broken, while *I* like them fried whole & the *Dr* likes nice juicy steak & strong coffee.

We are again cut off from the city by a crevasse just below the the other of Apr—about 5 miles below N. O.

It is quite an extensive one, but it is hoped, that it will be stopped in ten days or so. That cannot be however if these heavy winds & rains continue— on Monday there was a terrible wind, which extended very far from what we can learn— Many lives were lost at Sea & on the lakes. Dr R——& myself went 12 miles below— it was pleasant when we started— when we returned about half way home, the storm met us—& we had to shelter ourselves in a negro cabin. There was but little rain—after the hardest rain was over, we came on towards home but were sprinkled a little. I suffered very much fearing our new house would be blown over for there are no chimneys in it yet to steady it. You can imagine how glad I was to see it standing as firm as ever & the carpenters told us that it had not even *shaken*.

Georgy is not well— he has been growing poor for a week from disordered bowels— His father gives him medicines which help him & then he will eat something which puts him back again. I am obliged to watch him very closely. Plums are ripe & we have had some sent us twice, so that I have had as many as I want— Blackberries too are ripe & plentiful. We shall soon have the greatest quantity of ripe figs— our peach trees will bear none this year.

I hardly know what to do with myself now that my sewing is mostly done— one thing, I will do & that is write to Grandma— I can imagine Emma's visit there & almost envy her. Her dress is very pretty— I wear mostly blue & purple & those are Dr R——s favorite colors.

WEDNESDAY—NOON.

As I suppose the boat will stop to-day with freight, I finish this to give to the captain & he will mail it for me. — The mason has just com-

menced   he has the two high chimneys to build & the walls to plaster
& hard finish. He thinks it will take him 25 days. Dr R——thinks not.
Most of the painting is done & the carpenters have only mantles & fold-
ing-doors to make & banisters to the steps. I hope *they* will be through
in a week from now. Then the mason & painters can soon finish & *perhaps* we shall live in a *house* again— The cabin is very warm & for the
last two or three nights our sleeping-room has been very close. Write as
often as you can & tell Emma & George I am waiting for letters from
them. Good Bye—with much love from Your Affectionate daughter.

T. B. Fox.

I dont like the remarks of the Ed. of the Eagle about the rebels; he is
not a good judge in regard to their needing a *rope* about their necks. I
know a good many Yankees who deserved such a favor—for instance—
those who *shot* Pa's cows & left them lying in the field—others who
took ladies' wardrobes & tore everything they had to ribbons, & others
still who *cowhided a lady* because she would not tell them where her *gold*
was & a thousand others that I *know* about— it was not hearsay.

When Pa's *ten* cows were all shot in the field there were ten young
children under his roof depending upon *milk* for their food. we had
nothing but *corn* & *milk* left & you may know how we fared when the
cows were all so wantonly killed.

The Yankees had then already destroyed the *gardens*, the *orchards* &
killed *all* of Pa's hogs & sheep & broken into the store-room & carried
off all the meat   all the fowls were destroyed on the first day that
Grant's army passed.

☐ ☐ ☐

Dear Mother—   *HYGIENE JULY 22ND 1866.*

Once more I am *at home*, that is—*we have moved into the new house,*
and the first stroke of my pen is to—you. I wrote a lead-pencil line in
the city the other day but fear you can hardly read it—; in it I promised
to write again soon. We reached home very late, very tired and *muddy*.
All day Friday I was both busy working myself & superintending others. Dr R——& myself sat up till about eleven unpacking furniture &
setting it up. The next day we were up at daylight and at work again and
with the aid of Milly & a woman whom I hired to scrub the floors &
clean mattrasses by noon, on yesterday we were quite *settled*.

The young Creole carpenter who has worked so well & faithfully for us from the time he commenced hewing out the first cypress sill in the swamp until yesterday, when he gave a final finishing stroke to the windows, so that they would not fit so tight, and whom I cannot but rank as a friend, stayed & helped Dr Raymond & the servants to bring in the *piano*. It is very heavy and required all the strength of *five* persons to lift it up the steps; after that job was done I felt quite at ease and as I looked through one room & another could hardly realize I had been turned out doors so long & lived in so warm & uncomfortable a place. How I wish you were here— this writing is such slow & tedious work. You should have Dr R——'s arm-chair, near the sliding doors, between the North & South windows where there is a fine breeze & then I could tell you *all* so soon. The *hard finish* you see, is not well done— it is the work of a negro mason, who would drink his three bottles of whiskey pr day in spite of all we could do or say. He gave us a great deal of trouble & finally left without finishing— We hired a plantation hand who understood the business & he completed the job. I feel a little disappointed as we expended a considerable sum of money for plaster of Paris, sand, lime &c. This cottage furniture dark brown, with a scroll of white around the edge & gilt leaves with a cluster of strawberries in the centre, Dr R——selected for me & purchased with the bale of cotton sent by his father. Is it not pretty & does it not make my room look homelike & cozy? The mantle-piece is a design of my own; I laid it off to correspond with the arch over the sliding doors. This is rough, but may give you some idea of it [sketch included in original]; the parlor the same; both painted black. The mop-boards are painted dark mahogany—the rest of the wood-work pure white. All the door knobs are white. Every thing is simple, but altogether the house looks very pleasant & picturesque & is an extremely comfortable & convenient one. The set in the bedroom back of this is imitation oak & consists of a bedstead, with boster,[5] which cost thirty five dollars, a wardrobe $24. a wash-stand $6, a candle-stand $3, and two half arm chairs $6.. making $74. in all. Furniture is very dear—but we were obliged to have enough for two rooms. The parlor has only the piano & 6 half arm chairs. we have a new gilt frame for the mirror, which Dr R——will put on at his

---

5. This should read bolster.

first leisure & I suppose Mrs Hoyt will send my sofa & centre-table home now as I have need of, and room for them. The old sofa, centre-table one rocking-chair & the only sofa bottom one that was saved furnish the little sitting-room back of the parlor. [Sketch included in original.] This is a rough sketch. The sliding-doors between my room & the parlor are eight feet wide & 9 high. Both my room & the parlor open upon the gallery in front & a hall behind. a pair of stairs lead up to the dormitories commencing in the hall near the back door, and going up over the sitting room door. [Sketch included in original.] They are rather narrow but the best we could do. Until we can furnish the basement, for dining room, we shall use the room in the cabin, which we have occupied as sitting room. It is a little more trouble for those who *partake* to go over there, but a great deal less for those who *cook & serve*. It was no slight addition to the work here, in former times, to be obliged to carry all the meals across the yard & up a flight & a half of stairs. I never realized it, until since I have been living next to the kitchen & found with how much less time & labor a meal could be served there than it was before in the house. Now I must tell you how I came by my nice set of China— The Dr had a patient—a wealthy gentleman—last week, who required his services, until they amounted to $32; he cured him & the gentleman told him to make out his bill, which he did. It was paid & the Dr gave it to me for crockery—I merely intended to buy a dozen soup-plates, as I needed them more than anything else but after we reached the store, Dr R——said I might as well buy what I needed at once & get what was nice. Backed by such advice & the $32, of course it was more than almost any woman could withstand, so I have 6 tea-cups & saucers & 6 coffee-cups & saucers, a sugar-bowl, cream pitcher & soup-bowl, 12 soup, dessert, dinner, tea, & breakfast plates, & two cake plates & a tea-pot, excepting plates, of the most unique & elegant shape; & all pure white French porcelain. Of course it *corresponds*, with the old red deal table & faded, patched checked red & blue table cover. all of my linen table cloths were burned excepting the one you sent me & that I keep for *grand* occasions.

A little accident happened to Georgy to-day. He fell against the kitchen stove & burned his left hand & arm quite badly, but his father thinks it will not be anything very serious. He is waking, so I must stop.

LATER,

I did not think it would be so long before I finished this; but I have had
no chance of mailing it; if I had I would have sent it so— We have no
Post Office yet, but I believe our new P. M. (to be) took his oath yesterday & Dr R——the only *public* man on this side went his Security, so
you may direct your next letter to Jesuits Bend, Plaquemines Par. La, as
you used to do.

George's arm & hand pained him considerably for two or three days,
but are getting well now. Since writing, I have been very busy and yet
I can hardly tell you what I have done— *Some* mending & *some*
cleaning—had the dining room thoroughly scoured, all the medicines
& bottles overhauled & cleaned & made Fan a new calico dress & re-
trimmed her last summer's hat. We are enjoying most delightful
weather— I see by the papers, that the Philadelphians & New Yorkers
are complaining of intense & unusual heat; here the nights are cool &
the days really pleasant, from the breeze. We have had frequent slight
showers & crops & gardens are both in a fine growing condition. There
is but little sickness yet in the neighborhood. Dr R——is however absent a greater portion of the time visiting some one. Dr Wilkinson sent
for him early this morning to visit his grandchild— He will probably be
absent most of the day, being alone makes it seem long; the children are
out in front playing in the shade; Ann who is well again & has come
back to work is with them. Milly, I let go visiting yesterday, to reurn
to-day. She cleaned the house so faithfully & took such good care of the
children, on my two trips to— town that I promised her she should go
as soon as we were fairly settled. I am expecting Mrs Hally & her baby
over to spend a few days with me, the last of the week. She is not very
well— & the Dr thinks it will do us both good. To tell the truth, I don't
care much about company for awhile. I want to enjoy my new house by
myself & *take my ease*. I have been so hurried with sewing & worried
with ill health & anxiety ever since the burning of the house, that I feel
like resting for awhile. No matter how little company one may have,
you know it makes extra steps & thought for the *housewife*. But I cannot
give much extra thought to the eating line for we are living quite economically now & I dont intend to change the "bill of fare" for any one.
My sugar-barrel is too low to make many cakes and butter too dear, for
poor folks. Fortunately our garden is a good one & we have plenty of nice

vegetables, particularly beans, (shell) butter beans, okra & tomatoes. We have a "trot line" which gives us a nice fresh fish occasionally & we have shrimps two or three times a week; these with my chickens, which are now nearly grown, & fresh beef on Sundays give us a good variety & *keep us off* salt meat a part of the time. I wish you could have some of the fruit which we have in the greatest abundance—water & musk-melons & figs until we are tired of them. Not many peaches. The *hail* in the Spring injured nearly all the trees in the Parish. I have been making Fig preserves during the week; they are delicious, but wont *keep long* as the Dr says— you would *think* so, to see him & the children devour them. Have also made some nice *tomato* pickles— I pick the tomatoes green & about half grown. Wash & prick them with a fork, throw salt over them & let them stand three days. Then pack them in jars & pour boiling spiced vinegar over them. They are very nice in about a month. You see I am a busy body—always *fussing* with something & getting so that I read & write but very little—owe all my friends a letter, but can't tell *when* I shall feel as though I could spare time to write. Have a dress for Fan & two suits for G—— to make next week & a dress for myself *some time or other*—as it is so near August now, I shall not need it very much & may let it alone for this year. It is truly delightful here now—a little cloudy and a fine, cool breeze, the birds chirping & singing in every direction & little sail boats rapidly gliding by on the grand old Mississippi. Our new house dont need much more furniture, though of course a carpet & curtains would add much to the appearance of the parlor. & I would not object to a sideboard & safe. In this country where ants are so plentiful & *fingers so long,* a safe where you can lock up eatables & your sugar-bowl & put the legs of the safe into cans of water, is almost indispensable.

The little closet at the end of the cabin answers very well for a china closet, so I can get along without a sideboard. Milly is perfectly honest but I would not trust Polin[6] alone in my store-room for *two* minutes. & never expect to see any extra meat or lard that happens to be left in the kitchen outside of the safe, after he has been there. He is an impudent, lazy somebody & I shall be glad when we can hire some one in his place. As the Dr gives him only five dollars pr month, we rather put up with

---

6. A new hired servant.

his insolence as a matter of *economy*. I sometime wish that Sumner[7] had him for a *valet*. He has been ordered off several times, but he is too smart to leave a place where he knows he will get plenty to eat three times a day.

Although I have not said half that I have thought of telling you, when busy house keeping or sewing, yet I must close & write to some of my other friends—Sister Emily, particularly. She was sick when I last heard from her—much worried with her affairs— The estate is so large & left at just such a time that it would have required all of Mr Messenger's tack to have arranged everything to good advantage. & how can she be expected to do one half.

MONDAY A. M.

All well— I close in Haste having a chance to send.
All send love to *all*. Your Aff. Daughter

T. B. Fox

I shall be *32* to-morrow.

AUG. 7TH 1866..

As I have tried in vain to have my letter mailed, I open it to add a few words. Dr R——was too unwell to go to the City last Thursday—he had fever several days but *would* not or rather thought he *could* not give up to it, so took his medicines & visited his patients, instead of lying in bed— Persisted in crossing the river in the hot sun, & fainted away on the other side. He is better now but looks badly. He goes to the city to-morrow if well enough. I wished to go with him but was told yesterday that there was a good deal of cholera & of a severe kind & am afraid to go. It is mostly among the blacks yet, still many are leaving the city. There have been no cases upon the coast yet. Dr R —— fears that it will make terrible havoc among the negroes here. The riots of which you have doubtless heard are all quelled & everything is quiet.[8] Many persons express much fear that the negroes will prove hostile & that there will be an insurrection but we do not think much about the reports. If any such thing occurs, it will probably be in the City. Dr R——thinks we are perfectly safe here. I have not much else to tell you

---

7. Charles Sumner (1811–1874), abolitionist and radical Republican senator from Massachusetts.
8. See Gilles Vandal, *The New Orleans Riot of 1866: Anatomy of a Tragedy* (Lafayette: Center for Louisiana Studies, 1983).

than what I wrote on the other sheet. We have had no letters from our Miss. friends for some time, but as I have not written I do not deserve or expect any.

Our friend Dr Wilkinson dined with us yesterday; I was glad to see him, but was truly ashamed of my dinner—made a mistake, & the chicken pie was made of my old dark flour & *was* so tough & black that it required a good appetite & poor eyes to manage it— Of course, the biscuits were the same & as I thought only Dr R——would dine with me & the children I had no extras,— no soup of any kind & no dessert. We always have better dinners by ourselves— is it not strange how things will sometimes *all* go backwards & wrong? The rice looked dark, the Irish potatoes were lumpy & the squashes too greasy. Milly was busy ironing & Ann managed the dinner. Milly has turned out to be a splendid cook & I am quite proud of her as one of *my pupils.*

I hope Dr R——will bring me letters from some of you to-morrow. Much love to Emma & George. Remember me to inquiring friends if there should be any. I am sometimes very homesick for the sight of old familiar scenes & faces & sit & think of you all, long after every one else is in bed and asleep. Had it not been for the burning of the house perhaps I might have made a short visit home, now there is no hoping for that. Good Bye—From Your affectionate Daughter.

T. B. Fox.

□ □ □

Dear Mother,   HOME. OCT. 3RD 1866.

As I hardly know what to do with myself, I'll sit down in the confusion & answer your letter of Sept. 13th & that will rest me & take one duty off my mind. Emma's new situation gave me a sharp pang for a moment but when I analyzed the feeling it consisted mostly of wounded *pride*— I forgot that I was poor again & could not have everything my own way & that I ought to be thankful that she had so good employment, so near you & with such good wages. I am glad your boarders are good pay for I have sometimes been much worried fearing you were having all your hard work for nothing.— I can hardly realize that Mary & Semantha would have been so old— Fanny grows more & more like Mary every day & reminds me often of her. I think you would be struck with the resemblance—not only looks but in disposition & manners. Fanny is as kind-hearted and generous as one can be & so perfectly *unselfish* in disposition, that hers will be the lot through life to *care* for rather than be cared for. Even now she is of the greatest comfort to her Father, particularly when I am too unwell to notice household concerns & her watchfulness is the same as ever for Georgy. You say you do not think we shall ever see one another again — I hope we may for I want you to *know* my husband & children. But still the prospect is not very bright — I cannot leave Dr R—— & I am afraid he will never think he is "well enough off" to *leave his practice,* & take such a trip. It will take all of this year's & next year's practice to pay for the house & furniture & to make us comfortable. The fences are all falling to pieces & the stable needs repairing & there are so many things, that ought to be bought & done that there will be nothing for traveling very soon. My yearnings for home are sometimes very strong but I cannot make him unhappy by wishing for what is not now in his power to grant, so I try to content myself with my *own home* & living upon the pleasant memories of childhood's home & bright anticipations of what the future may bring. I am glad Grandma has such good health for so old a lady & that my letter afforded her any gratification — I will try to write again. I often think of her & those happy, happy days when we used "to go to Grandma's" — Last week I took the children to ride (with old Dick in the buggy) & all our time was spent talking about *"your* Grandma, ma-ma" & the old big rock in the orchard & *the brook* with its cowslips & the big echo in the woods. My children at least Fannie know the old place *by heart.* I received Aunt Mary's letter. — *Green corn & frost,* what a delightful country! & how I wish it were in my power to remove you from it to this one, where we have only begun to think of Jack Frost — Have not had a glimpse of him yet, though we did have to build a little fire for two or three mornings in Sept. We are busy *planting* a *new garden* — have young cabbages & turnips two or three inches high   lettuce growing finely, & roses lilies & verbena in full bloom. Had butter beans & okra, from the garden for dinner. We are eating corn bread made of this *years corn* — ripened & ground. Have an abundance of sweet potatoes, & pumpkins & might have had several other fresh vegetable had we not been so busy with the new house & the cholera & a good many other things. Then Polin is of no earthly account in the garden & when we send him there to work he does it by leaning on his spade or hoe or hiding himself under the fig-tree. The most I have ever known him to be guilty of doing from 9 to 12, was to *spade* up a piece about as *big* as *your parlor.* of course with such a help & the Dr gone almost constantly one cannot be expected to have a very good garden. The front yard is dressed up in weeds & tie-vines & everything on and about the lot looks untidy & *thriftless* except the new house & that does look nicely & one would think to ride by that that it was the coziest, shadiest, most home-like looking little place ever seen— The old oak shades it on the South & the three pecan trees make it look cool & pleasant on the North. But if that rider by could come in & stand on the back portico & peer into corners & under things as I can he would see enough to be done, & plenty of things to put to rights. I told you I was tired when I sat down— you ought to see me & where I am. The floor is all grease & dirt   the table-cloth so soiled I know you would n't eat from it & my kitchen—next room—such a sight as would make you northern ladies with your clean kitchens & shining tins, raise your hand in horror. Milly has been gone since Friday. Ann came & cooked & washed dishes & *cleaned kitchen* (you ought to have seen the stove & inside of the pots when she left on Saturday & Sunday & Monday sent me word she was sick. I could n't get anyone else until to-day. So have played cook & housemaid myself & tried to get off the first coat of dirt from everything I touched in the kitchen— The serve & bread-bowl were *all* grease   the safe shelves fairly black, all the *tin* ware dingy grey & everything else in proportion— You have no idea how little black people know of *true cleanliness.* So a thing is wiped over & *swabbed off* with something that is all that is necessary— Dr R——has had me a nice little kitchen made of the bed-room part of our "cabin home"—and as it is nicely ceiled with a glass window & good white pine floor   I am going to see if I cannot have it kept more like white folks' kitchen. It is very small, but I think will answer my purpose very well—just for cooking. There is a narrow door between it & the dining-room & also an opening which lets down & shuts up, where the meals can be served up— We have made this room by throwing up a partition where the large curtain used to be. It is a nice arrangement for me when I have to do my own work, but you just ought to see the condition of the three rooms just now. The carpenter has just finished in the new one & Lucy the washerwoman in the old one & I sit here in the dining room between the two thinking how much there is to be done before all will come out straight & clean & then there is all to-day's big washing to be ironed &c. &c. A body wouldn't mind these tight times coming once in a while if one could hire a woman when wanted but these free darkeys are getting so independent that they wont work for love or money & so we white folks *no account like myself* have to do the best we can— Not that I dont like to work—I do really love to work hard, but I *cannot*— it is not laziness— it is inability by the time I have cooked the breakfast, & cleaned up the breakfast things—dishes & kettles & swept the house & made the two beds I am completely tired out. I know you will think me no account sure enough but so I am. Last night I was so tired I could not sleep just from cooking & doing our little house-work. I suppose Milly will be back "on Sunday" & Lucy will come up & help me again to-morrow & perhaps next day, but it discourages me to think how dependent I am & sometimes I wish I had been kept at *hard work* all my life, I should be used to it & shouldn't mind what a smart New England woman would call *light work*. But I have been croaking all the way through my letter & now it is supper time & I must go & feed my big family— 4 hogs, 15 pigs, 60 fowls, 2 horses, old Polin, husband, babies & self, though I am not hungry & if all the rest didnt wish for any more supper than I do, there would be neither much to cook or give out—measure out— Fortunately my husband is not an exacting one & so I give him a good cup of coffee with & a cold biscuit & little fried ham he is perfectly satisfied. It frets him to see me fussing more than it would to go without supper. Well I'll write again when everything is all right & Milly has come back & I am up in my nice little sitting-room in a clean suit, instead of in this untidy loose gown & dirty skirts & hair combed straight back behind my ears & done up in a little wad behind. It is of no use trying to look like a lady when you are doing work in such a *nigger* kitchen as my old one when the floor & stove are both the same color &c. &c— Arent you tired of hearing it. Let me tell you a trick I saw to-day. Lucy took up an old dirty *pan from the floor—where the cats & chickens come & go*, dipped it into my water-pail, took a drink, dipped again gave her *greasy* mouthed child one, then *put the rest* of the water into a half-*washed* skillet to *boil* the *okra* in. I saw it, walked in emptied the *water out* & made her bring me some fresh & put it on *myself*.

SUNDAY A. M —

The Dr goes to the Office this evening so I finish my letter & tell you how *straight* & nice I & *matters* in general stand— Milly has returned, the week's vexation & fussing are over & sure enough I am up in my little sitting-room (where I belong, I'm thinking) looking & feeling quite decent. She came back last night just *after* I had prepared the supper & you can imagine I was glad to see her. My new kitchen was completed Friday & with Ann's help I moved everything as clean & bright as soap, ashes, & brick dust could make them yesterday & you ought to see how nice it all looks— I am not afraid to step into it with a clean dress on. Milly is very neat as a *black* person, still I shall have to watch her in it or she will soon have the floor all grease & *smut*— a darkey thinks nothing of lifting a stove cover & putting it anywhere on the floor or a greasy *kettle*. For some reason I do not feel right well this morning, but shall probably when I get rested. All the rest are well. Dr R——is complaining of a troublesome tooth-ache. You need not worry about *me,* in regard to the hint I gave you[9]— I expect to have just as easy & nice a time as *Old Bet* did the other night with her *nine* pigs. Dont you think of the matter again until next Jan & then you needn't till I write & tell you that I am the happy mother of *two bouncing boys*! & maybe a girl or two besides

Tell Emma many, many thanks for the pretty tatting. I wish I knew how to make pretties & then I would n't bother her. It may be that we shall all take a trip to town this week & will try to send you the 5. promised— Dr R——has employed his leisure time lately fixing up the old carriage & you dont know how nice it looks, in its mended dress & new coat of black paint & varnish. F——received the ribbon & wrote her Aunt Emma a note thanking her which I suppose she has by this time.

Good Bye— With love to all. I will write when I can but shall probably be quite busy for a couple of weeks, putting the yard in order, setting out my roses & strawberries & sewing when I can. Your aff. Daughter.

T. B. Fox.

---

9. Tryphena was pregnant with her fifth child, Frank Coleman, born January 14, 1867.

Dear Mother—   [? OCTOBER 1866]

I think that if you were to search the Union over you would hardly
find another such a busy little hive as ours— All hands are up at daylight & often before & such a walking to & from & picking up & cleaning & working generally, you can hardly imagine. Dr R——is very busy
every leisure moment he can command from his practice putting on the
laths to the rooms up stairs & gardening— let me tell you how hard he
has worked to-day. First cleaned out my stove-pipe & put it back before
day, then went into the garden & set out 200 turnip plants, watered
them & covered them with hay; helped Antoine (an extra hand whom
we are hiring for two days to trim shrubbery & spade in the front yard)
saw off the peach-trees, ate his breakfast, dressed himself, (or rather was
dressed by his wife & you ought to have seen the change in him as he
stepped into his buggy with his nice black suit, buff vest, snowy bosom,
well oiled hair &c, &c,) & went off up the road to make his several
Tuesday's visits—prescribed for all the ailing darkeys & white folks on
six plantations & returned home late to dinner   after dinner pulled off
the fixens, & went out on the river side & with *Polins* help picked up &
hauled in 6 cart loads of drift-wood, which the river is bringing to our
door now in great quantities. Then watered his turnip plants, measured
out the different *feeds* to Polin, ate his supper & threw himself upon the
sofa to rest— Dont you think it was time? We are around the centre
table now; he in a rocking-chair, reading with the aid of *spectacles*—
F——fussing with doll-baby things & this good for nothing in a low
sewing chair writing this on my knee, on the account book— Have not
done a stitch of sewing to-day except to work a scallop or so on a chemise sleeve as I walked about the yard *overseeing* a little & helping a little, & tiring myself a great deal. Have been with Antoine most of the
afternoon showing him what shrubs to trim & where & the orange-
trees & flowers begin to look quite clean. After he went away I cooked
the supper as Milly still had some washing to finish & all her big washing to bring in & wash-tubs, board &c &c to put in their places. At
noon I helped prepare the dinner as I wanted Ann to scrub the dining-
room & *privy* & wash off *my* carriage wheels so that the carriage could
be put away. You dont know how nicely the old concern looks in its
new coat of paint & varnish. It took all of Dr R——s leisure time for
three days to fix it up & me 1/2 day to make a cover for it with Milly's

help. I ripped up nine large oat-sacks, & we sewed them together carpet fashion, to protect the carriage from the dust & moisture & chickens when we do not use it. My new kitchen is a great convenience to me & you may be sure I have it kept clean— if Milly spills a drop of grease I tell her she must get a corn-cob & ashes & scrub it up & give *herself* a good scolding   She laughs & does as I tell her except the scolding— I have never heard her speak a cross word on the place yet— Good Night— I am tired of leaning over & will write more some other time. Spent yesterday sewing & almost finished those new breeches of Dr R——s.

Sunday P. M—

Your letter was brought to me to day—Emma's on Wed.— I get them in *8* days now that we have a P. O. I *would* have answered E——s but have been very busy all the week— Helping Milly iron & keep the house in order, so she would have an extra day to help me with my roses & strawberries— Have set out a large bed on one side of the front walk & Dr R—— laid the *bricks* on both sides— We have had an old man white-washing— he has finished about half the fence around the front yard & lane & the place begins to look like old times before war & fire. There is about another week's hard work yet—weeds to be hoed down old limbs & shrubbery picked up & the circle of roses to be weeded & manured. But I must not stop to write all that now— I took this up to tell you about E——'s coming. I should like to have her with me very much, both for *her* sake & my own—but I cannot see or devise any plan to raise the money to pay her expenses. Dr R——is in debt now to the *amount* of his yearly salary. His brother owes him nearly $700. & two other men $100. apiece. If they will all pay him this fall, he may think he can send Emma 100 to come on—if not, the plan will have to be given up. His health is very delicate & he often is very anxious about our future is much worried with his present debt & I shall be glad when the time comes round when he can pay it & be free from that care. I sometimes speak of selling my piano, which is a very handsome & valuable one & at present almost useless to me but he will not listen to it & says—no you may have to depend upon that & your education some day. He has had night fevers for several nights past— He has been at hard work all the week & is nearly worn out—not being accustomed to work of any kind, till the Yankees took Pa's negroes away. We were there at the time & Dr R——pulled off his professional suit & did the work of 6 men for as many weeks—until he saw it was of no use. The Yankees would pull down fences & scatter & kill the stock & do more damage in one hour than he could repair in a week so at last he was obliged to let thing go to ruin & go where he could be of some Service— He has never been strong since Our home now is pretty well fixed & I am determined to keep him from working as much as I can. Daylight never finds him in bed—no matter whether he has rested or not & he is busy at something all day.

Tell Emma I am more obliged to her than she can imagine for the pretty tatting— And yet I sometimes feel as if I had no business asking her to make it—when she is a young lady & needs all her leisure moments to embroider her own clothing. Never mind about the braid. I do not *need* it— it was only a fancy of mine.

The pantaloons were finished at sundown last night— This week I expect to make the coat at odd times. I think Milly can manage the down stairs work by herself— If well I can rise early & put all the house in order & dress self & children & be ready to go to sewing soon after breakfast. This last week besides making the pants & spending a great portion of the time in the yard or cabin, I have embroidered a chemise sleeve & hemmed *16 diapers*—at odd times when F——was out at play or asleep. he sleeve I kept in my key basket & worked a scallop or two when *waiting* for something or *somebody*. For instance the breakfast bell rings—I go down to the table, but Dr is not quite ready & must finish some little job first, or I go to the corn house door to count out the ears of corn for Polin & he has to stop & hunt up his feed box or shuck some corn so I haul out my embroidery & make a scallop or two— Dont you think I am getting economical in the way of *time*. —

SUNDAY NIGHT—

A guest with us to-night—an old friend of the Drs—as I have only my bed & the childrens, George is tucked away in my bed & Fan, in the lounge over in the dining-room. You don't know how I dislike having her so far off.— Still she is perfectly safe. Mr Hally takes Rebel & the buggy & leaves for town at daylight in the morning, so I send this by him. Tell Georgy I certainly will try to write to him soon— I think often of him & should like to see him & you & Emma so much. I see by the papers that each of his patrons were blessed with a daughter— My compliments to them & my congratulations— May my brothers Friends never be less. We were much pleased with Kate's Photograph—my love to her & tell her she *might* have favored me with one for my album. I think she would, could she have heard the Drs remarks—"good face"—"a woman of character" I do not think Le Roy's son[10] resembles our family. His forehead is a little as I remember brothers & that is about all of the Holder I see.

I remember the cosset lamb—what a pity it could not have lived for Grandma's sake. I had a fleece of its wool but it is gone like all my other little but loved relics. Give my love to Grandma & Aunt Mary— I would write if my underclothing drawer was not almost *empty*—one nightgown not patched & only 2 chemises (whole), besides all those little fixings & the time is flying by so fast— I cannot realize that it is the last of Oct— Fan must have some thick underbodies & drawers & it wont take long to make them. You can imagine I have learned to handle my needle rapidly. The Dr says if nothing happens, I shall have a sewing machine by this time next year. I hope so, for I have played sewing machine almost ever since I was married.

My paper is scarce or I would not send you a soiled piece written double. Emma's eyes are so good I reckon she will be able to *pick* it out.

MONDAY NOV. 5TH—

Did not send my letter by Mr. Hally after all— he started too early & I felt too unwell to get up— All are well this morning   Dr R——goes to the City & I enclose the $5 to pay the borrowed tax-money. Had a letter from Eliza yesterday. She will be down soon to spend the winter with me & I some[times] think Aunt Randolph will be with me *in Jan*— Good Bye once more   Love to all— Your Affectionate daughter.

T. B. Fox.

□ □ □

Dear Mother,   [JANUARY 6, 1867]

My letters are all short & hurried now for it seems as if I never had time for writing, & besides, it hurts me to lean over & write. I suffer a great deal but hope my troubles will soon be over—had quite a serious time about two weeks ago after standing up all day attending to the

---

10. Frank Wood Holder, born to Le Roy and Margaret McFraquhar Holder on May 28, 1859. *The Genealogy of the Cleveland and Cleaveland Families*, no. 438, 3:2018.

cutting up, & salting of a hog & trying out the lard—have not done much of anything since. Eliza & Emma[11] are still with us & seem to enjoy their visit very much considering the very bad weather we have had— it has been either cold, *snowing,* or *rainy* ever since before Christmas. But they sit in the parlor, & read or embroider or play on the piano (you don't know what a source of pleasure it is to me to have so nice a one for them as they are both splendid performers) & I try to give them as much of a variety in the way of eating as I can. Milly does remarkably well with her cooking & is just now, my only help for I became disgusted with Alice proceedings & last night paid her up & discharged her after putting up *three weeks* with her careless dirty ways & impudent replies—wont be bothered with darkeys now—used to be obliged to put up with it but feel free now. Did I tell you of my Christmas present? a *beautiful* 3 *ply carpet* for my parlor which cost $56—paid for by Brother James $33 & Dr R——$23 & sent as a surprise just before 6— Christmas on the S. Boat—have not been able to make it yet— it is too heavy for me just now—the colors—oak, green & crimson. Sister Eliza gave me a handsome copy of Byron in green & Aunt Randolph sent me a new pr of linen p——cases with the sheets she gave me two years ago & a new white spread, Georgy a beautiful large spread, *pieced* in stars & a red cushion—of course for my use—but to be given to him when he gets those *three* wives he talks about which he intends feeding on egg-*shells*— you ought to see the little fellow & hear him talk.

I hope you are all well & that the winter is a mild one with you— Good Bye write often & I'll make up one of these days. Love to Emma & George & yourself from all— Your aff. daughter

T. B. Fox.

---

11. Eliza and her sixteen-year-old niece Emma Newman arrived December 15, 1866. See TBHF to ARH, December 15, 1866, MDAH.

Write soon *about the sugar* where & to whom to be sent & how &c. &c.[12]

□ □ □

Dear Sister,   FEB. 7TH 1867. IN MY ROOM.

Yours in Mother's was received some time ago but I have not had much time for writing & what little there was has been spent in "posting the books" & straightening the acc's which had gotten sadly out of order, during the past two months. Yesterday while all were gone to town, I wrote to Sister Lucy as I had not written to her in a long time & she has always been one of my regular correspondents. The days are so short that with my late rising & young babe there is not much time for me to do anything. He is now three weeks & three days old & as fat & hearty as any Mother could wish. I think he has blue eyes while his hair is almost black. They say he looks like me & it seems odd enough that I should have a boy like me. Dr Raymond has named him after the Dr with whom he studied medicine, "Frank Coleman"— I almost hoped he would be named Frank Cleveland but did not like to say so after Dr R——expressed a wish to name him after Dr Coleman.

Fanny is quite delighted and you ought to hear the patronizing way that Georgy speaks of him "My little brother that belongs to me." It seems so odd for me to have a little baby to take care of & wash & dress that I can hardly realize that it is not all a dream; particularly as I am confined to my room yet and cannot attend to the housekeeping affairs. Milly has stood by me like a Trojan & though half sick sometimes has worked through it all & waited upon everybody & everything. Of course I have hired the washing & ironing done & Rachel helped keep the house in order while she stayed & dressed & waited upon George, still Milly has had a great deal to do & has done all faithfully without being told or without grumbling—has worked Sundays & evenings & all times. I am going to make her a present of a pretty barege dress which I have & I send you a .50 cts, & wish you would make or buy her some simple but pretty collar & send to her— she will be so proud of it as coming from my sister.

---

12. After the 1866 sugar grinding season, Dr. Fox received several barrels of sugar from planters in lieu of cash payments for his services. He planned to send a barrel of it to Anna. See TBHF to ARH, February 13, 1867, MDAH.

To-day she is busy trying out the lard & cooking the souse & cutting up the sausage meat. Dr R——had his last fat hog killed day before yesterday. & I wish I could send Mother some of the lard for I have a great quantity besides this last, & I should like to send you some sparibs & backbone too & souse. You would all enjoy it more than we do for this is the 3rd hog we have killed this winter besides a young pig. Monday before the girls left I had a nice roast turkey for dinner with vegetables, rice &c, &c, & boiled custard with sweet crackers for dessert, which all seemed to enjoy very much. As I could not go down to the dining-room I had dinner brought up to the parlor & then threw open the sliding doors between my room & the parlor & made a pleasant dining-room. My new carpet is still unmade— it only graces the *corner* of the room yet in a bundle. It seems quite lonely to have Eliza & Emma gone, but have so much to do that I do not expect to find time to be lonesome much. I have some garments to make baby yet & then a set of shirts for Dr R——which will probably take all my spare time for a month.

Dr R——got rid of old Polin yesterday morning to my greatest joy, & so we have no man servant just now but shall probably hire another in the course of a day or two. I have a new responsibility besides baby—a little negro girl about twelve years old whom Dr R——had bound to him for the next five years.[13] We are to feed, clothe, & take care of her & teach her to read & write for her services & fit her to be a competent house servant. I dread it, but as she seems a quick, good child I may have no difficulty with her. She came yesterday & has certainly been a great help to-day, in keeping up the fires & waiting upon George, who you know is just the right age to need some one to talk to him & amuse him— Fan had kept him amused for the last two months, but she commenced her lessons again on Monday & I cannot have her interrupted after she has gone to her room to study.

I enclose a photograph for Mother, the *best* that Dr R——has ever

13. Emily. For a discussion of newly freed minors bound out in apprenticeships after the Civil War see Rebecca J. Scott, "The Battle Over the Child: Child Apprenticeship and the Freedmen's Bureau in North Carolina," *Prologue* 10 (Summer 1978): 101–13; Barbara Jeanne Fields, *Slavery and Freedom On the Middle Ground: Maryland During the Nineteenth Century* (New Haven: Yale University Press, 1985); Peter Kolchin, *First Freedom: The Responses of Alabama's Blacks to Emancipation and Reconstruction* (Westport, Conn.: Greenwood Press, 1972).

had taken. You will see how much better he looks this year than last. The little pieces[14] are — the wine color, my dress which I have made into a Gabrielle & lined with dark calico, bound & trimmed with black braid & buttons & which makes me a very pretty & warm garment for my room; the other woolens are baby's socks. The white scraps of his little long sleeved, high necked dresses — called here *camisole* — They keep them on the babe until a month old, then put on regular baby dresses. I did not make but 5 camisoles. & but 3 new dresses as I had several left of George's.

The little figured dark calico is like his crib cloak lined with red flannel (very fine) & bound with red braid. It is the most useful garment he has for he is always wrapped in it or has it thrown over him.

Eliza & Emma each made Fan a white apron & scalloped them. Eliza made hers high in the neck with long sleeves, worked around the bottom, the collar, cuffs, & pockets with white floss. Emma made a short bib apron scalloped with red all around with little pockets. They also helped me make her a new dress & sack & made & worked Georgy 2 shirts one with white floss & one with red for this summer. It has helped me very much. — I have had nothing new for a long time excepting some night-gowns, chemises & stockings & a work-basket for which I had paid .60. It is the first one I have had since my first straying away from home in '62, when I left mine here on the wardrobe shelf & which some darkey bought at the sale for a mere trifle. But I must not write any more now; I am trying to answer all letters so Mrs Dewey will hear from me soon. I hope she is through with her troubles by this time. Tell Georgy I'll try & write but he will have to read yours & imagine it to him, as what I write to one of you I know all will hear. With much love to all — Good Bye — As ever — Your Aff. Sister

T. B. Fox.

FRIDAY EVENING

I gave the pink ribbon to Emma & cut the blue into four book-marks for Bible & P. Book.

---

14. Tryphena enclosed swatches of fabric. See samples in the Fox Collection, Department of Archives and History, Jackson, Mississippi.

Dear Mother,   HOME, MAR 8   67.

You shall have the *first* written on my new desk — a beautiful present from my kind husband, prized all the more highly from being a perfect surprise and given at a time which — but I cannot tell you now — It is Monday & there is much to be done for I am general cook & housemaid again. Milly wanted to go to town last Thursday to see her sick god mother and I have played her part & my own too since with Emily's help — Breakfast is over & the rooms in order, but Dr R — is going to the city and I must help him dress & then baby will wake up & need his bath & breakfast & then dinner must be under headway, so you see I have not much time to write — We are all well & jogging along nicely. Dr R — has not succeeded in finding a waiting man yet — He hired one last week who stayed two days & left at night without an cause whatever that we could find out — No one has seen him since & had he not taken all his clothing I should be alarmed fearing he might be drowned.

The blacks are all growing more & more unreliable every day, & we are becoming very tired of them. I fear they will be an extinct race in a few decades of years. Dr R — is so disgusted with them that he will hire a white man & his wife the first chance that he has.

My spring sewing is getting along out of my way — have made me one new calico & altered one, made over my white shawl, (ripped it to pieces & had all but the border washed) Dr R_____ a new pr. of pants, & two shirts & Fan one new calico & new skirt, 2 prs. of pillow cases, 10 napkins   6 towels & 1 tablecloth besides my new carpet & some other things since baby's birth — Had a girl to help me sew last week but she is very slow with her needle & I don't think she helps much only she is better than nothing.

I forgot to enclose the $1.. to Georgy the next morning & send it now — also $1. to buy a little singing book such as Georgy & the other children used to sing from. I want to teach my Georgy for he has a decided taste for music. Can you not buy me one, — do it up securely, & send it out by *mail* — If I remember right it was a book about the size of this sheet, an inch thick & had piano *accompaniments* — to the songs — had in it a song ending — "murmur God is good" — & "oh merrily, oh merrily my moments fly" & others — ask Hat about it & if you cannot buy that one send me something of the kind, so that I can play the music & the children sing—mine were all *burned*. If I send to the city Dr R——will not be able to find what I want & will pay five dollars perhaps for some costly one that we ought not to afford now.

I send Fan's [letter]—it is all her own—only she would ask me to spell some of the words— With much Love to Emma & Georgy & much to yourself— I am as ever— Your Aff. Daughter.

T. B. Fox.

You have no idea how much company the little clock is for me — I try to have the whole establishment regulated by it, but it is almost impossible to have anything regular in a physician's family— that is if we wait meals for him. But since George is getting old enough to go to the table, I think he as well as F—— need their meals at regular hours, so we have come to the conclusion it is best to have them served whether he is here or not & keep his warm in the steamer, but I dont like it & always think of the verses written by some doctor's wife "Oh the horrors of a saved up meal" which I presume you have seen. So having a clock we are to have breakfast at 7 dinner at 1 & supper at 6 & Fan is to study at regular hours & practice 1 hour every day. She can already play 3 little tunes right prettily & I am very ambitious for her to play well— I sometimes think of taking some little girl of her age, as company for her both in study & play & it would take no more of my time to teach two than one if both were in the same studies & it *pays* well — I could get 30 or 40 a month for board & tuition— So you need not be surprised should you find I had another scholar—not that I intend opening a school, & would not take any one if it were not for Fan's benefit. Besides you know, I love to teach. Poor Lui, my former pupil, is faring badly— her husband grows worse & worse & her own health is again delicate   she has two children already. I am going to write & ask her to come & pay me a visit though I think it is doubtful if she can raise the money to come.

I have had to give up my town trip, on account of the bad weather & bad roads.

Am feeling much better than when I last wrote & of course am not low-spirited.

We hear from Pa's people & Lucy occasionally— Are all well & prospering notwithstanding their great losses by the war.

Pa finds it difficult to hire hands to carry on the place. Jimmy had cut his leg badly but it was healing when he last wrote. Mrs. Messenger is very busy making arrangements for this year's crop & seems to be quite in her element—managing her large plantation. Good Bye again

T. B. F.

□ □ □

SAT. EVE. MAY 25TH 1867.

Dear Mother— Frank is handed over to Fanny that I may write you a short note in answer to yours of May 16th which Dr R——brought me last night & tell you how *very* sorry I am that I wrote that pencil note in such a way as to hurt your feelings & make Georgy regret his truly brotherly kindness to me. I feared after the hastily pencilled letter was sealed that it was not worded as I intended, but though I was very much fretted when I wrote I did not mean that you should be fretted too. Dr R——& myself had been out upon the st. together & he found a bill of $53.. for medicines at Cousin John's which he did not expect to find & he was saying how fast he was spending money & all that & ended off in this way — & "there's that $70.. must go North to-day & I expect that will be lost & there will be that bill against me— all the year — " & of course I went back to my room feeling uncomfortable— He said he should be uneasy all the time until he heard from it &c, &c. I don't know that I wrote that I wished to sell any of the things— I thought some of selling or rather exchanging for *white* check the black & white plaid as I thought it too thick & warm but on examining it find it as you say just the thing for riding in & home wear & wish it was made up— I would have it on now for we had a hard rain all day yesterday & it is cool to-day. It is thinner than I at first thought. The bonnets I had already sold for $10.. as Fanny & I both had new & did not need them. I felt that morning as if I could have *sold* my *head* if it would have made Dr R——feel any better— I even came home without having my teeth fixed & would not tell him the reason until afterwards— Of course it all passed over in two hours & could you have heard him talk & seen him fill up my purse you would have thought, that he never was fretted with money matters in his life & he isn't very often. He is now talking of taking me to the city to buy a sewing machine! as he thinks I have too much to do— I hope he will but shall not say much about it— He

enjoys buying me things so much *himself.* George's shoes are too large
& I shall have to exchange them   All the other things we are very much
pleased with & you had better believe I shall hold on to them.

Have you one of those Balmorals, if not get one & charge it to me for
the one you sent me before is as *good as new* & you can have the new
one— I will not send *it* back but let someone have it for *three* dollars &
send that to you to buy you one— I don't need two you know— Now
don't misunderstand me & read my scribbling wrong. If you could have
seen how your letter pained me last night you would not have been fretted with that lead-pencil scratch enough to have sent back the *$1.00*—
you might have kept it & bought you some new book & read it for my
sake— but never mind I'll send it back & you'd better *mind*— & *let it
stay there*— now that is not a very respectful way of talking to one's
Mother I know but I can't help it. I say & do just as I please at *Hygiene*
& if you do send it back I'll go all the way to Pittsfield to carry it — so
there! As to the carriage blanket Dr R _____*never* had any idea of *selling*
it & if Georgy knew *how much* Dr R—— thinks of it he would not feel
hurt I know.[15] I had it thrown over the rocking chair one day & he
wanted me to put it away because he was afraid it would be soiled &
that was something remarkable for *him* to say. He says— "Tell Georgy
I never *sell presents* & particularly one made to me as that was made. The
reason I asked the price of it was because we were comparing the prices
of things & that among the rest & concluded it would cost about $25
here. I received one Sun paper last night the first in a long time— Now
dont get out of patience with me again because I sometimes feel a little
fretted because Dr R——is & *that bill of Cousin John's* (and he charges
exorbitant prices for his medicines) was at the bottom of all the trouble.
It is paid now & forgotten. You know Dr R——had paid him $125.00 in
full in Jan. & $25. only a little while ago & supposed he owed only $15 or
$20 instead of $53..— & the *fun* of the thing is this that the medicines
cost us a great deal of money & are the same as *given away* for the negroes never have ready money to pay for them & have to be *credited* &
there it stays *charged* on the books. not one tenth is ever paid—so Dr
R——has declared he will not credit any more— Frank is beginning to

---

15. Dr. Fox received the blanket, probably made at the Pontoosuc woolen mill, as a gift
    from Tryphena's family.

fret for he is hungry—slept all through dinner like a good child that he is & let Milly help wait upon table—

I have had my hands full since Thursday night— 3 gentlemen came unexpectedly for supper & lodging after 7 oclock when the kitchen fire was all out, Milly gone to her room   not a *biscuit*, or piece of cake on the *premises.* only one spare bed! didn't I fly around— Milly made a fire & *biscuit*,   Emily went to the nearest grocery & bought soda crackers, sweet crackers, & butter (*mean* stuff) (we never buy it, bring it from town but it was all gone) & Fan put Frank to sleep & to bed, while I played hostess, & hunted up extra sheets & pillows & a bar for the lounge which we moved from my room into the spare room. Milly soon had a nice supper—cold roast pig, souse (for we had killed a half grown pig the day before) tea, coffee, preserves &c &c. One is a New Yorker & 2 Bostonians. They are taking the negro *registry*— no one would or could entertain them so Dr Fox told them to come here & he would do the best he could for them for said he to me I believe a Southerner should show his enemies that he has not lost his hospitality if he has his property & freedom & so looked to me of course to help him out. I have had nice breakfasts, dinners, & suppers but Milly & I are both nearly tired out for the washing had to be put off this week until Wednesday because it rained & that pushed the ironing & cleaning all to this part of the week & then company too. I ironed half the time yesterday & helped her with the dinner— We made bread & cake after breakfast, had a roast ham, pea soup, peas, beans, beets, Irish p & sweet p. & dressed lettuce for dinner with coffee & cake served in the parlor after for dessert— To-day I had ham, baked [. . .] vegetables *6 kinds*— & a nice pudding with dew berry preserves. Dr R——bought a nice extension table not long ago. & when it was all set   ready for them to come down I wish you could have seen it— I keep my silver & china *shining* & felt just a little pride as I sat at the head of the table in my pretty but old muslin with white Swiss waist trimmed with green ribbon & with my children looking nice & clean. I can tell you Mother it is no easy thing to keep *all* straight & right—house, husband, children & all, & sometimes I blame myself for not doing more than I do but I cannot without setting up nights to sew & that I find I *must* not do because I am sure to have a chill or be sick in some way if I do. They are to leave to-night. are you not glad for me? Good Bye— I wish you could see Frank— he is the admiration of every body besides his Mother!—so smiling & lively—the baby I mean, not the Mother. Good Bye—with much Love from Dr R——who is sitting by reading a paper & from all— Your daughter

T. B. Fox.

I have been reading my letter over—don't think I am pushed to death from what I have written—Am *generally* lazy & good for nothing but having had a little extra to do in the last few days had to tell about it

□ □ □

Dear Mother,   HOME AUG 3RD 1867.

I believe it is time for me to write again, though I have nothing new to say in the way of news, politics— neighbors, crops or weather. We still have *daily* showers, but we cannot complain of them for they keep us delightfully cool these warm summer days. The Crops look pretty well & promise fair notwithstanding the wet season— The rice crop is an excellent one throughout the parish— it has been extensively planted through the parish this year and is found to be more profitable than either cotton or sugar. The land is flooded through flood gates from the river and it requires but few labourers or mules to raise a fair crop; the expenses are estimated to be about 1/4 which you see is very little. New corn is just ripe, and we have our first load from our place— the tenant paying part of her rent by furnishing the Dr corn & fodder. I am afraid she will make a failure there this year. Last year she did well & paid quite promptly; so far, she has only paid $100..— there was one due in July which she is sending the corn & fodder for, & then there will be one hundred due at the end of the year. She may be able to pay it by raising sweet potatoes & other vegetables but I doubt it. The Dr says he expects he will have to take a mule or something of the kind for payment. He will rent it to white tenants next year; the negroes are too filthy and take no care of the house or premises. It is a nice little cottage house and looks quite home-like & inviting when properly cleaned & kept in order— it has a front gallery, 2 front rooms, 2 back rooms and a back gallery with one end closed in for a store-room   There is a good kitchen, chicken-house & barn & a large garden, in front & the same

[in] back besides the field of——acres[16] running back to the swamp—
The Dr thinks of renting the house & front garden to a white tenant &
the back premises to some one else or else cultivate it on shares. So
much for the lower place.— Perhaps it will be confiscated by this time
another year— there is no telling what those smart radicals will do in
the course of another twelve months. Is it not a glorious Union? I mean
that part of it, this is a *Union*— we poor rebs are kicked out now, & it
will be a good while before we knock for admittance again. The talk
here is to vote *no convention.* The Dr—says he would rather be governed by an intelligent military ruler than be in a state, governed by ignorant negroes, as Louisiana will be when we are readmitted.[17]

We have not been into town for some time— the cut-off is still impassable & the river road very bad. I do not care to go it is so very
warm, any where excepting here at home   The house stands so high &
is built with so many openings that you can always find a cool spot
some where in it & I dont keep any of the rooms shut up for
company— Always try to keep them in as good order as I can & if any
one comes I am not much frustrated.

Have been very smart this morning   Had the whole house swept
dusted   & *scrubbed,* breakfast cooked as usual, Dr R—— a linen suit
washed & ironed, dressed him in it, greased his hair, *pulled* his whiskers,
gave him a couple of crackers and sent him off for the day. Then made
a cake, superintended the cleaning of the dining room, took a bath,
combed my hair very *elaborately* & *fashionably   nursed my baby & here I
am*— Of course I had Milly & Emily to help & Fan, amused Frank
while I was busy & Emily washed her own clothes & the diapers. Milly
is to get us something to eat for dinner & clean the kitchen & then as I
laughingly told her she can play the rest of the day but "I'll be bound"
(did you ever hear that expression before)   She'll find something to
do, for she is the most industrious somebody I ever knew.— Georgy
has been unwell all week with influenza, accompanied with fever, he is
better to-ay than usual. Frank has recovered from his and is as jolly as

---

16. Tryphena left a blank space as if she intended to supply the number of acres later.
17. As a result of the Military Reconstruction Act of 1867, Louisiana became part of Mil-
    itary District No. 5, initially under the command of General Philip H. Sheridan, who
    was succeeded by General Winfield S. Hancock. The state regained admission to the
    Union on June 25, 1868. See Foner, *Reconstruction: America's Unfinished Revolution,
    1863–1877,* 307–8, 331–33.

ever again — the most frolicsome, laughing baby you can imagine — we call him "old Jolly".

Fanny is nearly well — I am quite so & the Dr as well as usual. His health is quite good this summer, in comparison with last, and I hope he will have no fevers this fall. His practice keeps him quite busy now — there are a good many cases of bilious fever which is very severe. He fears a great deal of sickness when the dry weather sets in. As I have scribbled my time out as well as my sheets, I must be off about my business — that is, mend my muslin to wear to-morrow & then try to finish F——s sunbonnet which I cut out yesterday evening & nearly made with Milly's help — I cut it out of that piece of green & white plaid gingham that you sent — it also made Frank a short low necked *slip*, and a josey. I made Georgy two shirts of the pink striped calico & Frank a nice full *dress* & josey. The early part of the week I sewed on Dr R——s nice black sack & finished a pretty purple calico for Frank — and made Georgy a new pr of pants out of the skirts of a dress coat — nice black summer cloth which was not at all worn — only stained with medicine & paint. I made it up the other side out & you have no idea how nice they look with his little embroidered shirt. Wednesday my birthday, I wrote to Grandma, a long letter. I thought of writing to you but the Dr came back from his usual trip quite early & was reading aloud to me & talking & I don't care to go off by myself & write when he is here.

SUNDAY EVE —

I have an opportunity of sending for stamps & mailing this so Good Bye — all well except Georgy who had another fever this morning but is out playing now — we shall have to give him quinine to-morrow. Love to G. & E. — Much to yourself. your aff. Daughter

T. B. Fox.

□ □ □

Dear Emma,   HYGIENE. AUG. 6TH 1867.

I hope this letter will give you as much pleasure to read and *obey* as it does me to write — A large package of letters from all my friends & the Drs, received this morning have gladdened me no little, but with all the pleasure there was a sharp *pain*, for from Mother's I leaned that you had gone back to Pontoosuc. and for what — a mere pittance and have to work so hard too & to be in such company! I ought to have helped you before—why cannot we see matters in their true light until nearly or quite too late? Mine are opened and not too late I hope, for this will soon reach you before you make yourself sick and as soon as you have read it, just quietly fold it up, and quietly fold your *parapharnalia* and quickly take yourself *home* and with the accompanying order, which I presume the Messrs Friends will take and which Dr R—— will pay before many days, procure yourself what clothing you need and remaining at home with Mother, & helping her make it up at your leisure. As Cotton Cloth is cheap now, I wish you would make yourself 4 fine bleached chemises and 2 or 3 good full underskirts. As you will have time, trim them all prettily with something pretty on the bands & sleeves. Put some little but heavy edges on the skirts, either crochet or tatting. I would also advise you to make 2 dark pretty calicoes & 3 nice night-gowns long & full, if you have no nice ones already it will take nearly or quite a bolt of cotton but as you can get it cheap now you had better spend 10 out of the 25. for underclothes, as I think it more or as necessary for one to have them as outsides. Have them ready so that *if there should* be an opportunity & *funds,* you can start to come to me, without much delay, and if I cannot have you with me, the things will not be amiss any where. Here, one needs a good many underclothes and I like to see pretty ones & servants always *respect* the *embroidered* or *trimmed* ones— The 25, is as much as you could earn in 3 mos, if I understand Mother about your wages 1.95 pr week, so you may consider yourself paid off, for that time. If then I cannot have you with me & cannot help you, we will see what is to be done, but I hope we can manage so that you will not have to put your foot in a factory again. Not that I think it necessarily degrading to work in one, but it is too hard for you and the company you find in one these days cannot be congenial. I hope the 25.. will be sufficient to fit you out quite respectably.

You must write often & tell me what you are doing and how you are getting along. Mother is too old now to do much, so you can help her for you & *me* too. All the pretty tatting and crocheted edging that you have made me I have trimmed mine & the children's clothes with and it has come very apropos, for I have had no time so far this summer to do any thing but plain sewing. Now I am at my leisure—that is, I can take up a piece of work & sew awhile & put it down without feeling that I must hurry its completion as there is something else just as much needed. I have on hand now a little embroidered shirt for Georgy which Eliza scalloped last winter but did not make and a nice white petticoat for Fanny. I am having Emily hem it, when there is nothing else for her to do and she hems very prettily when I baste, and also a pr. of fancy pillow-cases, which Milly is to sew up & hem, while I am to do the trimming. F——s skirt is to be nicely tucked & finished with fine serpentine braid on the bottom. I let them do the plain work on one piece while I work on something else. Fanny does not say lessons regularly now— she is not well & the days are most too warm to study much. They are all playing under the house this morning while I am writing— it is very cool & pleasant there. I had a fever on Sat. & another yesterday & took blue mass last night and am regaling myself with quinine this morning. Georgy has been very unwell for a week, and looks pale & puny, but I hope will improve now— I gave him quinine this morning— I dread giving it to the child— it is *so* bitter & leaves such an unpleasant taste in the mouth for such a long time after. The Dr makes it into pills for me so that I do not taste it. Besides two letters from Mother & one from George enclosing his photograph (you do not know how much I prize it, does it look like him?) I had an envelope from Aunt Randolph containing embroidered collar, cuffs, and bands for another shirt for her boy (G) one from Sister Emily & one from Eliza—was I not rich? & they all do me so much good, breaking in upon me like a group of pleasant guests & giving me new food for thought which is certainly most desirable here when our life is so monotonous particularly in the summer. In the winter we can go to the city & have our friends with us. & I love to live here & like it *as a home* in summer, for it is very pleasant here, but we need society—perhaps the plantations will change hands in a few years again, so that we may have neighbors as we used to do when I first came here. Good Bye— I must not write any more to *you* now or I shall neglect some of my other good correspondents. If there is any trouble about the order let me know immediately. I shall mail with this a letter to Mother containing a $5.. one-half of the $10.. which Dr R——sends to help pay the taxes. I mention it so she will be on the look-out for it. With much love I am as ever Your aff. Sister

T. B. Fox

Dear Mother,   SAT. MORNING. SEPT. 7TH 1867.

Enclosed you will find the other $5.. I received yours of Aug. 15th some time ago & ought to have answered sooner, but did not find any suitable time. A Mrs Hally an old neighbor who lived opposite when we first came back & whom I liked very much came unexpectedly and made me quite a long visit—from Tuesday the 27 until day before yesterday— of course she brought her baby now 21 mos. old & a servant— I enjoyed the visit from her very much but it was not as pleasant for her as she anticipated for the baby acted just as Fan did when I was with you & gave her mother a great deal of trouble & had two chills while they were here. She is a spoiled little thing and made Georgy stand out in fine contrast—for as she frequently remarked—"he is the best child I ever saw & Frank is the best baby". You say Frank must be a beautiful child— no I did not mean to write that, but is a good baby & very lively & extremely good-natured & has very fair skin & deep blue eyes & a fine shaped head but no one says what a beautiful baby as they used to do of Georgy. Both of them are still unwell— Frank has been free of fever since I wrote to Georgy until yesterday— it lasted him until daylight this morning— Georgy has had none for a week, but is very pale & feeble— I am giving him tonics. There is a great deal of sickness every where throughout the South-west— it was reported yesterday that 100 a day died in N. O. during the past week & the bayou people (back of us where Dr R —— sometimes goes) are dying at a fearful rate of a combination of diseases—malaria with cholera & congestive fevers. The Dr is run nearly to death here in his own beat but thinks of going over to-morrow for humanity's sake— I dread to have him go for he is not strong & those trips always make him sick.

We still have daily rains— the Dr says it is the most rainy season he has ever known here in 14 years— The rice crops which are about being gathered will be much injured. The cane looks & promises well. —

I received Uncle Brague's letter & will try to answer soon. Am sorry to hear that he is an Abolitionist & Radical— "if he only *knew*" he would not be— I am sorry not to hear from Emma   I am afraid she thought me too dictatorial— I am not disappointed with Georgy's photograph— I am very proud of it & proud to tell people "that is *my* brother "when they ask me who that fine looking young man is. I cannot stop to add more for this must go to the Office now to be mailed before the 10 o clock boat comes— The Dr is gone for all day   I wish you could come— I shall hear Fan's lessons & try to finish her petticoat & G——s fine shirt— As it too rainy & muddy to scrub, Milly will help me take care of Frank & cook our little dinner. I hardly know what yet for the garden produces nothing & I have only rice & macaroni besides the flour, lard, sugar, salt pork & fish of the store-room. I sent out & bought vegetables while Mrs H & Rose & Kate Wilkinson were with me & with fresh beef, duck & chickens managed to give them nice dinners & I have taught Milly to make *very fine rolls, light bread* & batter-cakes & pastry so she set a nice table all the time they were here—   I wish you could have a loaf of my bread   it is like baker's only *better*— Cant I brag?— Good Bye— Love to all— I have many little items to write but have not time. Write often. Next Friday is Fan's birth-day. If her father can leave to go to N. O. she is to have for birthday presents—a Bible from him, a Prayer Book from me— a plain gold ring from Georgy & a little pretty work-basket from Frank. George was 4 years old on Sunday last—the 1st of *Sept.*

[unsigned]

□ □ □

Dear Mother,   HOME. OCT. 8TH 1867.

I write to acknowledge your of Sept 19th containing the vaccine   it came the same day that I wrote to Emma & I was glad to hear that you were better. We are much obliged for the vaccine & presume it will take after-a-while— Frank seems to be a hard *case* & refuses to *take* so far but we shall try again. I am not in a letter writing mood to-night but am answering yours so as to ease my conscience for to-morrow is mail-day. Since receiving yours, I have often thought of the expression in your last—"I could not bring up another family of children" & well may you say it— I am probably only 1/4 the way through my journey or say 1/2 and even now I am very weary sometimes & look upon everything as a task. It is a great responsibility that girls unthinkingly take upon them-selves, and there is no shirking or shrinking from it— I expect more of myself because of the advantages I have had & so the thought is ever-before me— A daughter to be so brought up & taught that she may be a good & useful woman & two sons to be sent out, intelligent, high souled, honest, noble men fitted for some high position & I am constantly fearing that I am not doing my duty— But it is not their future welfare alone that occupies me— their everyday needs of the present moment must have attention and it is these which demand most time & patience & self-denial now—for what mother with a family of little ones has time or right for self-gratification? But I am not going to write you an essay on a mother's duties & rights, but will merely add that *I* for one mother have not played a tune upon the piano for weeks & written no letters for months almost—just a few hurried scrawls to one & another in answer to theirs. & I love both music & writing, you know.

All have been quite well since my last until to-day. Dr R— has been complaining all day & has gone to bed nearly sick. The truth is he needs *rest*—for the past six weeks he has been almost constantly on the road— fevers are abundant & almost every family has one or more member sick with fever, either bilious or intermittent— We have had no more cases of yellow fever in this vicinity. A few cases died about forty miles below— one of them spent a short time in town, went home & communicated it to the rest. We have had a terrible gale, farther below there was much damage done to crops, stock & buildings, while here it only kept us on the "qui-vive" wondering *if* the house would stand it— it shook a little once or twice but proved itself in the end a very solid & substantial shelter, though the rain did beat in at one place & wet my new parlor carpet pretty badly. — It had hardly cleared off yet. There must have been great suffering out at sea & we shall probably hear of many ship-wrecks.

The 'little world' of Hygiene moves on just about "so-so"— we had a nice hired man, whom both Dr R—— & myself liked very much— He worked hard & faithfully & would soon have had the premises in nice order, but all of the sudden yesterday morning without rhyme of reason, he rolled up his few new clothes which we had given him & *left*. The Dr had told him to bail out the skiff so that they could cross the river if the wind lulled but we suppose that as he did not understand English well that he mistook the Drs intentions & concluding that he could not cross, had better *leave*. I am very sorry for it thrown double duty on the Dr again—waiting upon himself & every body else too. Besides his waiting upon the Dr so nicely & knowing how to work the yard & garden he was a good *tailor* & one Saturday when he was too unwell to work out he took a little black sack coat for George to his room & made it all himself even buttonholes. All I did was to cut it out and the Dr told him that he might make a pr. of pantaloons for him the first rainy day. Now they are on my hands & I am so tired of sewing, but I have not very much to do this fall. My new black check is nearly done to-morrow's work will probably finish it— I made both sack & waist to it & gored the skirt & made that separate so that I can wear it with a white waist if I wish. Fanny has one more new calico to be made & a delaine to be altered & some joseys made for every day wear but they will not take me long. I gave out two chemises for myself to a poor woman who owes the Dr a bill & she is to make me two calicoes as soon as we can get the material from the city. At present no one ventures in unless absolutely necessary & Dr R——does not think it quite prudent to bring goods from there.

As I have come to the bottom of my sheet I will stop, though I could write much more now that I have "*got started*" —elegant expression, is it not?

Fanny has written quite a respectable letter to her Aunt just while I have been writing this— it is childish but well done & I should like to have you see it. Good Night & Good Bye

Love to Emma & George & yourself Your daughter

T. B. Fox.

□ □ □

Dear Mother, & all   [HYGIENE DEC 18TH 1867]

I have not heard from any of you in some time & am becoming quite anxious to hear from you. I see by the papers that you are having very cold weather & terrible storms. I am very sorry to hear it for we are having the most delightful weather & have had no *hard* frost yet. The doors & windows are all open, the fires all out, roses in bloom & self & children in their summer clothing, and it has been the same nearly all the fall & winter. I wish you could be here with me to enjoy the season. All are tolerably well. Dr R—— has been very unwell so that I have been much worried about him. He attributes his fever & prostration to dyspepsia, but I sometimes fear it may be something else— You know his mother died of quick consumption. Sometimes the future looks very dark to me for besides individual cares & anxieties, there is a feeling of doubt & anxiety in all minds occasioned by the terrible condition of *the whole country south*, & perhaps north too—*no crops, no businesses, no money* every body seems on the verge of distress. You perhaps will think *me* a little blue this morning, but I am not & have not as much reason to be *as others*.

The Dr——has had a good practice & will collect a greater part of it. We have plenty to eat, a home over our head & nearly enough clothing for a year & that ought to make one contented. There are many who do not know how they will get next year's living, having failed this year & run into debt trying to make cotton & other crops.

But as I have not much time this morning let me tell you how busy I have been & who have been my guests— *Brother Jimmy* from Ala——came on the 9 & returned the 10th. Then Mrs Guider & Mrs. Dyer & *Pa.* all came on last Wednesday's boat to my surprise for Pa. had written that he was not coming. Mrs G—— & Mrs D. only stayed over night & left on next day's boat. Pa stayed till Monday & I *enjoyed* the *visit from him very much*. Sunday morning we all *fixed up* (you know, what that means when a mother has herself & three children to dress & be off for a twelve miles ride by 8 o clock in the morning) & went to Dr Wilkinson's where Pa. held service christening the Dr's grandchild & *our boy*— just eleven months old that day. He behaved very well only persisted in trying to pull Pa-pa's spectacles off his nose while he held him. His being christened relieves me very much, for I think it the first duty of a parent.

Saturday I worked hard all day making cakes & pastry & preparing & partly cooking a *mammoth turkey*, for the next day, expecting to have service here & have Frank christened at home & have some friends stay to dine with us, but the gentlemen thought it best to have the service at Myrtle Grove as it was more central.[18] There was a number present, but mostly Dr W——s family & their near neighbors. Miss Logan is Frank's godmother by proxy as she could not be present.

Pa enjoyed the turkey for his two breakfasts & Sunday night supper & it was so large we have had turkey ever since. I thought of you often during all the time my guests were with me & I was bustling about & having good things for them & wished you were among them.

---

18. Myrtle Grove, originally a sugar plantation belonging to the Theodore S. Wilkinson family, covered some fifteen miles along the Mississippi river front. See J. Ben Meyer, *Plaquemines: The British Empire* (Laborde: Meyer, 1981), 60.

We are expecting the *Bishop* of La——down to stay over night with us the day after Christmas— He is anxious to get up a church here but I think it almost impossible— most of the whites are Catholics & the blacks nothing but shouters. Good Bye— Much Love to all of you. From Your Aff. daughter & Sister.

T. B. Fox.

The box has not come. Write soon.

□ □ □

HOME, Oct. 2ND 1868 4 O CLOCK P. M.

Dear Mother— As I have been thinking of you so far of the day I may as well humour myself a little & write awhile, although I came up hurriedly leaving the dinner things for Emily to clean & put away, for the purpose of mending a pr. of *socks* & *drawers* for my gude man— he having just put on his *last* of clean, whole ones. You see those two prs. over the chair, dontyou envy me those big holes in the seat? and then big holes in the socks & that basket behind my bed is full of them. You will wonder at my *laziness* maybe—but you would'nt if you had seen the three prs. I *darned* after eight last night, & the two prs of drawers I folded & put up for him about this time yesterday & then could see & hear this driving wind & pouring rain & see the wet things around the fire *trying* to dry. So you perceive it is not my good-for-nothingness this time & it wont take me long to scribble you a few lines & then I'll hurry & mend before he needs another change. He was called up at eleven last ng. to go across the river to visit a very sick lady & as it rained very hard there, he came home quite soaked. To-day he has been out until about an hour ago & came home again ditto; it is the last of the week & there are several suits in the dirty-clothes bag, so you do not wonder at his being out & my having to haul out *old* things? I had hoped not to have any more use for them; only I make over the best of the old socks for Frank & George. (Georgy has come in & is sitting beside me he says who are you writing to Ma ma—"? "Grandma". "Well, wont you tell her I say—"Please to come—?" Yes. well then suppose she says I am not able to come what then? The little fellow seems very anxious to see you; so far in his life he has seen but few of his relatives.

Your letter—one from Aunt Mary directed by Georgy, and one from Sister Emily Messenger all came to hand yesterday. I was very glad to hear that Emma had been confirmed— it has long been upon my mind. I wrote to her not long since & will try to do so again soon. The *pins* & *needles* were safe, Thank you m'a'm— how did you know that my paper of pins was just out & that I was grieving because I had forgotten to send by my Doctor to get some when he went to town? Having misplaced your letter I do not remember all the items in it to be answered but remember you seemed much shocked at F——s accident & "almost feared to open our letters lest they might give you some bad news," I do not wonder at it but there's nothing bad to tell you this time; the house shakes terribly in this strong wind, almost hurricane, and I *should not be surprised if it went over some day*—though it has stood some terrible gales & surprised me very much. It stands very high, & the strong east wind sweeps across the river & full against it, with unbroken force & sometimes I cannot help being somewhat alarmed. Perhaps you wonder how I happened to be thinking of you more than usual, because, I *did so* much wish you & G—— & E—— could come & dine with me & because I was my own cook for I am again without a servant as I wrote to Emma on Monday. Tuesday "Old Aunt Sally—the *elite* of the next plantation, and of the old Virginny stock, hearing of my inability to get any one volunteered her services & came & cooked dinner & washed for me & the next day cooked & ironed & yesterday cooked the breakfast & dinner & picked & cleaned my turkey & left early, expecting to come to day & cook it for me—but it has rained so hard, I suppose the old woman didn't like to venture out— She is a mighty wise old body and it seems like "old reb times" to have her in the kitchen calling me "Miss Blanche" & Dr R——"Mas'r Ramon." "You knows Miss Blanche—I would'nt cook for every body cause my son can *sport* me, but you knows I *would* come seein twas you & Mas'r Ramon." That is the way she apologized to her *pride*, & freedom when she came down the first morning. But I've gone off to Aunt Sally, when I intended to tell you about my nice dinner all prepared by myself & I can tell you I was quite proud of it when we all sat down & Dr R——said it was as nice a turkey as he ever saw or tasted   my first attempt you know— It was delicately browned & nicely seasoned & stuffed— the breast with rice & butter,—& the body with light bread & hominy thoroughly mixed & highly seasoned with onion, sage, pepper &c. &c. Then I had macaroni baked with cheese, stewed apples, rice plain, & sweet potatoes

& nice light bread—my own make too—but with all this cooking & fussing, Fan's lessons are going to the dogs & I never read or play a tune now & only write letters to you regularly; once in a while I manage some of Sister's letters, & my hands are getting so black & rough & my face so tanned that a stranger wouldn't think me the Dr's wife; only a servant; well as I cannot help it, I don't mind it & hope we shall live some day where we either can control or command labor, or where it is the fashion for ladies to do their own work— I heard yesterday that Milly's god-mother died on Tuesday & was buried Wed—so I suppose I shall soon hear from Milly— I have come to the conclusion I would rather have her than any one else & the Dr says he would if he does have to hire the washing extra for Milly is so much more like white folks than any other black one I can find— You know she is my scholar—not knowing anything when she came three years ago. But I believe I have told you this a good many times before.—

5 O CLOCK—

The Dr has gotten up from his nap, the children have all come up from the dining-room, through this soaking rain, & it is all noise & hurrah, so Good Bye for the present— I wish you could hear Frank say "Dorg'e'e"—Dor-g-e-e, calling Georgy from the steps, when he is in the yard— he whips Georgy & makes him mind as if two years the oldest.

FRIDAY NIGHT OCT 9TH

I did not think this would stay so long unfinished, but my thoughts & occupations have not been suitable for letterwriting this week. I am in more trouble than ever about a servant. Milly is in the neighborhood—has been since Tuesday. Last evening came to see me with a broad & smiling face *apparently* delighted to be here— Told me she would come & take the place on the 1st of Nov. I was *surprised* & very much *displeased* for I have kept her place for her & worked like a darkey rather than hire a fresh hand & *teach* them & I might have had one pretty well trained by this time, but Milly kept sending word that she would like the place & would be back as soon as possible. She is too independent—thinks I cannot get along without her & so stays up there in the Quarters, till the 1st of Nov, knowing I have no one upon whom I can rely to cook my next meal—*working* myself & waiting for her. So after a long struggle—last night, (for she *is* better than any of the rest of them) I sat down & wrote an advertisement to be put in a N. O. paper for a white woman & to-day wrote a note for Milly telling her to "come & take her things from the cabin as I do *not wish* to hire her *any more*"— If nothing happens I go to town next week to see what *I* can do in the way of *hiring*. Were I to wait till the first of Nov. for Milly she would probably put me off another month—for the *whole race* is *treacherous, difficult & unreliable*. Her Godmother died about the 1st, left her two lots in Algiers & a small house, with all new furniture & clothing so Milly will be of no account as a servant any more & would not probably stay more than a month or two anyhow & I might as well *wean* myself first as last. I suppose she will be much surprised at my resolution & letter for she bade me Good-Bye last night, in the best humour imaginable little dreaming what was passing in my mind at the time. I showed neither surprise nor displeasure when she told me.

The storm was terrible here— it lasted three days— We have no news from the sea yet— I hear that some portions of the city were flooded & much want & discomfort produced among the poor classes.

My carpet was so wet that I had to have it taken up & dried— & the rain was beat into several places in the house so that the rooms were damp & in many places badly wet. My parlor & spare-room are in disorder—my fall sewing quite behindhand but I hope all will turn out straight after a little.

Good Night   With much love   I think much about you as the cold winter creeps upon us. I fear we shall have a severe season as it is already very chilly here. Give much love to G. & E. & believe me as ever Your aff. Daughter

T. B. Fox.

□ □ □

SAT. EVE HOME FEB. 13TH. 1869.
Dear Mother— Though I do not feel in a letter-writing mood just now, yet I cannot let the day pass without a line to you, for to-morrow being Sunday I do not allow myself to write & there is no telling if I can take time next week. I have been reading over the 2 Suns that came together this week, and am surprised that there are so few names in them familiar

to me— Dr Todds[19] calls up his kind face & I see a few others, Mrs Justin Merrill among those) who are of old acquaintance but the rest are strangers. Yours of Feb. —came day before yesterday— that night I was sick & had to go to bed as soon as I came home & last night again could not summon energy to sit up & write so here it is Saturday afternoon & as usual I am hurrying, though I have not much else that ought to be done. You say you would not care to leave your old home & come to me & that I must come & see you— well perhaps I may this summer. The Dr has been very successful in making his collections & we are to have enough on hand to pay off the last of the debt to Brother Jimmy   He does not know yet what bargains he will be able to make for the coming year but I suppose they will be about the same as this last year— if so, I think it will not be extravagant or out of the way to make you a visit which I suppose will have to be early in the spring if at all—for this constant *nausea* & *chiliness* & feverishness & general good-for nothingness make me fear that I will not be at liberty to go & come as I would the latter part of the summer; still it may be nothing but a general debility after all & a trip somewhere may shake it off. For two weeks I have had a very bad cough seeming to come from the lower part of my chest keeping me hoarse all the time & much increased by exposure to the wind or the out-door air; still I think it is nothing more than sympathetic—would not have mentioned it if I had. Now for fear you will worry (*you* needn't, Dr R——*dont*— you know he is a good physician & understands the *sympathies* of *woman nature*, pretty well). I must tell you how relieved I am from house hold duties & cares. I have a *most excellent* woman & her daughter a light mulatress about 13 years old to do my work— the mother does the cooking, washing & ironing & anything else I need done) & the girl sets table, cleans the rooms & minds Frank when he wants to be down in the yard & garden. The husband is as black as the ace of spades, but fat & good-natured, waits upon the Dr & takes such good care of Dear Old Dick & Reb & the chickens & cow as they were never taken care of before. We pay them *three* $300.. pr year & give them their board & room rent, "Victor" 13,

---

19. John D. Todd, Doctor of Divinity, Congregationalist clergyman, served as president of the Maplewood Institute Board of Trustees and as a member of the school's board of examiners, in addition to his position as biblical science lecturer at the institute.

Celestine 10 & the girl Rosella 2, pr month. It is about the same as we have always paid, but we are waited upon 3 times as well as ever before— Celestine is a good cook & I am happy to write to you, quite equal to my *ideas* of *neatness* & *cleanliness,* in all her arrangements. Keeps my kitchen & dining room in such order that I am not afraid of soiling my dress by walking through them & does her work with that promptness & dispatch that I have often thought it might be done in. You ought to see what a great fat, muscular good natured somebody she is & see how she seems to want to please me— She has lived in N. O. all her life & understands her business well & has good judgement— can make & bake my bread & parch the coffee & make cake & pastry without my standing by to help & so far as they have been with me (for 3 weeks) I have found her perfectly honest—but I do not trust her yet in my store room— I have been so deceived in Milly that I shall never trust any other so again. I told Celestine to-day when I went down to show her my new way of making sweet-potatoe pies, that I wanted her to learn my measures & tastes so that I could leave her to keep house for the Dr while I made my mother a little visit— she said she'd try & I would nt feel so badly on leaving him knowing that I left someone at home, who could do his cooking as he likes it. But I have written all this & not told yet, that he & Georgy are not at home, that they have been gone since Monday to pay Pa a visit— The old gentleman was badly injured by the limb of a tree falling upon his *knee* & has been confined to bed ever since. There were no bones broken, but Mother wrote that he suffered the most intense pain from the sprain & bruises & that he was almost sleepless notwithstanding the copious use of anodynes & that they would all be so glad to have Dr R——come up; so he hurried through with his collections & I hurried through two complete & handsome suits for Georgy (which took me nearly a week shirts & all) & they started on the Monday's boat. I suppose they will be back if nothing happens on Monday next or at the outside on Wednesday. The days have seemed somewhat long, though I have tried to keep busy & have had company one afternoon & been visiting one. The mornings I have spent in the garden helping Victor— he spades & breaks up the beds while I plant & cover— I have since Tuesday planted 2 long rows of Irish potatoes, 2 of peas, 2 of green corn, 3 of spinach, some cucumbers, cabbages & beets & have some more ground ready to set out some cabbages in case of rain, which it looks very much like. So far I have not done much in the poultry line — Fan having a taste for domestic affairs rather looks after the eggs & chickens & she seems persevering & interested I let her have her own way — she has set two hens & is picking up eggs every day for a third. The Dr bought me a gobbler before he left, so I am going to try raising turkeys again. The old cow is surpassing herself since the Dr left & has given such quantities of milk that I have made butter twice about a lb. both times yesterday & to-day. Besides gardening I have been house cleaning some — Yesterday had all the cobwebs swept down (not a few) & all the bare floors scrubbed & *all* the furniture dusted & washed where needed & you ought to go through the establishment & see how nice it looks just for once. But I have done *no* sewing — for a whole week little Friend has stood unmoved & my work basket uncovered & I ought to be ashamed of myself too, for I need new night-gowns & Dr R——needs new shirts & it will soon be time to make the spring suits

When I have had a leisure moment I have been practicing "Rock me to sleep Mother" & reading "Barnaby Rudge"[20] which the Dr bought for me last week for company while he was gone. To show you how thoughtful he is & how he humors me — I said I wished I had a book of sermons to read on Sundays so when he was in the last time he brought me 3 — all excellent collections by good authors. Some are for Lent — you do not know how keenly I feel being deprived of all church companionship in keeping Lent & wish I could come home & spend it with you & in my native church. I suppose it is cold with you yet, while we have open windows & fireless grates & hearths excepting for a little while morning & evening.

Fan has had another holiday from lessons but still gets along tolerably well — is now busy reading her book Mary Gay[21] which came by mail Thursday. Frank is over in Celestine's room, with her & Rosella. I often look at Celestine & wonder why I could not have found such a woman before, for though Milly tried to please me, she did not know much & I had to be always teaching & showing. I was amused at Ce-

---

20. Charles Dickens published *Barnaby Rudge: A Tale of Riots of the 'Eighties* in 1841.
21. Dr. Fox allowed Fanny to order Jacob Abbot's *Mary Gay Work for Girls for Winter* (New York: Hurd & Houghton, 1867) and promised others from the four-volume series "if she would be a good girl." See TBHF to GH, January 26, 1869, MDAH.

lestine yesterday— I was telling Victor how anxious I was to get the seeds planted before another rain & all the cabbages & beets hoed & she not having much to do, just pitched into the garden & hoed away for dear life & soon had all that done & then helped me plant the corn— You know there are so few that will do that— they just want to do certain things for certain wages & no more & look terrible grum if anything else is demanded of them. I promised her I would each Rosella an hour every day as there is no school about here & she is very anxious that she should go to school & I call it worth $2 dollars more so that no one can say we do not pay her enough— That is generally the cry from somewhere, if you get a servant to suit you— Somebody puts it into their head to demand *more*— we have had it understood that we shall give no more— Oh how! I wish I could step in & spend the rest of the afternoon, for I feel very lonesome— Mrs Hally has gone on a visit to the city & I have no other neighbors excepting Mrs Wilkinson who is five miles away— It was she whom I went to visit the other evening— she has a second little son, only 13 mos. younger than the other— she is a nice little woman & promises to be more sociable when she gets up— Before they had no means of coming but have had a pair of horses given them recently I believe.

I suppose next week I shall have company to stay for a month or so— she that was Jenny Fox (now Mrs Shute—Dr R——s cousin & her husband— Dr R——tells me that the Shutes live in the finest style in N. O, but I know Jenny & *her* home so well that their coming will not put me out in the way of style & hope the visit will be pleasant to both of us.

The boat has passed— I had half hoped as I watched her slowly puffing this way, that the gude man & Georgy might be aboard, but now they cannot come home until Monday any how.

Ma ma Ma-ma (with a huge push of the stand) where's my little papa, *my* little papa & brudder Georgy— I forgot to tell you that *strangers* find a striking likeness, between Georgy's photograph, & Frank's Phiz & I believe if you were to see Frank you would almost think it your two year old baby.

The violets are all out— I send two & the jonquils too— & the clover is beautiful [. . .]

SUNDAY EVE.

Dr R——& Georgy both came safe & well on a little boat late last night, much to my surprise & joy. They left Pa, better & all the rest well & brought many tokens of love with them from our friends in that neighborhood   Aunt Randolph sent me a beautiful *snuffbox* (a relic in the family) containing a handsome gold *pin* for myself, a ring with *seven* pearls for Fanny & 2 gold shirt-studs for Georgy. Some books also & some from Mother.

Sister Em. has saved me many a stitch by giving Dr R—— a lot of nearly new shirts of Mr. Messengers—

You can hardly imagine my feelings on being told that he had *Mrs* Messenger's two wigs which had been handed to him to be disposed of in N. O. I started to undo the bundle & look at them but could not. How many times that stolid face & cold eye has looked at me from un-der that same unfeeling wig—old memories how they hang around cer-tain objects & only they will call them up.[22] All send much love— Mr. Hally who goes in to-morrow promises to take my letter so good Bye— Yours affectionately.

Blanche

Get a little *Sulphurick* of *Potash*—wash the *dog* in it 4 times, keep him tied up & he will soon get over his mange. First use soap & water— I am sorry to hear of [. . .] death— with love.

□ □ □

Dear Mother—   [SEPT. 7TH 1869]

Your very short but welcome letter reached me Sat. A. M. & as the mail will probably go up to-morrow, I will try to write you a few lines in return. We have had a touch of gale, which we feel has been terrible out at sea, & below us but have not been able to hear yet. We only know that at "Pointe a la Hache"—a settlement 40 miles below   the water was from 2 to 7 feet high all over the cultivated portions of the land & that the rice planters have lost their entire rice crops, some just gathered & stacked, others still unreaped. Many lost all their stock, chickens, &c &c & had the lower parts of their houses inundated: here the storms

---

22. This seems to refer to tensions created in 1858 when Harriet Mead made remarks about the Holder and Fox families while working as a tutor for the Messengers. The comments annoyed Tryphena, who told her mother to ignore Mrs. Messenger's "haughtiness." See TBHF to ARH, June 13, 1858, MDAH.

began about midnight sat night & lasted all through Sunday & Sunday night incresing in violence until about 10 P. M. Sunday. Monday morning it turned off as clear & calm as though there had been no sign of wind or rain. The bath-house, wharf & skiff were utterly demolished & thrown up on shore near the next neighbors— fortunately for us, our levee is low, so we suffered from no fear of breakage there. We always feel somewhat concerned about the house as it stands so high & exposed— it stood firm until about noon Sunday when I felt it tremble a little   The rain beat in at every possible crevice—soaked the parlor floor & so dampened the mortar in the spare-room as to cause it to fall from a large place under the window a yard square. The mosquito-house on the gallery had all the netting torn off so that it is of no further use this year; but it is so late in the season we shall not be troubled much more with mosquitoes. I regret the loss of the bath-house on the children's account— they used to have such nice frolics there every day.

As the Dr needs a skiff as much as his buggy he had to send for a carpenter to have the one repaired which has been lying useless under the house for a long time. It was a present from Mr Robinson, but as he has just built a new one & did not need two he kept it there out of wind & weather & it comes in play now, you can imagine. He is still very busy with sick folks & has but very little leisure for rest or home affairs. Our meals are terribly irregular & it keeps some one busy looking out for his clothes, comfort & welfare generally. You say you would do the work yourself before being troubled with these helps— I could not do it & put up & dont see many an *insult* rather than not have them to do menial service of such an establishment as this. Celestine is a *good worker,* so I tell her what I want done & keep away from her, & have less trouble than almost any other lady in the neighborhood. Mrs Hally is still without a servant, having had about a dozen in the past six months. One must'nt be too particular & stand on having things just one's own way— for instance—I like the cow milked about 1/2 past five, so I can have fresh milk for the children's supper (as milk turns quickly in this climate) & Victor knows it, but it is often 1/2 past six & 7 before I can get a drop, without making a fuss & rather than do that I pacify the children & get along the best I can, often giving Frank his cup full in bed. Celestine knows the Dr likes early breakfast always when he is here, but it is often nearer 8 than 7, when we get it. I could tell you of many curious freaks, but it would only make you out of patience & worry while they do not affect me in the least. I teach & sew & help keep my house & children clean & wait on my gude man & attend to my side of the business & leave the cooking & washing & scrubbing & dishes & ironing to her & Rosella & dont bother my head with it or them. But it is so dark I cannot see, so Good Bye till morning.

TUESDAY NIGHT SEPT. 7TH.

Morning came & found me busy till lesson-time & after that dinner & then I was too tired to write—threw myself on the bed for awhile & then bathed, dressed & mended & fixed for Dr R——s two days trip to town. He came home late, helped him make a "lot of medicine, then came up & put the children to bed &c &c & it is now nine & I am *again* tired so you'll have to excuse any thing more. Have had letters from Pa & Lucy: the latter talks some of coming to stay with me— Sister Emily is to be married about the 1st of Oct I suppose; my frolic will probably come off about the same time.[23] The Dr will send you off a P. O. order for $10.. while he is in the city— Tell Georgy many thanks for his nice long letter & the photograph. I like to be kept familiar with his *phiz*, for I should nt have an idea of his looks otherwise. The Dr says "he has a good face & gaps at him long & admiringly—but you need'nt tell him that—

With much love to you both I am as ever   Your Aff. daughter

T. B. Fox.

□ □ □

Dear Mother,   HYGIENE NOV. 4TH 1869.

Babe is one month & a day old and I wrote to you soon after her birth but have received no tidings from you in all that time & am growing anxious to hear from you. Both of us are quite well & doing finely, only we are so delicate & weak— I am good for nothing excepting to eat & sometimes dont care to do that & baby is still too feeble to suck & has to be fed with a spoon; so far I have given but little milk but hope to do better after a little. The others are all well. Dr Raymond & Lucy left for the city before day-light this morning, Lucy having been with me, nearly three weeks— I cannot tell you how much I have enjoyed her

---

23. Tryphena was pregnant with her sixth child, Blanche Cleveland, born October 4, 1869.

company & how loth I was to part with her nor can I give you an idea
how lost & lonesome I have felt to-day. As she came when baby was
nine days old & I did not need her as nurse or to help keep house, I
insisted upon her playing visitor & made her visit as pleasant as possible
for she has had a hard time at home this summer; fighting want & nursing an invalid daughter & consumptive son-in-law & taking exclusive
care of their little one—a son of premature birth that has been able to
nurse but very little & of course had to be fed night & day. She is very
fond of oysters & you ought to have seen Dr Raymond's endeavour to
provide them for her. We had fresh beef twice a week & I had 2 of my
turkeys killed & gave her chicken quite often. The housekeeping did
not progress very smoothly while she was here   The washing & ironing were constantly behindhand the house not kept at all in order & the
breakfasts were very late, but as I could not help & saw no use in fretting I let matters jog along as they would content if we all had enough
to eat & the beds were made sometime during the day. Rosella was sick
quite often, with chill & fever & had not nurse Rachel taken it upon
herself to clean the bedrooms, they would have gone unswept & un-
dusted many a day. Celestine is a good worker when I am about & can
be *head* for her, but not worth much to go a head for herself. I was
astonished & often worried to see & hear how behindhand the work
down stairs was, when it all goes on in such good order when I am
about, although I do not raise my hand to do a thing down there. But
it is all over now & on the whole it is the most pleasant month of confinement to look back upon that I ever spent. I was in too big a hurry to
go down when baby was only 18 days old, which gave me a severe back-
set, which kept me in my room all that week & from which I am not
entirely well yet. Dr Raymond has been very kind & attentive & I have
felt so differently from what I did after Frank's birth that I cannot be
thankful enough for having been spared a repetition of what I suffered
then, both bodily & mentally. His prescription now is ten drops of iron
3 times a day & a wine glass full of sherry; of course I enjoy the latter
very much & hope soon to be as strong & hearty as a mother of four
"youngsters" ought to be.

Fan has done so well, that I am quite proud of her & yet it seems as
if her faults were more glaring while her aunt was here, than ever
before—one fault above all others is her heedlessness, but I suppose she

is like most other girls of that age & I hope she will outlive it; I can't say out-grow for she is almost as tall as I am already. Both hers & Georgy's lessons have been altogether neglected so I suppose as my holiday is over, that I must buckle on my harness again next Monday & assume old duties, which I dread no little — a good deal of sewing stares me in the face, but I hope with the aid of the machine & long evenings to be able to get through with it, in spite of a new baby. At present she sleeps most of the time, but the naps will grow shorter & shorter, so I shall have to improve the time now while she is so young.

She has no name yet — we have talked of several — I wanted to name her 'Blanche Raymond' (making Raymond a family name but her father never did like his name & says no) then I have thought of naming her 'Blanche Cleveland,' the *latter after grandma*, & 'Emma *Cleveland*' & Blanche Angell (this being Pa's mother's family name, but we only talk them over & can come to no decision. Emma, was the name of Pa's second wife who ws a true mother to Dr Raymond & I think it would be paying Pa a compliment as well as all the girls who idolize the memory of their mother to name her Emma & all of whom I love very much, though I do not like either of their names Lucy, Emily, & Eliza sufficiently to name my baby after them — then too, it being my only sister's name makes it a preferable one, though I cannot say that I like the name itself very much. I think Dr R——likes the name of Blanche Cleveland best, but he will not say & always leaves the matter entirely with me. Which do you like? I thought of Blanche, because he & all his friends have always called me that & I wanted the name *legitimized*; having always somewhat regretted being *called* so, when not christened so. Frank is as delighted with her as at first & will allow no one to monopolize her but himself. Fan grabs her up at every chance & often gives me the fidgets, fearing some accident will happen from her heedlessness.

I received Emma's letter about a week ago, but wont promise to answer it for fear I might break my promise — Give her much love & tell her to write to me — as long as she has n't four chicks to look after, besides the darkeys, & turkeys, & husband's old coat & breeches which need mending & *cleaning* right often.

Tell Georgy "howdy" (the Southern for how de do) for me & *command* him to write also & all of you be sure I want to see you just a little & would come & spend this pleasant afternoon with you if possible.

With much love for yourself & all of our friends I must bid you Good Bye for this time. Your Affectionate Daughter.

T. B. Fox.

I saw the notice of your plants & premiums in the Sun & was pleased for you.

Seeds of magnolia, a little shrub when Fanny was a baby — 20 feet high now.

□ □ □

My Dear Mother,   [THURSDAY DEC 30TH 1869.]

I know I have done very shabbily in not writing but I could n't. The day after my last to you Celestine *left suddenly* taking Rosella with her, without any *provocation from* me or *notification to* me. My baby lacked a day of being a month old. Every other negro woman in the neighborhood that *could* be spared from her own family, had engaged herself to work in the cane fields during the taking off, of the crop at 75 cts pr. day. The Dr would have given it but we searched the coast up & down — & for a week we could not get a soul to wait upon us — A mulatress near took my washing & ironing home & Fan & I & *The Dr* managed to get something to eat & keep the baby from crying — no we didn't for the little thing took cold the next day but one after & had a rising in both ears which fretted the little thing terribly — they are not well yet. After a week the Dr succeeded in getting a woman to come & do anything I needed cooking house work &c &c, until I could find some one — She did tolerably well, but proved too much of a *lady* to suit the Dr   She could n't get up till long after daylight, could n't *scrub*, could n't wash a few pieces & cook dinner too, so that I had just about as much to do as before she came & the Dr got all out of patience with her. If we had been giving her, her board & a much obliged to you every night, it would have done but we paid her $8 dollars pr. month — & she had no washing to do only one day I wanted her to do up a few pieces for Fanny who was going to a party the next day & the common diapers for the *baby*. So at the end of the month as she thought the work too hard for her (Fan & I cleaned up nearly all the house) we parted, good friends, for I could not help her any more & thought I might as well try some one else. Milly used to do the cooking half the housework, all the ironing & then nurse Georgy for me every evening except ironing day & Saturday & this woman never found time to hold her excepting while I *bolted down* or sat down for a meal. The last week of her stay Jimmy & his wife & two children & servant came & you can imagine I had my hands full. They only stayed from Sat. Eve. till Tuesday. I thought they would stay a week or two but I expect Jimmy left sooner than he would when he found how I was situated   The woman knew nothing about cooking excepting a few plain dishes so I attended to all the roast meats fowls & soups and cooked all the oysters myself; for I was determined to set a nice table for him, if I could n't keep the house clean & in order. Fanny (his wife) seemed to enjoy her visit & I was sorry they would not stay longer if it did give me a little more to do. The woman left the next day & I was again alone, only Fanny is equal to *two darkies* any day; can cook as nice a breakfast as you ever ate & put a room in as nice order, but of course being nothing but a child in strength I would not let her overtask herself—as it was, she did too much & had a very sore throat which laid her up for two days & was seriously threatened with *quinsy.* We had promised to let her spend the holidays in the city with Alice & as she had looked forward to it for so long I could not disappoint her though her father said he did not see how I was to get along without her. Her clothes were unmade & she had nothing fit to be seen in, but by hiring a woman from the next place last week (the day after they finished grinding) to help about the work & another to help me sew & baste for the machine & ask a little help from Mrs Hally who thinks almost as much as I do of Fan we managed to get her ready. Made her two new chemises   1 pr new drawers, a new flannel skirt, put new bands on two cotton ones, finished off her scotch plain which had been begun some time & was all *flounces* & ruffles, made her a white alapacca waist trimmed with folds of the same & blue velvet, & made her a new black sack, with belt trimmed all around with two rows of *blk* velvet to wear with a red & blk plaid skirt for a traveling dress; hired another woman (her old nurse Mary Cox) to do up all her underclothes & had her all ready by Friday at 12—*packed* & off, did not commence till Tuesday the 21st—sat up 2 night till 12—was n't I smart? Her father goes up on the Bradish Johnson for her to-day—to return to-morrow   takes Georgy with him   Matters jog more smoothly with me as Rosaline a very good woman comes down from New Hope every day & waits on me till about 5— she has a husband working there or I would try to hire her for next year. she is sensible as any of them & works quick & willingly & is good to the children. Yesterday she scrubbed my room & the dining room—which were terribly dirty & to-day is cleaning the spare room & hall which are *ditto.* The Dr. & Fan being gone on Christmas, & it being a dark & rather stormy day & Mary Cox's baby being too sick for her to come & cook my Christmas dinner as she had promised, I laid my turkey on the *top shelf* & I went up & dined with Mrs Hally, Mr Hally coming in his carriage for me himself— it sprinkled a little & rained hard after we got there & baby took cold & has had sore eyes ever since. Dr R——came from town & stopped & took a late dinner that Mrs H had saved for him for I had *nothing* cooked down here & then we all came home. He brought a little Santa Claus with him; but it did n't seem at all like Christmas. He bought Georgy a nice *stereoscope,* & a pocket-comb with a looking-glass in it, Frank a little cart & a trumpet, & his wife a handsome Alfinide butter-dish & a new *silver thimble* as mine which he gave me when we were first married was worn & bent & hurt my finger as he had heard me say a few days before. Cousin John sent me a beautiful powder box with puff & Jimmy had left *each* of the children a beautiful silver spoon to be marked with their initials & presented at Christmas— then came one for F. O. F., one for G. R. F.   F. C. F & B. C. F. so you see the baby is named Blanche Cleveland— the latter *in* compliment to Dear Grandma as I could not call her Tryphena   Emma's letter of the 23rd has been just handed in— The boat is in sight so I cannot write much more, only tell you how hard I have tried to harden myself & do my own work by putting the washing & ironing out but it is useless to try. I am not a hardy plant certain the first week by myself I had fever after 4 days *exercise,* this last time, had an attack of erysipelas & you ought to see my hand where the Dr. had to scarify & cauterize the "pustule malign" as the French call it— it is all sore & black. The poison had gone to my arm-pit but was stopped by the cauterizing & my arm is better to-day— Will write again soon   Please say to Mrs Merrill to write to Hannah to be sure to come & spend some time with me— please send me her address— With Love to *all* in haste— Your daughter—

                                                              T. B. Fox.

HYGIENE FEB. 10 [1870]

Dear Mother— Having a little more leisure now-a-days, theres no excuse for my not writing to you oftener.

Yours of Jan. 28th reached me a few days ago & though short was
very welcome, for I am always very glad to hear from you & thinking of
you so much as I do, a *line* is sometimes sufficient to alleviate the homesickness & break up the monotony of my country life. It is now almost
a year since I have been out any where, or had much pleasant to occur
& ever since baby's birth my life has been all hurly burly, until I had
almost begun to think that a home & a family were not the treasures I
had always thought them, after all. At present we are all very well &
matters jog along quite smoothly though a little *strangely*. I say
strangely because it seems odd to have a *man* serving about the house &
it certainly was a novelty to me, to be able to call upon *someone* to come
& take the baby. You write that you hope that I have good *help* & I am
very happy to write that I think we have. The English people whom I
write to *Georgy* about (I hope he has the letter before this) have turned
out to be quite good helps though not what the Dr hired them for. The
man after 3 weeks trial could not do the Drs. work, so as the Dr had
concluded to look for some one else & "ship him" & as we needed a
cook, washer & ironer & as his wife was too feeble to do that I told him
I thought he had better go to the city & look for a situation suitable for
himself as dining-room waiter; he replied that he would rather not look
for another place that he had been out of work for a long time, that he
liked here & intimated that he would take less & do what he could. That
same day Old Peter (the old Negro who has been doing the Drs work
off & on ever since Victor[24] left came to me with a long story about the
man who was hiring him would not let him & his old wife stay there
any longer, if he did n't stop coming here to wait on the Dr, so I

24. Dr. Fox discharged Victor in September 1869. Tryphena described the interaction
between Vcitor and Dr. Fox when she wrote: "The man whom we have is very often
contrary & impudent to him & cross to his horses which is a serious thing with him.
Old Dick is nearly as dear to him as one of his children & he has not thrived well this
summer—has been lamed twice in some unaccountable manner (I think Victor
struck him & ran him out of the stable too fast one rainy day & his foot slipped on
the planks in front of the stable door, which slant down.). The Dr. has not been able
to drive him for two weeks & the roads are heavy & the calls numerous Just now. He
dont care to drive Dick much anyhow but he can go short rides which rests Rebel."
TBHF to ARH, September 28, 1869, August 6, 1869, MDAH.

thought the matter over & as the Dr had left in the morning for me to
settle with Wm during the day, just concluded to change all around—
hired Peter for $8.. pr. month to do the Dr.s. work—attend to horses,
cows, stable, buggy, *boots*   orange trees   garden at lower place, skiff,
row across the river cut the wood & bring water &c &c
&c——s Offered Wm & Martha $12.. to stay (he *jumped* at the offer)
& Wm to do the cooking, dining-room & *office* work, & gardening &
any job I needed done such as scrubbing, washing windows, cleaning
furniture, &c &c. & Martha to nurse baby & keep the parlor & bedrooms clean. Nan still takes the washing & ironing home for $5.. pr.
month, so we pay out $25.. pr. month for servants hire & are better
waited on than we expected to be at $30. for the Dr thought we would
have to pay these people $25.. pr. month & $5.. for a housegirl   Perhaps you wonder how we can have so much to do—with so small a family; well I cant tell you, unless you could be here & see how for yourself.
All I know is, that I was nearly worn out *trying* to do & then after working so hard all day. I could not see that I had accomplished much of
anything. Wm is a tolerably good cook, though I have to notice him
more than I would like, for he has evidently been brought upby slovenly people, is a very good dining room hand & a tolerable gardener—
 he is apt to *slight* every thing, but "where *are* we to find *perfection* in
servants if it is not to be in superiors"? & *I* have lived long enough to
find that one needn't look for it— *The Dr is not quite of my mind & seems*
to think that a servant is the very one to do everything in the right way, the
right time & the right place & does n't know how to forgive if they dont. — if
you will notice those lines carefully, you will understand where the
trouble is in our household & will no longer *wonder* if as Emma wrote
I am fretty—for I am not. For peace sake, I often stand between him &
them & take their part to him & then turn around & take his to them,
for he does fret most unnecessary sometimes—but as I told you before,
not at me. He has much to worry him outside, sick patients, contrary
patients & patients *friends,* who you know always advise something
contrary to what the Dr has left— he is often gone all day without a
mouthful to eat, of course it is very natural for him to feel irritable when
he comes home & perhaps speak sharply to any one, particularly if they
have n't done as he wished during his absence. *I know how he feels,* but a
servant dont or wont & of course feels that the "Dr is cross for noth-

ing". Old Peter is about the only one whom the Dr can get along with & you dont know how glad I am to have secured his services— The Dr & Wm never could have 'gee'd' for they had already had a falling out— for Wm slighted washing the horses feet one night, when the Dr drove home late & they were terribly muddy & he neglected giving them hay when he fed two or three times, &c. &c. &c. Of course the Dr did not feel very pleasant about it & *spoke* as he *felt* & Wm was mad & refused to eat any supper— He does a good many things wrong & backwards for me, but you know a woman has a different way of governing & *finding fault* from what a man has— as for scolding I gave up that long ago & not to boast or brag, I never have had much trouble with any of our servants since I came from the Confederacy & would n't have had with Celestine if it had n't been for Victor who was certainly the worst piece I ever dealt with. This Wm is about like that Lorenzo we used to have & seems to like me very much & runs his legs off to wait on me. Martha is a nice body but too feeble to do much more than light work such as I can do, but she is just the woman I want & says she wants to stay with me the rest of her life. It is so much better than having darkies to watch & look after. I can trust her to take my keys & go to the store-room & attend to my milk without feeling that perhaps she will help herself to a bowlful of sugar at the same time she gets mine or take a pint of milk for herself & put the rest away for me. Things go along so smoothly that I hope the Dr will not feel fretted anymore with home affairs for a long time & I shall be able to resume my duties which have been much neglected of late— The children have gone back to their books & hope to *grease & start my machine* next Monday. Another thing I forgot to tell you which is a great gratification to me— Both Wm & Martha are *good* to *all* the children & make much of *Frank* particularly, & keep a little watch for him, down in the yard, when I am in school with the others, & then I feel so much easier when this woman has the baby than I would trust her to a darkey & perhaps a young careless one at that.[25]

There has been a great deal of smallpox all around us & as the Dr was constantly called on to see some of the cases, he thought it best to vac-

---

25. According to Tryphena, Celestine did not "take that Motherly care" of the children, "who did not like her very much." Besides, she was "very domineering" to Fanny, who wanted to bake cakes and cookies. Tryphena kept Fanny away from the kitchen and Celestine to avoid tension. See TBHF to ARH, May 24, 1869, MDAH.

cinate the baby, which he did on both legs & made very bad sores, but they are nearly well now & so is her head which has been very sore— her ears run a little yet, but do not seem to pain her & she is getting fat & hearty & begins to look like a decent baby. I am obliged to feed her entirely now. There have been a few nights since her birth that I have been able to nurse her enough to satisfy her until day-light, but not many. I am generally up & broken of my rest an hour or more. Up in bed for the Dr never lets me get out on the floor; he gets up & makes up the fire & warms her milk himself. I hope now to have more appetite & perhaps have more milk— we are to go to the city as soon as the roads will permit.

I have no news to tell you. Hygiene is my world & what transpires outside I know but little of. Our neighbors Mr & Mrs Hally moved into the city on the 1st thus depriving me of my only near neighbor.

I had a nice long letter from Hannah M——a few days ago which was a very pleasant surprise though I was sorry to learn that she could not come see me.

I forgot to tell you that *I* sold $19.. worth of *turkeys*— aren't I getting to be an old market woman indeed. We milk three cows now & I make all our butter & sell all the skim milk for *5 cts a quart. Have lots* of eggs & have to set over *100.* Also 13 duck eggs. Have 8 turkey hens & 4 gobblers for $3. As I could not send you a turkey for your Christmas dinner, I send you the $2.. in the place of it— I sold the hens for $2 & the gobblers for $3.

Have that dress made & come & make me a visit some of these pleasant spring days. I want you to see all my *babies* (Fan is as tall as I am) & I want to *talk.* I shall not be able to come home this summer. The Dr's practice will not allow of our travelling or being extravagant. He is anxious to lay up some thing every year & buy a house & lot in town so we can live there when the children are older.

Good night— I will try to add a few lines before the mail goes out. If the Dr could afford it, he says he would send money to Emma for her to come & stay with me if she would like to, but he does not feel as though he could spare the $100. this spring—he has to put up a cistern which will cost about $120, & make some improvements in the fences which are tumbling down on the south & west sides. I hope he will feel able to

send for her by next year, though I do not think it would be very pleasant for her here, particularly after the novelty of the place had worn off.

You see I have forgotten how to mind—but I was so anxious to have
one baby named after Grandma— you'll have to excuse my disobedi-
ence this time. Give much love to her & to *all* when you see them. Tell
Georgy about the long letter I wrote him, in answer to the one containing the earrings. One of my ears grew up in the Confederacy. It was
made sore by my wearing my pearl earrings to a party—forcing one in
& taking a little cold in it, which brought on a violent attack of erysi-
pelas, which had affected that whole side of my head & face, when Dr
R——became alarmed & ran a streak of caustic from the part of my hair;
down through the middle of my face, under my chin, & around my
neck, & at the same time gave me active internal remedies— I was very
sick for a few days, but he managed to conquer it & you ought to have
seen my face— there is a scar from my mouth under my chin now, quite
plain, when I am a little unwell.

Well I must n't *gas* any more for I have Hannah's letter to answer,
Hattie Dewey's & Sisters Em's (she that was Mrs Messenger), &
Eliza— Dr R——is opposite writing to Pa & Lucy— her son-in law
died, after a long illness & confinement of consumption on the 2nd of
February—thus leaving her daughter only 18 now, a widow with only
one child & she has had a sad time ever since her marriage   With much
love for yourself G & Emma I am as ever Your Daughter.

T. B. Fox.

□ □ □

Dear Mother,   JULY 19TH 1870.

Yours of the 11th reached me yesterday & relieved me very much; I
was becoming very anxious to hear from you, it being over a month
since I had heard. I feared you were sick & was not surprised on reading
your letter to find that you had been & was glad you were better. I have
not written for a long time & feel ashamed of myself for not doing so;
not that I have been idle but I might have neglected some of these mul-
tifarious home duties & devoted a little while to you; I have been hoping *the leisure would come* & hurrying to arrive at it, but it is like the blue
lake in the story book that deceived the little ones, still far in the distance
matters are jogging along a little more smoothly now & I will add

satisfactorily than for a long time before—(since Wm & Martha were fully established & before they fell back into their old previous habit of drinking, which must have been the secret of their poverty & distress. After they had been doing well about three weeks they began to take a little more & a little more until we could do nothing with them.

I shall not write you a very long or readable letter for these *chiluns* & the Dr bother me & talk to me constantly— it is so all the time; there is never an hour I can call my own till after eight & then I am completely worn out & ready for bed instead of anything else though I often *have* to sew as *I did* last night—work the button-holes to G——s new suit, so he could have it to put on his others being all dirty & out to the washer woman & she never brings anything home until Friday or Sat. Well *thank fortune*, I am almost done all the worry now for all have suits enough to keep decent. The Dr found I could not swim through & get to his drawer to fill it & so went to the city & bought ready-made a black alpaca coat, two shirts, & two prs drawers (the first of the latter he has bought since our marriage) & for which I was not sorry, buying the coat saved my making two linen ones—but enough of clothes— you'll think it is all I think of or do but it is n't— We are all well now & you ought to see how the baby is growing & coming out—has one tooth just through—has on short clothes at last & is very proud of her little shoes. The Dr is not very busy so you may know it is remarkably healthy for this season— I see by the papers that you Northern people are enjoying excessively hot weather   you will doubtless be surprised to learn that we have managed to keep cool this far, though it has been a warmer summer here than for several years—at present we are having frequent showers & the crops are looking & promising very well.

All of Pa's family are well— Jimmy has another little daughter— did I tell you they lost their youngest a little son, just after they left here? it was a terrible blow to both him & Fanny as they almost idolized the child

Lucy has given up coming to us this summer I suppose— I have not written to any of them for a long time—had a letter from Emily last night— She & the Dr were going to celebrate the anniversary of their engagement day by a big dinner on the 12th & wished I could be there[26]— Next to a trip home, nothing would please me more than a visit to Baconham & I would not be surprised if I made a visit there before the year is out.— though how I am to leave home to go any where is more than I can see. Like all children I sometimes get tired & think a little variety would do ever so much good but the mood dont last long— I am only too thankful to have a pleasant, comfortable home, a good, thoughtful husband & dear, healthy obedient children to allow myself to be discontented

At present I have two helps—both negro girls about sixteen — both *very* slovenly & careless & prone to be idle & yet very good girls for blacks— one has been nursing children all her life but has never lived in a genteel family until Mrs Wilkenson took her about two years ago   she suits me tolerably as a nurse & house-girl— The other was never in side *"white folks house" until she came here about a month ago,* so you can imagine what a *watchful* time I have had for the last month & *how much* I have had to do myself—yet she does pretty well is strong & stout & healthy & can wash clean & scrub the floors well & has learned to cook a good many things & learned to manage my new Charter Oak so that I am not afraid to leave her with it two hours by herself while I teach the children   Then I go down to see how she & the dinner are coming on & cook any additional dish I think desirable. Is it not a little singular that *her* name too should be Milly? I do hope she may prove as good as my old Milly, though she has not the same kind disposition & is inclined to be deceptive & *thievish*— Saturday I left the cookies for her to bake; which she did & kept 3 for herself—was in the habit of keeping back some of the biscuits & the batter cakes but I believe I have about talked & shamed her out of that   always give her plenty of every thing we have but tell her if she does so & so again I wont give her any.

well that is enough for her—only—her father has given her into my hands as long as I want her provided I will teach her to cook, wash & iron & be a good house servant— I find her better then nobody & *much better* than some old, hard headed, impudent, stealing woman whom I

---

26. James A. Fox had written that his daughter Emily Fox Messenger was engaged to a Dr. Howard and planned to marry in the fall of 1869. See TBHF to ARH, August 6, 1869, MDAH.

couldn't manage — this one is easily governed only she requires a great deal of noticing or she forgets or is sure to do something backwards or up side down.

I have made *no* visits & seen no callers for a long, long time. The Dr is so kind as to take magazines & papers for me & buy me nice books but they often lie untouched for the want of time— He still reads aloud to me so I manage to keep posted on the current affairs of the day.

I must not forget to tell you of the *delicious peaches,* which we are & have been enjoying for a month— two that were gathered yesterday were perfect & measured 8 1/2 & 8 3/4 *inches in circumference*— large yellow juicy freestones! The tree hung quite full— they are most all gone now but there are plenty more almost ripe   the figs too are ripe & plentiful & I never have a plate full that I do not wish I could hand it over to you   We have had a few melons & cantaloupes which were very nice. The Dr planted none as he had not room for them but his patients & friends keep him supplied

The garden don't amount to much just now. There are beans beets & tomatoes plenty & a few cabbages— that is about all. I have good luck with turkeys— have 7 old + 32 half grown + 3 1/3 grown + 14 young = 56 & about as many chickens old & young.

When you go to grandma's give her much love for me & tell her I want to be there too, but am afraid I never shall be— With much love to all others & particularly the home-folks— you & G. & E. believe me as ever— Your Daughter

T. B. F.

□ □ □

Dear Mother,   [DECEMBER 28, 1872] THURSDAY A. M.[27]

Now that the excitement & frolic are over, I must write you a few lines to tell you of our happiness & the many wishes we all uttered & thought that you might be with us. I hope it was a merry Christmas for you all & your absence alone prevented it from being a Merry Christmas for us. The *box* arrived safely *just in time*— it was delayed somewhere & I looked in vain by every steamboat, for Cousin John promised

---

27. There is a gap in the extant correspondence from July 19, 1870, to July 14, 1872. During that time George Holder visited Hygiene. See Fanny O. Fox to George Holder, July 14, 1872, TBHF, MDAH.

to forward it as soon as he got it   How can we all thank you all enough for the many pretty things in it, besides for so kindly & tastefully filling out my order— Most of the things are much cheaper than could be bought in N. O. I wish you all could have seen the parlor & *the tree* & been here to witness the children's delight & surprise for the *tree* was actually loaded & there were presents enough for a dozen children & as many old folks instead of 7 little ones & 5 old ones— Every member of the family had been remembered by all the others & then with the addition of yours   Emma's & Georgy's you can imagine the variety— the parlor was like a *fairy* scene—Fan poor child who was laid up this morning with blistered feet & general *malaise* superinted & *did* almost the whole of the work—she will write & tell you about all the affair in a little while— She enjoyed it all so much I was delighted for her sake— May they all always have as merry a time. Dr R——& I sat back in our room with the folding doors open after the ceremonies were over & enjoyed ourselves witnessing their joy & I ought to have been a happy wife & mother, for the children had all been at work for me & Dr R——had remembered me by putting a handsome pair of chased gold sleeve buttons in a conspicuous place on the tree. They are very heavy & neat & will do for a family *heir loom.* Fanny had worked me a pair of slippers & had them made & braided a beautiful pattern on a *night-gown yoke.* all her own work & neatly done. I had not seen it; she says she was nearly six weeks doing it at leisure times. Georgy had *netted* me a nice large patch-bag which I prize highly, it being all his own work. Cousin Mary gave me a crocheted shoulder cape corn color with blue border & cord & tassels all her work. Even *Christian*[28] had a gift for me, a pr of nice gray gloves lined with pink flannel — just my size— you may know he thinks a great deal of "the Missus." It was rainy & cold & none of our invited guests were present excepting Blanche Stackhouse.

The exercises opened with a little speech from Fanny—her own composition & beautifully worded & spoken, thanking her parents for the pleasure we had given her in allowing her to arrange the tree & having her *sway* for the evening— Then Georgy came forward with a pretty little speech. Then Frank, & then all sang a Christmas Carol while I played the piano for them. Then Fanny began to distribute the pretty

---

28. A servant.

things while Cousin Mary who is tall, unpinned & untied them for her. All this time as a kind of *subdued accompaniment* Little Blanche & Johnny[29] had kept up a perfect round of exclamations Oh! See the doll, see the little doll, & the drum & the man—"look mice" "see the engine" for Johnny says everything) & oh! I want my Dolly I want my dolly, &c. &c.

Then we older ones partook of some egg nogg & cake which I had placed beforehand on the round table in my room & each of the children cake & milk & then the boys were set out for show— The fire engine like to have run over every body— Johnny's jumping-jack was in every bodys face   poor little Blanche was almost overcome with her two dollys & seated herself by the grate in her little rocking [chair] to sing them to sleep & singing at the top of her voice, 2 military gentlemen, suddenly appeared in uniform, with drum   sword, gun & trumpets & it was amusing enough to see all & *hear the noise*— Do you wonder I wished you all were with us. The pretty verses from Georgy graced the front & center of the tree & are beauties indeed— I cannot describe all the things—perhaps Fanny will give you a better idea of the matter. Though I must tell you of a remarkable piece of *embroidery,* by *Georgy*   it is a newspaper holder made of black broadcloth upon which he worked in worsted a beautiful rose with leaves & buds & a bunch of roses with [leaves and roses]   it is about 18 inches from top to bottom & 16 wide— Of course Cousin Mary drew the pattern & showed him the stitch & helped him a little but it is a remarkable piece of work for a *boy*— it is of this shape   I cannot draw the flowers on so small a place. [illustration in the original] Fanny had worked a beautiful bag for him to carry his tooth-pullers in, but it is too pretty for use— it is on black broadcloth with forget me nots in applique on the front & D. R. F. in a vine of gold braid on the back. The girls were delighted with their new dresses—poor things.[30] I cannot but be sorry for them—though we all try to make them feel as members of the family & they seem satisfied & happy, yet, I think what if my children should be left so. I do not think they could have found a better place   particularly here at the

---

29. Tryphena refers here to her seventh child, John Angel Fox, born December 17, 1870, according to *The Genealogy of the Cleveland and Cleaveland Families,* no. 438, 3:2018.
30. The servants Olivia and Margaret.

South, where there is a *latent* feeling which grew out of old slave labor that *work* is more or less degrading & whoever does it must be of the *menial* class— But I think the feeling will gradually die away, for too many nice ladies & their daughters have to do their own cooking washing & ironing who never used to even fill their own pitchers, to allow of its being prevalent long. The girls work for me & I watch them & make them keep everything clean & nice & Olivia has got so she can do most of our cooking by herself, still when their work is done I send them to comb their hair & put on clean dresses & have them work with me & Fanny evenings & treat them like young ladies not like servants. & they are very good girls— Martha who helps me clean house & then takes care of the two young children, is a very superior girl & is so kind to the little ones, that I am much pleased with her. Her mother was evidently a *lady* of true Christian principles— the other is of a little coarser parentage but thinks much of me & minds me well & tries to please me. The Dr is inclined to find some fault with her because she is apt to forget & he says she requires too much overlooking & helping from me, but you know all young folks are more or less heedless & no one has ever trained her much in little nice ways

With Christian our *Dane*, we are more & more doubly pleased — I dont think you ever met a person so devoted to the Dr & Missus "as he is—is always hard at work & never grumbles or finds the least fault. We feared he would get drunk Christmas — but not a bit of it— he went to the shop to carry Mr Sarpy a bowl of egg nogg & a basket of assorted cake for me & came back all straight having only taken one drink, though he treated *13* darkeys—ah Missus that trip to the store cost me money   why now Christian "— all the negro men there ask me for Christmas gift, Christmas gift & I give all a drink & it take one dollar & 30 cents out of my pocket—" & he laughed as though it had done him good to treat the lazy rascals. I cautioned him against them & told him not to treat any more of them. He was much pleased with the silk handkerchief from the Dr but more so with a nice old-fashioned housewife" which I made & put on a tree for him, with his initials C. N. worked in yellow silk on the cover. He can sew as *good as a woman* & *nicer than a woman* would have done. — so dont you think I have a treasure in the way of a serving man & do you wonder that Dr treats him better than any one White or Black has ever been treated before.

It is bitter, bitter cold & freezing every moment my feet have not been warm to-day— the sun has come out a little after 4 dark, chilly days—most miserable Christmas weather out of doors— I have stolen off here to the dining-room, where there is a nice fire in the little stove to be with you & watch your preserves—for I am making you a jar, of *some lemons* from Dr R——tree which was planted by our front gallery 15 years ago & this year bears us, its first fruit—nice large lemons of the most fragrant kind. The Dr has watched them with the greatest care & now we have the pleasure of not only enjoying the pretty sight of full grown lemons, half hidden among the rich evergreen leaves, but we have & some of the nicest punches you can imagine & when I want a lemon for any of my fancy dishes all I have to do is step to the gallery & pick one. Yesterday Dr R——gathered 13 for you which I am preserving in some of our Louisana sugar made on Mr Stackhouse Belle Chasse plantation & which I hope to forward to you soon with a jar of orange preserves also grown on our lot.

LATER—

Having stopped to *help Fanny* make her papa an egg-nogg & *help Martha* give Frank a hot foot-bath & orange-leaf tea, for the poor child had a chill just after school began, & help Olivia fix the fish for din-ner I am back again—just in time to save the preserves from burning; they did scorch a little at the bottom of the kettle, but not enough to hurt; they are made of a lemon which has a very thick rind called the *Bergamot* lemon & I made then after a recipt in Marion Harland's Com-mon Sense, which I presume means *Sicily* lemons— mine have a slightly bitter taste though I hope it will not affect their goodness— any how you must take them as I *intended* & not as you may find them. I took a great deal of pains with them & they & the Xmas doings & cold weather & all sent me to bed yesterday at 4 with a terrible toothache— I put chloroform in it & breathed some & went to sleep & had a nap of two hours—never heard a sound— the first time I have been absent from the table since Cousin Mary came— The Dr often fusses at home because I wont try to rest in the day-time but I never feel as though I had time.

Now my winter sewing is nearly over— Little Blanche has some dark calicoes to be made over & that is all— should you not think I should feel *free* & *easy* at last— but I dont dare think of it for fear something will turn up. I worked very hard before Xmas to get everything done & help the girls some with their little fancy works for the tree & last of all made the three flags & two blue military jackets trimmed with yellow *braid* & a nice Xmas present for the DR — in the shape of a *saddle blanket* — made of *oat sack* first — that covered with strips of black broadcloth from his old breeches, bound with blue poplin trimmed with red flannel points & hearts with J for Jack & R——for Reb. in the hearts (worked large sampler stitch in the hearts with blue worsted.

It took me nearly two days to make it — but the Dr is much pleased with it.

As I have come to the end of my paper I must close for the present. Tell G——I am *chawing* some of the gum — very *secretly* — thank you — *mister* — did I not laugh when I found it? Fan. is writing to him & Emma, but I will mention here too, now much pleased I am with the pretty tidies & cushion & scrap [. . .] thank you.

The Springfield Republican has come twice & I am much obliged for it. The views are like some I have   Some are different   I was glad to receive "Dr Todd in his pulpit". I will write again soon & if I have neglected thanking you all for all the pretty things it is not because I am not grateful but because I have no more time to write at the present. Good Bye with love from all to all from all— Your daughter

T. B. Fox

□ □ □

Dearest Brother—   [DECEMBER 23?, 1873]

My spirit has been with you all day & I feel that you must have been thinking of me more than usual; every where I have gone something has more than ever reminded me of you — the croquet box, under the spare bed, the pretty vases on the parlor mantle, the piano stool, Scribners [magazine], the little engine in the nursery play-box, all have brought you vividly before me & I can not let the day pass, without a little pen chat with you — but what would I not give could we only meet, even if but for one short hour— I presume you have been to church and realize the benefits of our beautifully devotional services & been strengthened for the coming week by the good advice of your kind pastor & had your heart raised above worldly pursuits, with their many pretty anxieties by the solemn litany & the almost divine strain of the

organ & choir—if I could have been with you! My soul so longs sometimes for a little food from without—such as we find in the holy tem-
ples, for that at our own private hearthstone does not have the
nourishment that a mother needs to help her on another six days of life's
journey, when so many fruits of the spirit are needed to guide & govern
the little ones aright.

But I am sermonizing & I did not intend it— It has been a windy
day—cold & cloudy & promises bad weather for Christmas— & we
have had a most delightful season heretofore; a little fire in the morning
& then open doors & windows & bright sunny hours for the rest of the
day—no clouds, no dampness & but little fog at night—

There is no business going on with us at present— the rice crops are
gathered & the planters have finished the half sugar crops. The negroes
are mostly paid off, & being out of work, will soon be out of money &
then I do not see what is to become of them— many of the plantations
are not to be worked this next year; on others only a little seed cane will
be cultivated. The Drs prospects are more gloomy than ever—& we
shall probably do one of two things, remove to California or—rent a
rice plantation & try to make enough to build up our waning fortune—
strange that the golden spoon from which we have heretofore been fed
should now be turned into an iron one, when there are so many more
little mouths—is it not?— It has gone very hard with the Dr to lose his
little fortune for the *third* time, but I believe he is rallying from it as but
few men would have done & his health is improving, so that he begins
to look something like himself again— I bear it resignedly though I feel
it is *hard*, on all of my children— & it is for them that we are making
an effort to go where they may have church & school & some congenial
society— To show you how earnest we are about removing to Cal.— I
have already sent *five* letters—the Drs photograph— letters of inquiry
in regards to the needs of growing towns & what a physician might be
sure of— they are written to influential men — if we receive favorable
answers, we shall probably rent or sell & go in the Spring. We should
prefer to sell if we could get good cash payment— Do you know of any
physician there who would like the place & could pay say $3500.. one
who could be contented with 10 or 12 hundred a year & has no young
children to educate would find it an excellent place— I thought some of
advertising it, in the *Springfield Republican* but concluded to wait &

hear what you thought about it— the rest of the payment of 3500 could be paid in three payments in three years with a mortgage on the place— the orange trees are doing nicely— the other fruit trees were somewhat injured by the hail— you know there are six acres in all—& you know of the improvements— if any one should make inquiries of you—

We have been "pretty well" since I last wrote— Georgy is still feeble from malaria & has a chill now & then & has to take quinine— the others are tolerable   We are beginning to retrench in our expenses   Martha went with her oldest brother to Thibodeaux,[31] week before last— I did not feel able to keep her any longer. Olivia will go as soon as I can find a good place for her & Dr R——thinks he cannot afford to pay Cousin Mary, more than one more month. By that time we shall know whether we go to *Cal*— or not[32]— if we are not to go there, I am anxious that Fanny should go North with Cousin Mary & hope I shall not be disappointed— the poor child leads a terribly lonesome monotonous life here— An old woman like me can *endure* it—but for her it is too hard—. It is getting too dark to write more at present—so with *Much Love*, I must say, Good night Yours affectionately

Sister B——

Emma's letter to F——& your Scribners to Dr R——both received— for which many thanks from *all*.

□ □ □

Dear Mother,   WED. EVE. JAN 3RD, '74

As Fan has taken Burt[33] to watch for a while I'm going to spend a few minutes with you before dark. I have been thinking of writing to you several days, but somehow I could not get at it — not that I dawdled around & read a novel, when I might have been writing but because there's always something else to do— have been busy for two days mending—Fan & I both, for it seemed as if every garment in the house needed some repairs and I have "let things go"—considerably lately while trying to make a few new clothes to eke out the old ones— we are

---

31. Thibodaux is located southeast of Baton Rouge on Bayou Lafourche in Lafourche Parish.
32. Only John A. Fox moved to California. See David Raymond Fox, Probate Records for 1894, Plaquemines Parish, Pointe a La Hache, Louisiana.
33. Tryphena's eighth child, Burt Randolph, was born March 9, 1873. Fox-Holder Genealogy, original in possession of Mrs. J. A. C. Birchett, Vicksburg, Mississippi.

pretty nearly through patching to-night & will probably make shirts & pants for the boys the rest of the week—then all the children will be pretty well of for clothes and I can find time to make a set of shirts for the Dr & some new chemises for self, all of which are much needed. My new gray calico is done excepting the overskirt. Fanny made her one last week & one in Vicks[burg]. so she is pretty well off with those she had.

The clothes Emma sent me for Burt & Blanche helped me more than I can tell you & removed quite a load from my mind. I thought perhaps I could have a bonnet & polonaise made in P—— & sent to me, but left it entirely to Georgy's judgement— I suppose he has the letter by this time—(if he does conclude to send them I wish he or Emma would have two morning sacks or basques made for me of some white material like Blanche's or cross-bar muslin & trimmed like the children's dresses with Hamburg & put them in with the others if & if &c &c &c)— They would be nice to wear to breakfast with some figured linen skirts I have, half-worn—the waists all gone) But enough of clothes, you will think, I have no other ideas I have—once in a while—but I regret clothes do occupy much of my time & thoughts for the present If you were to see these frolicsome boys & how *sharp* their knees are you would not wonder & the Dr is very careless with his—

I have no school this week—think some of going to town with the Dr—but—have no hat or bonnet—perhaps I'll make over an old one to-morrow. Dr R—— wants me to go to keep him company & — it is our wedding week & we, like John Gilpin & his wife, like to celebrate the day a little, or one near it. We shall have been married 18 years to-morrow—& on the whole, we have passed it as happily as any couple ever did— we have had many misfortunes & had much trouble, but they have not separated us, as they have many. I feel that I have many blessings & try to be thankful for them, but know I am not as much so as I should be always. Separation from old friends & scenes doubtless gives me feelings of discontent, which I cannot always restrain, but I don't allow them to have sway long. It is getting late, so I shall be obliged to close on account of the mosquitoes; they are very trouble-some now at night fall— We put up our mosquito room, in my room on Sat. & I could have no peace after lamp light were it not for the bar. Besides these night pests we have red-bugs & *chicken lice* — the latter are terrible—worse than ever we knew them before—they trouble the children terribly, for every time they go to play, they are sure to brush by some place infested with the lice The cistern has been dry for some time & I dislike to use the river water.

□ □ □

Dear Bro. G.   TUESDAY APR. 6TH 1875. "WREN'S NEST"

Though I am not very well this morning I am going to "stretch a point" & write you a *few* lines anyway, to *thank* you for so kindly & promptly executing my demands in the way of *socks* & *anticipating* my *wishes* by sending me this pretty wrapper. I was sitting up & *partly dressed*, writing to Sister E—— Blanche went to the Office to carry the letter & returned with a bundle. I knew your hand, but never dreamed of the favor contained, till I read your letter You can imagine I was *all dressed*, in a few minutes—the very thing I wanted & it fits in every way as if I had been measured & *tried* on a dozen times—& so cheap too—I would have had to pay a dollar for the making here after cutting & fitting it myself & then wait till May probably before its completion So I believe I will trouble you to send me another—*made just like this*— Lilla, who was down yesterday with her mother to spend the afternoon with me; was telling me about the solid calicos with bright borders such as gray with blue border, buff with black &c &c— I think I should like a gray or slate with contrasting border, but if there were none at Colby's you need not bother about it, *any one you may select will suit me.* I am provoked with that last smart Congress for adding to *our* postage, but even with the heavy postage it is cheaper for me to get my calicos in that way, than to try to make them, for with this little additional care I dont expect to find much time to sew beyond patches, buttons & strings. The socks are wonderfully pretty considering the price & will answer nicely for a change, though as you say; there's not much wear in them. Here comes Aunt Rachel & she says please remember me to *him* with my best respects— she is such a good, faithful old body! But like all the rest of us begins to show her age.

Dr R——has gone to Pointe a La Hache—the county seat—to give his testimony in this suit against Recorder Thibaux, in his Trufant case— I do not know whether I told you, Dr R—— has sued this Recorder for giving him a false certificate of the mortgages on the Star—if he had a true certificate of the prior claims he would not have lent the money to T——. McCaleb, the lawyer employed, is very sanguine that the Dr will gain, but if he does, I fear Thibaux has no property which can be of any account to the Dr

We have had reason to fear that this five acre property was to slip from us, through some illegality, of sale & ownership, but the gentleman who last purchased, has promised the Dr all right, title & interest which he *might* legally claim, knowing that the Dr purchased it in good faith from Mrs Stackhouse, & paid its full *cash* value.[34] He wants the Dr to purchase the acres back, but we dont want it, because any spare funds that may be ours, after all expenses are paid, the Dr wants to put into a house & lot in the city, so we can send these children to school, in those happy days to come, when Louisana will be her old self again & N. O. the queen city of the South. These *poor* boys (happy, they consider themselves to be so free) have been going to school about 1 day in 4 ever since my return—something is all the time happening—so that "school dont keep to-day". & the consequence is, they are forgetting what little they did know, in place of learning any thing more—as soon as I get out once more, if nothing happens, you may be sure I shall make an effort that nothing more shall interrupt school hours, for a long time.

Fanny has had so much to attend lately that she is about half sick, but manages to keep up & look after everybody. As baby is twelve day old to-day,[35] I hope soon to be out, but it seems as if the harder I tried to get out, the more I am put back. About every two days I find myself on the back track, so that I am almost discouraged sometimes & fear it will be a month after all before I can be housekeeper again.

All the children are very well— You ought to see Burt—a great, stout looking fellow   always trotting & forever jabbering—talks about every body & every thing, but in such an incomprehensible style that only ma ma or Sister Fannie can understand him; there's not a baby look about him now.

---

34. Raymond Fox purchased the property from Sarah Stackhouse on September 21, 1872. See Probate Records, June 22, 1899, 34:682–88; June 5, 1912, 46:680–82, Plaquemines Parish, Pointe a La Hache, Louisiana.
35. Emma Catherine, Tryphena's ninth child, was born March 25, 1875, according to *The Genealogy of the Cleveland and Cleveland Families,* no. 438, 3:2018.

I am so glad that Mr Hubbell would not listen to your objections & *I do hope you* will continue in the choir, you will never regret it & that is where you belong or rather where that voice of yours belongs.

Fanny says give much love to Uncle G——& tell him to stay & sing in the choir for *her* & him too & that she does so much wish that she could go with you & Aunt Emma to the rehearsals. The desire to go with you too, almost makes me a little *homesick* so you must go & sing for all of us.— I have dated this "Wren's Nest" because we have had it painted brown   it looks so cozy & comfortable, and all the shrubbery has "put out" & is growing so beautifully this Spring. The orange trees are splendid one grand bouquet & the roses & oleanders are one mass of blossoms. How I wish I could send you some of the many pretty bouquets we could gather at any moment.

The Dr has made a good many improvements this Spring & if our pretty home were only a little nearer town, I would n't exchange it for any in the Union— Tell Mother that after I had written the letter about the *names* & was telling Dr R—— about it, he says why you could n't find a prettier name than Emma Catherine & it was the names of two of Pa's wives too & would be paying the old gentleman a compliment if you were to name her that, so if Mother don't mind, my "taking back" her choice, I think I would rather she would be named that rather than the other—Aunt Catherine was always with Grandma in my day & the name will be to me a memento of the dear old place & *all* its inmates— Well I must stop for I am tired— Give Much Love to Mother & Sister E——& some to Bruno[36] & with much for yourself believe me ever
    Yours Affectionately

Sister T.

---

36. The family dog

F——has just come in again & says did you give him my love? Well Give him my best Love & tell him I'll write soon.

P.S. When I first put the wrapper on F——exclaimed Oh! ma ma how nice & young that makes you look! Dr R—— says—
Why that's fine! is it n't!

□ □ □

Dear Mother,   9 O CLOCK—SUNDAY EVE JAN. 2ND [1876]

I promised myself a letter to you yesterday morning as a kind of New Year's treat, but the day with its many cares & duties came & went & found me at *eight* o clock a tired mother trying to hush a fretful baby & finally falling to sleep in my rocking chair with Katy in my arms. The lamp was out, the fire burned down and the room too damp & chilly for me to sit up in so I thought it best to wait until to-day but there has been no time for letter-writing— now the babies are all asleep & how I should like to step in & stay a little while with you! but as that cannot be I will wish you a very happy New Year, hoping that *you* will be with me, before it shall turn to an old year. I wonder if it is cold weather with you— we are having warm sunny days, roses, oleanders & open windows; were it not for frequent rains & heavy fogs, we should hardly need a fire but a little is indispensable morning & night on account of the dampness—

Strawberries & dewberries are in bloom & the garden looks as if it were Spring.

Most of the planters have finished grinding and the rest will soon be done— the crop is a tolerably fair one, but the juice *ferments* more than usual & there is much waste— The Dr told us Friday on his return from the city that all the molasses on the levee is in a state of fermentation & it is running from the bbls. so as to six & eight inches deep in places & all the poor—black & white are squabbling over it & trying to save all they can.

Dr R——is not very well—has taken a bad cold & is quite tired out from his trip to town Friday—had to get up at three to be ready for the boat which came along 1/2 past four—went in to get my *new cooking stove*— family too large—stove too small, so Pa & Mother made me a Xmas present of *forty* dollars for one larger than the one I had—bought a No 88—Charter Oak, two sizes larger than the other. this is far more suitable for my family— It came at 8 o clock at night & the next morning we had it set up cooked the New Year's dinner in it & had our roast turkey at 3 o clock—was n't that smart? had no trouble whatever in making the change & am truly thankful, you may imagine, for the useful gift. I hope to sell the old one for about half price, it is a real nice one yet.

Fanny & Johnny are both unwell with chills every now & then & Katy has been half sick for about two weeks— I think she is about to cut teeth & has a bad cold besides— She is a cunning little piece & as good as she can be & dont make me half as much trouble as one would suppose— I wish every day that Em could see her & some of her baby tricks— I think she would be amused—

The boys are well & growing so fast that they astonish me— You would hardly know G——He is writing a letter to Eddie Dewey[37] which I suppose he will have ready to send with this to-morrow. The P. O. is not established here yet, although Dr R——has the key & his commission— he is waiting for the mail bags books &c &c which belong to the Office & have been carried some where below. I shall be rejoiced to get my letters & papers once more for now they take a long time to get here & some have not come at all. G——had the money for a scroll saw, & F a handsome Prayer Book from their Grandmother. G—— & F—— both a nice trunk from me, G——a writing desk & F—— a box containing a fancy pen holder, pens paper. I had a *present*, that was indeed to be prized, by a poor body that finds time to sew excepting after all are settled for the night, & that was 4 new *chemises*, all nicely made & trimmed from Fanny, who made them up stairs evenings & down in the schoolroom at odd times, so that I knew nothing of it, till the bundle was opened from the Xmas tree. Dr R——gave me a book Coxes "Thoughts on the Service" & Olivia made me a present of a gold chemise button, handsomely enameled. I gave her a nice lamp, the Dr gave her a writing desk & Fanny made her a present of a nice cravat—

Fanny had a silver thimble, a braid, & a piece of music.

Mother gave Aunt Sally a nice head hkf., the girls gave her a nice cal-

---

37. Possibly the son of Harriet Murray Dewey.

ico & I presented her with a large frosted cake which she thought splendid—

Fanny & Olivia cooked the Xmas dinner, made all the cakes, which were very nice & arranged the Xmas tree, so they deserve all the credit for our pleasant time—

Since Katy's birth it seems as if I could n't do much of anything, only take care of her & "keep moving on"—forever looking after something or somebody & *doing nothing*— come when you might you would doubtless find me walking about with Katy on one arm or over my shoulder hunting up something or seeing to somebody's work or finding out "what's the matter"? Johnny crying, or Burt yelling, or the papa wanting some article indispensable at the moment or the boys in some fuss or dilemma so *Ma ma* goes all day long called here & called there, with no rest & no quiet & no time to sew or read or write & sometimes none to eat in peace—but hope bids me look forward to this year as a more settled one, with not quite so many cares for all things to take up one's time & interrupt one's duties, a little babe can do the most—& Katy has had a full share of the past year. As she is now old enough to play with the older children I hope to be able to do more sewing & less nursing, & introduce a little more order & regularity in my somewhat upset household.

Pa & Mother will probably stay all winter with us— Pa had improved wonderfully & looks & acts quite strong again— He seems to like to stay & so Dr R——& I told them they had better not go home but remain with us— I suppose they will go to Hot Springs later. If Emma does not get better or if she should grow worse I want her to go there— it would be almost a certain cure for her neuralgia— We will see after a while— As it is getting late I will not try to write anymore tonight— All send Love— let me hear from some of you soon

                                                    [unsigned]

Epilogue

In many ways Tryphena Blanche Holder Fox was an ordinary woman living in the nineteenth-century South, facing housekeeping chores, the births and deaths of children, seasonal visitors, and intractable servants. In other ways she was a "stranger in a strange land." Throughout her correspondence, the reader sees a woman who pushes herself beyond reasonable limits to maintain a comfortable life in an alien environment. She persevered and fulfilled the role of a dutiful daughter, caring sister, faithful wife, and loving mother.[1]

Tryphena kept the familial ties bound between Mississippi and Massachusetts through letters. Visits were not frequent because of numerous financial crises in her household, which thwarted her desire to rescue her mother from poverty. That was only the distaff side of the story. When Tryphena wrote about traveling to Pittsfield in 1866 she mused, "I am afraid" Dr. R——"will never think he is 'well enough off' *to leave his practice,* & take such a trip." Well off or not, he and Tryphena traveled to Pittsfield in 1877. Nearly twenty years after his marriage, Dr. R——met his mother-in-law and many others whom he had known only through letters. The trip to Pittsfield was not quite the dream-come-true that Tryphena had always wanted. The cost of travel for themselves and the children, Fanny Otis, George Randolph, Frank Co-

---

1. See Virginia I. Burr, "A Woman Made to Suffer and Be Strong: Ella Gertrude Clanton Thomas, 1834–1907," in Carol Bleser, ed., *In Joy and in Sorrow: Women, Family, and Marriage in the Victorian South, 1830–1900* (New York: Oxford University Press, 1991), 215–32, for similarities in the lives of Mrs. Ella Thomas and Tryphena Fox.

leman, Blanche Cleveland, John Angel, Emma Catherine, and James Torrey, was prohibitive.[2]

Tryphena did not fulfill the dream of having all her children know their grandmother firsthand, but some of her other aspirations for them came to fruition. She took her duties as a mother seriously. She wanted her children to live outside the "rather rough & *weedy domains*" of Plaquemines Parish, where attempts to cultivate "society" were generally "trampled down & overgrown." She was especially concerned about Fanny remaining in Louisiana. "An old woman like me can endure it," she wrote, "but for her it is too hard." She succeeded in sending some of them away from the "penitentiary of the U. S." The older boys, George and Frank, attended Louisiana State University in Baton Rouge. Fanny went to school in Massachusetts.[3]

It is not clear if Fanny and Tryphena had agreed to write frequently and freely as Tryphena and Anna had done a quarter of a century earlier, when Tryphena left home. It is demonstrably apparent, however, that Tryphena's letters to Fanny contain a genuineness that never appeared in those to Anna. These candid letters show that the mother-daughter nexus had given way to sisterhood. Tryphena could now trust Fanny with her carefully guarded emotional secrets. When Tryphena's "spirit seemed under a nightmare" due to a misunderstanding with Dr. R—— in 1881, she wrote to Fanny rather than to her mother.[4]

In the correspondence to Anna, Tryphena carefully painted David Raymond Fox as a kind, patient husband. She chose a different brush with Fanny. "Between you & me," a phrase never used with Anna, "I think Papa exacts too much of [John] seeing he is such a willing mind," she wrote, intimating that Dr. R——worked the boy so much it interfered with his development. The letters to Fanny portray Dr. R——as domineering, impatient, and given to shouting. She and Fanny had shared the same sphere and knew his behavior firsthand. Fanny sympa-

---

2. TBHF to ARH, October 3, 1866, MDAH; George Fox to GH, October 29, 1877, MDAH. James Torrey Fox, Tryphena's tenth child, was born February 22, 1878, according to *The Genealogy of the Cleveland and Cleveland Families*, no. 438, 3:2018.
3. TBHF to ARH, August 1, 1881, MDAH; Register of Cadets of the Louisiana State Seminary of Learning and Military Academy, 1865–1927, Louisiana and Lower Mississippi Collections, Louisiana State University, Baton Rouge, Louisiana; TBHF to Fanny Otis Fox (hereafter cited as FOF), February 21, 1881, MDAH.
4. TBHF to FOF, August 8, 1881, MDAH.

thized with her mother's complaints, as evidenced by her description of
the abrasive tone her father had once used in the presence of others.
Although Fanny said she was "so surprised," Tryphena was embarrassed "& *angry* too." She did not respond in kind: "I went into the
room and shut the door," she wrote, "& then told him he musn't yell at
me that way that I thought he had given it up long ago." Tryphena
never mentioned this kind of behavior to Anna.[5]

When Tryphena divulged this private matter to her daughter, Fanny,
exhibiting a strong character, was more concerned with caring for
someone rather than being cared for. Tryphena graciously rejected the
proposition for she believed her spirit would heal and all would come
out right in the end.

Fanny understood the world her mother inhabited as well as the
realm Tryphena longed to live in. She appreciated her mother's fondness for beautiful surroundings and recognized the extent of her labor
to make her living conditions pleasant. Fanny commemorated her
mother's forty-seventh birthday in 1881 with a gift that Tryphena saw as
evidence of her success in creating in the young woman an appreciation
for aesthetics. Fanny alone remembered that it was Tryphena's birthday
and it was this thoughtfulness that caused the mother to confide in the
daughter.

Since Fanny did not remain in Massachusetts, Tryphena did not have
the anxieties of being separated from her children by great geographical
distances. Fanny married Louis Bartholomew Bennecke on November
20, 1883, and lived near her parents in Plaquemines Parish. She and her
children, Louis Raymond and Fanny Caroline (Carrie), visited frequently. George married Corinne Caco, became the father of nine children, and practiced medicine in Moreauville, Louisiana. Blanche
Cleveland married J. A. C. Birchett in 1889 and made her home in
Vicksburg, Mississippi. Only one of the children, John Angel, lived far
from Jesuit Bend; he relocated to San Diego, California.

After her husband's death in 1893, Tryphena left Hygiene and made
her home in Warren County, Mississippi with her daughter Blanche
Cleveland. Moving to Warren County around the turn of the century
was quite different from the move some forty years earlier, yet it was

5. TBHF to FOF, August 8, 1881, MDAH.

similar in that Tryphena left her beloved home and possessions behind. A prized asset, the piano, remained in Louisiana in the care of Tryphena's granddaughter, Carrie, who resided at Hygiene. After Carrie's death, her brother cleared the furnishings from Hygiene and sold the piano to an antique dealer in New Orleans, who later sold it to a couple who planned to have a table made from it.[6]

The disposition of the piano, which meant so much to Tryphena, gives pause when considering her efforts to have and keep the instrument. These struggles were a reflection of the ebb and flow of her life. "So it is with all of us," Tryphena wrote, "Sunshine & Shadow. Heaviness for the night but joy with the morrow."[7]

---

6. Emma Katherine Birchett to Wilma King Hunter, September 2, 1989, in the possession of Wilma King.
7. TBHF to FOF, August 8, 1881, MDAH.

Bibliography

MANUSCRIPTS

Alderman Library, University of Virginia, Charlottesville
    Mary T. Dyer Diary

Berkshire Athenaeum, Pittsfield, Massachusetts
    The Genealogy of the Cleveland and Cleaveland Families. No. 438, vols.
        2, 3
    Family History File

Department of Archives and History, Jackson, Mississippi
    Tryphena Blanche Holder Fox Collection

Louisiana and Lower Mississippi Collections, Louisiana State University,
    Baton Rouge
        Register of Cadets of the Louisiana State Seminary of Learning and
            Military Academy, 1865–1927

Southern Historical Collection, University of North Carolina
    Launcelot Minor Blackford Diary
    Caffery Family Papers
    Everard Baker Green Diary

Miscellaneous
    Berkshire Eagle
    Fox-Holder Genealogy, original in the possession of Mrs. J. A. K.
        Birchett, Vicksburg, Mississippi
    Pittsfield Cemetery and Crematory Records, Pittsfield, Massachusetts
    Probate Records, Berkshire County, Pittsfield, Massachusetts
    Probate Records, Plaquemines Parish, Pointe a La Hache, Louisiana
    Records of Birth, Marriage, and Death, City Clerk Office, Pittsfield,
        Massachusetts
    St. Stephen's Episcopal Parish Records, Pittsfield, Massachusetts

NATIONAL ARCHIVES, WASHINGTON, D.C.

Bureau of Refugees, Freedmen, and Abandoned Lands, Record Group 105
    Report of the First School Division, Louisiana
    Weekly Statistical Reports
    Report of the First Superintendent, State of Louisiana

Confederate States of America Service Records for Louisiana

Log of the U.S.S. *Sassacus*

Muster Rolls of the U.S.S. *Sassacus*, 1863–1865; U.S.S. *Satellite*, 1863; U.S.S.
    Saugus, 1864–65; the U.S.S. *Kenwood*, 1863–1865; U.S.S. *Keokuk*, 1863;
    U.S.S. *Keystone State* 1861–1865

Rendezvous Records, Civil War

Southern Claims Commission

U.S. 7th Census, 1850, Agriculture

U.S. 7th Census, 1850, Population, Plaquemines Parish, Louisiana; Berkshire
    County, Massachusetts; Warren County, Mississippi

U.S. 7th Census, 1850, Slave Schedule, Plaquemines Parish, Louisiana;
    Warren County, Mississippi

U.S. 8th Census, 1860, Population, Warren County, Mississippi

U.S. 8th Census, 1860, Slave Schedule, Plaquemines Parish, Louisiana,
    Warren County, Mississippi

UNPUBLISHED SOURCE

Huber, Jo Anne Sellers. "Southern Women and the Institution of Slavery,"
    (M.A. thesis, Lamar University, 1980).

BOOKS

Beers, Frederick W. *County Atlas of Berkshire, Massachusetts.* New York: R. T.
    White, 1876.

Berlin, Ira, Thavolia Glymph, Steven F. Miller, Joseph P. Reidy, Leslie S. Row-
    land, Julie Saville. *Freedom: A Documentary History of Emancipation, 1861–
    1867*, ser. 1, vol. 3, *The Wartime Genesis of Free Labor: The Lower South.* New
    York: Cambridge University Press, 1990.

Bleser, Carol K., "Southern Planter Wives and Slavery." In *The Meaning of
    South Carolina History: Essays in Honor of George C. Rogers, Jr.* Edited by
    David R. Chesnutt and Clyde N. Wilson. Columbia: University of South
    Carolina Press, 1991.

Burr, Virginia I., "A Woman Made to Suffer and Be Strong: Ella Gertrude
    Clanton Thomas, 1834–1907." In *In Joy and in Sorrow: Women, Family, and*

Marriage in the Victorian South, 1830–1900, 215–32. Edited by Carol Bleser. New York: Oxford University Press, 1991.

Censer, Jane Turner. *North Carolina Planters and Their Children, 1800–1860*. Baton Rouge: Louisiana State University Press, 1984.

Chesnut, Mary Boykin. *A Diary from Dixie*, edited by Ben Ames Williams. Boston: Houghton Mifflin, 1950.

Clinton, Catherine. *The Plantation Mistress: Woman's World in the Old South*. New York: Pantheon Books, 1982.

Cowles, Calvin D. *Atlas to Accompany the Official Records of the Union and Confederate Armies*. Washington, D.C.: Government Printing Office, 1891–1895.

Fields, Barbara Jeanne. *Slavery and Freedom On the Middle Ground: Maryland During the Nineteenth Century*. New Haven: Yale University Press, 1985.

Foner, Eric. *Reconstruction: America's Unfinished Revolution, 1863–1877*. New York: Harper & Row, 1988.

Fox-Genovese, Elizabeth. *Within the Plantation Household: Black and White Women of the Old South*. Chapel Hill: University of North Carolina Press, 1988.

Gates, Paul W. *The Farmer's Age: Agriculture 1815–1860*, vol. 3 of *The Economic History of the United States*. New York: Holt, Rhinehart and Winston, 1960.

Gray, Lewis Cecil. *History of Agriculture in the Southern United States to 1860*. 2 vols. Glouchester, Mass.: Peter Smith, 1958.

Holland, Josiah Gilbert. *History of Western Massachusetts*, vol. 2. Springfield, Mass.: Samuel Bowles, 1855.

Jones, Jacqueline. *Labor of Love, Labor of Sorrow: Black Women, Work, and the Family from Slavery to the Present*. New York: Vintage Books, 1985.

Kemble, Frances Anne. *Journal of a Residence on a Georgian Plantation in 1838–1839*. Edited by John A. Scott. Athens: University of Georgia Press, 1984.

Kett, Joseph F. "Adolescence and Youth in Nineteenth-Century America." In *The Family in History: Interdisciplinary Essays*, 95–110. Edited by Theodore K. Rabb and Robert I. Rotberg. New York: Harper, 1973.

Kolchin, Peter. *First Freedom: The Responses of Alabama's Blacks to Emancipation and Reconstruction*. Westport, Conn.: Greenwood Press, 1972.

Leavitt, Judith Walzer. *Brought to Bed: Childbearing in America, 1750 to 1950*. New York: Oxford University Press, 1986.

McPherson, James M. *Ordeal by Fire: The Civil War and Reconstruction*. New York: Alfred A. Knopf, 1982.

Mergen, Bernard. *Play and Playthings: A Reference Guide*. Westport, Conn.: Greenwood Press, 1982.

Meyer, J. Ben. *Plaquemines: The British Empire*. Laborde: Meyer, 1981.

Mintz, Steven. *A Prison of Expectations: The Family in Victorian Culture*. New York: New York University Press, 1985.

Savitt, Todd L. *Medicine and Slavery: The Diseases and Health Care of Blacks in Antebellum Virginia*. Urbana: University of Illinois Press, 1978.

Sitterson, J. Carlyle. *Sugar Country: The Cane Sugar Industry in the South, 1753–1950.* Frankfort: University of Kentucky Press, 1953.

Sixth Annual Catalogue of the Instructors and Pupils in the Young Ladies' Institute. Pittsfield, Mass.: Hanford, 1847.

Smith-Rosenberg, Carroll. "The Female World of Love and Ritual: Relations between Women in Nineteenth-Century America." In *Women's America: Refocusing the Past* 2d. ed., 167–90. Edited by Linda K. Kerber and Jane De Hart-Mathews. New York: Oxford University Press, 1987.

Stowe, Steven M. "The Not-So-Cloistered Academy: Elite Women's Education and Family Feeling in the Old South." In Walter Fraser, Jr., ed., *The Web of Southern Social Relations: Women, Family, and Education.* Athens: University of Georgia Press, 1985.

Strasser, Susan. *Never Done: A History of American Housework.* New York: Pantheon Books, 1982.

Vandal, Gilles. *The New Orleans Riot of 1866: Anatomy of a Tragedy.* Lafayette: Center for Louisiana Studies, 1983.

Winters, John D. *The Civil War in Louisiana.* Baton Rouge: Louisiana State University Press, 1963.

PERIODICAL PUBLICATIONS

Anderson, John Q., ed. "A Letter From a Yankee Bride in Ante-Bellum Louisiana." *Louisiana History* 1 (Summer 1960): 245–50.

Bartlett, Joseph Gardner. "Ancestry and Descendants of Rev. John Wilson of Boston, Mass." *New England Historical and Genealogical Register* 61 (January 1907): 36–41, 127–33.

Beales, Ross W., Jr. "In Search of the Historical Child: Miniature Adulthood and Youth in Colonial New England." *American Quarterly* 27 (October 1975): 379–98.

Beasley, Jonathan. "Blacks—Slave and Free—Vicksburg, 1850–1860." *Journal of Mississippi History* 38 (February 1976): 1–32.

Bellingham, Bruce. "The History of Childhood Since the 'Invention of Childhood': Some Issues in the Eighties." *Journal of Family History* 13, no. 2 (1988): 347–58.

Bernard, Richard M. and Maris A. Vinovskis. "The Female School Teacher in Ante-Bellum Massachusetts." *Journal of Social History* 10 (March 1977): 332–45.

Bonner, James C. ed. "Plantation Experiences of a New York Woman." *North Carolina Historical Review* 33 (October 1956): 384–412, 529–46.

Bruce, D. D., Jr. "Play, Work and Ethics in the Old South." *Southern Folklore Quarterly* 41 (1977): 33–51.

Cashin, Joan E. "The Structure of Antebellum Planter Families: 'The Ties that Bound us Was Strong.'" *Journal of Southern History* 56 (February 1990): 55–70.

Church, Virginia. "Solving the Problem." *Southern Workman* (July 1911): 402–9.

Clinton, Catherine. "Equally Their Due: The Education of the Planter Daughter in the Early Republic." *Journal of the Early Republic* 2 (April 1982): 39–60.

Cohen, William. "Thomas Jefferson and the Problem of Slavery." *Journal of American History* 56 (1969–1970): 503–22.

"Dr. Washington On the Servant Problem." *Southern Workman* 34 (May 1905): 200-201.

Dye, Nancy Schrom, and Daniel Blake Smith. "Mother Love and Infant Death, 1750–1920." *Journal of American History* 73 (September 1986): 329–53.

Faust, Drew Gilpin. "Alters of Sacrifice: Confederate Women and the Narratives of War." *Journal of American History* 76 (March 1990): 1200–1228.

Fox, Vivian C. "Is Adolescence a Phenomenon of Modern Times?" *Journal of Psychohistory* 5 (Fall 1977): 271–90.

Gundersen, Joan Reznen. "The Double Bonds of Race and Sex: Black and White Women in a Colonial Virginia Parish." *Journal of Southern History* 52 (August 1986): 351-72.

Hall, D. D. "A Yankee Tutor in the Old South." *New England Quarterly* 33 (March 1960): 82–91.

Herndon, Melvin G. "The Unemancipated Antebellum Youth." *Social Science* 23 (Summer 1984): 145–54.

Holder, Ray, ed. "My Dear Husband: Letters of A Plantation Mistress. Martha Dubose Winans to William Winans, 1834–1844." *Journal of Mississippi History* 49 (November 1987): 301–24.

Kondert, Nancy T. "The Romance and Reality of Defeat: Southern Women in 1865." *Journal of Mississippi History* 35 (May 1973): 141–52.

Lichtenstein, Alex. " 'That Disposition to Theft, With Which They Have Been Branded': Moral Economy, Slave Management, and the Law." *Journal of Social History* 21 (Spring 1988): 413–40.

McLean, Robert C. "A Yankee Tutor in the Old South." *North Carolina Historical Review* 47 (Winter 1970): 51–80.

Margo, Robert A., and Richard Steckel, "A Dreadful Childhood: The Excess Mortality of American Slaves." *Social Science History* 10 (Winter 1986): 427–65.

Mitchell, Martha Carolyn. "Health and the Medical Profession in the Lower South, 1845–1860." *Journal of Southern History* 10 (November 1944): 424–46.

Norse, Clifford C. "School Life of Amlanda Worthington of Washington County, 1857–62." *Journal of Mississippi History* 34 (May 1972): 107–16.

Padgett, James A. "A Yankee School Teacher in Louisiana, 1835–1837: The Diary of Caroline B. Poole." *Louisiana Historical Quarterly* 20 (July 1937): 651–63.

Prichard, Walter. "Routine on a Louisiana Sugar Plantation Under the Slavery Regime." *Mississippi Valley Historical Review* 14 (September 1927): 168–78.

Pryor, Elizabeth Brown. "An Anomalous Person: The Northern Tutor in Plantation Society, 1773-1860." *Journal of Southern History* 47 (August 1981): 363-92.

Rogers, Daniel T. "Socializing Middle-Class Children: Institutions, Fables, and Work Values in Nineteenth-Century America." *Journal of Social History* 13 (Spring 1980): 354–67.

Scholten, Catherine M. ' "On the Importance of the Obstetrick Art': Changing Customs of Childbirth in America, 1760 to 1825." *William and Mary Quarterly* 34 (July 1977): 426–45.

Scott, Rebecca J. "The Battle Over the Child: Child Apprenticeship and the Freedmen's Bureau in North Carolina." *Prologue* 10 (Summer 1978): 101–13.

Scott, Ann Firor. "Women's Perspective on the Patriarchy in the 1850s." *Journal of American History* 61 (June 1974): 52-64.

Sergmann, Linda S. "The Contemporary Letter as Literature: Issues of Self-Reflexivity, Audience, and Closure." *Women's Studies Quarterly* 17 (Fall/Winter 1989): 128–39.

"The Servant Question." *Southern Workman* 40 (July 1911): 394–95.

Shainess, Natalie. "The Structure of the Mothering Encounter." *Journal of Nervous and Mental Disorders* 136 (February 1963): 146–61.

————. "The Psychologic Experience of Labor." *New York State Journal of Medicine* 63 (October 15, 1963): 2923–32.

Sides, Sudie Duncan. "Southern Women and Slavery," pt. 1. *History Today* 20 (January 1970): 54–60; pt. 2 (February 1970): 124–30.

Stampler, Anita. "One Woman's Work: Clothing the Family in Nineteenth-Century Mississippi." *Southern Quarterly* 27 (Fall 1988): 95–104.

Stowe, Steven M. ' "The Thing Not Its Vision': A Woman's Courtship and Her Sphere in the Southern Planter Class." *Feminist Studies* (Spring 1983): 113–30.

Suitor, J. Jill. "Husbands' Participation in Childbirth: A Nineteenth Century Phenomenon." *Journal of Family History* 6 (Fall 1981): 278–93.

Sutherland, Daniel E. "The Servant Problem: An Index of Antebellum Americanism." *Southern Studies* 18 (Winter 1980): 488-503.

————. "Looking for a Home: Louisiana Emigrants during the Civil War and Reconstruction." *Louisiana History* 21 (Fall 1980): 431–59.

————. "A Special Kind of Problem: The Response of Household Slaves and Their Masters to Freedom." *Southern Studies* 20 (Summer 1981): 151–66.

Tandberg, Gerilyn. "Decoration and Decorum: Accessories of Nineteenth-Century Louisiana Women." *Southern Quarterly* 27 (Fall 1988): 9–31.

Whitten, David O. "Medical Care of Slaves: Louisiana Sugar Region and South Carolina Rice District." *Southern Studies* 16 (Summer 1977): 153–80.

Wren, J. Thomas. "A 'Two-Fold Character': The Slave as Person and Property in Virginia Court Cases, 1800–1860." *Southern Studies* 54 (Winter 1985): 417–31.

Index

LaVergne, TN USA
11 January 2010
169532LV00004B/1/A